D0906563

ENGLISH-
CANADIAN
LITERATURE
TO 1900

AMERICAN LITERATURE, ENGLISH LITERATURE, AND WORLD LITERATURES IN ENGLISH: AN INFORMATION GUIDE SERIES

Series Editor: Theodore Grieder, Curator, Division of Special Collections, Fales Library, New York University, New York, New York

Associate Editor: Duane DeVries, Assistant Professor, Polytechnic Institute of New York, Brooklyn, New York

Other books in this series:

MODERN ENGLISH—CANADIAN PROSE—*Edited by Peter Stevens***

MODERN ENGLISH—CANADIAN POETRY—*Edited by Peter Stevens***

AMERICAN FICTION TO 1900—*Edited by David K. Kirby*

AMERICAN FICTION, 1900-1950—*Edited by James Woodress*

THE LITERARY JOURNAL IN AMERICA TO 1900—*Edited by Edward E. Chielens*

ENGLISH PROSE, PROSE FICTION, AND CRITICISM TO 1660—*Edited by S.K. Heninger, Jr.*

ENGLISH DRAMA TO 1660—*Edited by F. Elaine Penninger*

ENGLISH DRAMA, 1660-1800—*Edited by Frederick M. Link**

OLD AND MIDDLE ENGLISH POETRY TO 1500—*Edited by Walter H. Beale**

THE ENGLISH LITERARY JOURNAL TO 1900—*Edited by Robert B. White, Jr.**

*in press
**in preparation

The above series is part of the
GALE INFORMATION GUIDE LIBRARY

The Library consists of a number of separate series of guides covering major areas in the social sciences, humanities, and current affairs.

General Editor: Paul Wasserman, Professor and former Dean, School of Library and Information Services, University of Maryland

ENGLISH-CANADIAN LITERATURE TO 1900

A GUIDE TO INFORMATION SOURCES

Volume 6 in the American Literature, English Literature, and World Literatures in English Information Guide Series

R. G. Moyles

Associate Professor, Department of English University of Alberta

Gale Research Company
Book Tower, Detroit, Michigan 48226

Z1375
M68

**Library of Congress
Cataloging in Publication Data**

Moyles, R G
   English-Canadian literature to 1900.

   (American literature, English literature, and
world literatures in English; v. 6) (Gale information
guide library)
   Includes bibliographical references and indexes.
   1. Canadian literature--Bibliography.
2. Canadian literature--History and criticism--
Bibliography. I. Title.
Z1375.M68   016.81'008   73-16986
ISBN 0-8103-1222-0

VITA

Robert Gordon Moyles is an associate professor of English literature and associate chairman of the English Department at the University of Alberta, Edmonton, Canada. His M.A. was taken at Memorial University of Newfoundland and his Ph.D. at the University of London, England. Professor Moyles specializes in Canadian literature, analytical and textual bibliography, and Milton. He has been Secretary-Treasurer of the Association of Canadian Teachers of English and is the Associate Editor of MODERNIST STUDIES. His publications include ENGLISH-CANADIAN LITERATURE: A STUDENT GUIDE AND ANNOTATED BIBLIOGRAPHY and "COMPLAINTS IS MANY AND VARIOUS, BUT THE ODD DIVIL LIKE IT": NINETEENTH-CENTURY VIEWS OF NEWFOUNDLAND.

CONTENTS

Contents

INTRODUCTION

"Of books published in the Colony," wrote Susanna Moodie in 1853, "we have very few indeed; and those which have been issued from a Canadian press have generally been got out, either by subscription, or at the expense of the author."[1] Thirty-eight years later, almost at the end of the century, Archibald Lampman observed even more severely that "a good deal is being said about Canadian literature and most of it takes the form of question and answer as to whether a Canadian literature exists. Of course it does not."[2]

An assertion of the nonexistence of a Canadian literature before 1900 is perhaps the first encountered and most recurrent fact of Canadian literary history. Its corollary, often repeated, insists that Canada was a singularly philistine nation, where the whole community was engaged in the pursuit "of the necessities and comforts of life" and cared nothing for the pursuit of literature. "There is," charged Edward Hartley Dewart, "perhaps no country in the world, making equal pretension to intelligence and progress, where the claims of native literature are so little felt, and where every effort in poetry has been met with so much coldness and indifference, as in Canada. And what is more to be deprecated than neglect of our most meritorious authors, is the almost universal absence of interest and faith in all indigenous literary productions."[3] As Daniel Wilson more succinctly put it, "we want our pine trees for lumber, and so long as they spare us a surplus for kindling wood, we ask no kindling inspiration from them."[4]

And yet, despite the abundance of such commentary, it is a provable fact that, between Colonial times and 1900, Canadians (native-born and immigrant) wrote thousands of books of poetry, fiction, essays, and descriptive literature. Moodie could have boasted that British and American publishers considered Canadian writers such as Haliburton and Richardson, well worth publishing. By the end of the century Canadians had supported, from time to time, more than a hundred magazines and journals, of popular, scientific, belletristic, and humanistic natures. Archibald Lampman's remarks to the contrary, between 1880 and 1891 more than a dozen very good books of poetry and fiction had been published by Canadians.

But this, it might be suggested, is too simplistic an answer: the implicit qualification attached to all assertions of the nonexistence of a "Canadian" literature before 1900 was "a literature of merit...; a body of work of sufficient excellence as measured by the severest standards, and sufficiently marked with local colour."[5] Compared with the English masters, the Canadians Sangster, Mair, Heavysege, Richardson, and perhaps even Haliburton, were at best but third-rate writers. And the answer to that charge, if indeed it can be answered, is too involved to tackle in an introduction; only a thorough investigation of all the primary literature listed in this bibliography and an acquaintance with the best literary histories will suffice.

What can be maintained, however, is that the student of early Canadian literature desires to read it not only (or even primarily) for its literary merit or for aesthetic pleasure, but because it provides insights into the attitudes and manners which formed both his literature and his nation, into the hopes and fears which its writers felt for both. For that purpose (one can assert without fear of contradiction), Canada has a large and well-filled storehouse of literature, some examples of which are:

1. Many hundreds of books of travel and description (some of them classics of their kind), offering the willing reader a lifetime of exciting (even if vicarious) adventure.

2. The sensational quasi-historical and romance novels of James DeMille, Lily Dougall and J. M. Oxley, who strove so hard to entertain.

3. The oratorical outbursts (and the occasional poetry) of the incomparable Joseph Howe and Thomas D'Arcy McGee.

4. The works of such emigrant writers as Frances Brooke, Susanna Moodie, and Catherine Parr Traill, who wrote to understand the land they had adopted.

5. The poetry of Goldsmith (nephew of the English novelist and poet), Heavysege, Mair, and MacLachlan, who tried to chronicle the hopes and dreams of the colonists.

6. The poetastery of the many unknowns who published in such literary journals as THE LITERARY GARLAND, ROSE BELFORD'S MONTHLY, THE BRITISH-AMERICAN MAGAZINE, and several others.

7. The novels of such emigre writers as Gilbert Parker and Sara Jeannette Duncan, who gained worldwide acclaim.

8. The early novels of Charles Gordon (Ralph Connor), the phenomenal success of which amazes literary historians even today.

9. The humour of Judge Haliburton, whose Sam Slick became universally known and loved.

10. The short stories and sketches of Charles G. D. Roberts and Ernest Thompson Seton, the acknowledged "fathers" of the realistic animal story.

11. The poetry of Bliss Carman, Charles G. D. Roberts, Archibald Lampman, Duncan Campbell Scott, and Wilfred Campbell, which ushered in a new and dynamic era in Canadian literature.

Not only does this literature exist; it is being read and studied with greater energy than ever before. In the past two years, four full-length anthologies of nineteenth-century English-Canadian literature have appeared; reprints from the same period now number in the hundreds. In nearly every major critical journal some aspect of early Canadian literature is treated; the Summer 1974 issue of THE JOURNAL OF CANADIAN FICTION, devoted entirely to this era, is an excellent example. The present bibliography represents another example of current attention to this literature and, hopefully, will be a catalyst to increased interest and awareness.

In ENGLISH-CANADIAN LITERATURE TO 1900 I have attempted to provide a list of all the important primary and secondary sources necessary for a thorough study of this literature. As one will learn from my table of contents, I have not included every writer of this period, but I have indicated, in the appropriate places, where the reader may pursue a more intensive investigation of an omitted writer. I have, however, included every writer of note and many minor writers, basing my choices on a personal knowledge of the period and on the critical advice implicit in the best literary histories and anthologies. I have also provided a comprehensive and classified list of Canadian travel and descriptive literature which, as presented here, is unique. My annotations have been applied only to those areas which are not well known, primarily the descriptive literature, and I have, for the author sections, opted for general introductory statements rather than individual annotations for each item.

It probably goes without saying that, with all other Canadian bibliographers, I owe a great debt to R. E. Watters for his CHECKLIST OF CANADIAN LITERA-TURE and to Watters and Bell for their ON CANADIAN LITERATURE. To the Canada Council, which provided a Leave Fellowship, to the various libraries which aided my research, particularly the Library of the University of Alberta, and to several friends and colleagues who gave advice, I offer my sincere thanks.

R. G. Moyles
Edmonton, Canada

FOOTNOTES

[1]Susanna Moodie, "Introduction to MARK HURDLESTONE," in CANADIAN ANTHOLOGY, ed. Carl F. Klinck and Reginald E[yre] Watters (Toronto, 1974), p. 58.

[2]Archibald Lampman, "Two Canadian Poets: A Lecture, 1891," in MASKS OF POETRY, ed. A. J. M. Smith (Toronto, 1962), pp. 26-44.

[3]Edward Hartley Dewart, "Introduction" to SELECTIONS FROM CANADIAN POETS (Montreal, 1864; reprint ed., Toronto, 1973).

[4]Daniel Wilson, "Review of Sangster's THE ST. LAWRENCE AND THE SAGUENAY," in CANADIAN ANTHOLOGY, op. cit. (note 1), p. 70.

[5]Lampman, op. cit., p. 27.

Chapter 1

GENERAL REFERENCE GUIDES

Chapter 1

GENERAL REFERENCE GUIDES

Listed below, in alphabetical order within sections, are the bibliographical and general references (indexes and biographical references) essential to the study of Canadian literature. Some of the items have long been out of print, but are listed for the serious researcher who can borrow through inter-library loan facilities.

A. BIBLIOGRAPHICAL REFERENCES

Amtmann, Bernard. CONTRIBUTIONS TO A SHORT-TITLE CATALOGUE OF CANADIANA. 4 vols. Montreal: Privately printed, 1971.

> A private venture based largely on booksellers records, with sale prices listed. No introduction; method unexplained; alphabetical arrangement; a continuing project.

Ball, J. L. "Theatre in Canada: A Bibliography, 1606-1959." CANADIAN LITERATURE, 14 (Autumn 1962), 85-100.

> "A list of materials outlining theatre history in Canada." Arranged chronologically.

Bell, Inglis, and Jennifer Gallup. A REFERENCE GUIDE TO ENGLISH, AMER-ICAN AND CANADIAN LITERATURE. Vancouver: University of British Columbia Press, 1971.

> A bibliography of reference materials to "meet the specific needs of the undergraduate specializing in English." A list of the major sources, excellently arranged and lucidly annotated.

Berton, Pierre. "Gold Rush Writing: The Literature of the Klondike." CA-NADIAN LITERATURE, 4 (Spring 1960), 59-67.

> A bibliographical essay with extensive footnotes indicating the scope of the literature relating to the '98 gold rush and after.

CANADIAN BOOKS IN PRINT/CATALOGUE DES LIVRES CANADIENS EN LIBRARIE. Toronto: Canadian Books in Print Committee, 1967--.

Compiled from Canadian publishers' lists. Useful for finding reprints of early Canadiana.

CANADIAN LITERATURE. Vancouver: University of British Columbia Press, Summer 1959--. Quarterly.

The annual supplement (in the Winter issue up to 1966; in the Spring issue up to 1972) provides a checklist of critical studies of both English and French literature for the preceding year. The section entitled "Individual Authors" is especially useful, with pre-1900 authors receiving extensive coverage. The "Annual Supplement" was suspended in 1972, and similar bibliographies are now carried by the JOURNAL OF CANADIAN FICTION and JOURNAL OF COMMONWEALTH LITERATURE described below.

CANADIANA. Ottawa: The National Library, 1951--. Monthly.

Published monthly with annual cumulations. This catalogue of all publications received by the National Library is the most comprehensive guide of its kind in Canada. Classified table of contents, number 800 being "Literature." Also includes lists of microforms. Useful for locating reprints of early materials.

Edwards, Mary Jane. "Fiction and Montreal, 1769-1885: A Bibliography." PAPERS OF THE BIBLIOGRAPHICAL SOCIETY OF CANADA, 7 (1969), 61-75.

Fiction published in Montreal during those years.

Fulford, Robert, David Godfrey, and Abraham Rotstein. READ CANADIAN: A BOOK ABOUT CANADIAN BOOKS. Toronto: James Lewis and Samuel, 1972.

A series of thirty brief essays dealing with a wide range of Canadian books in various fields. The essay entitled "Nineteenth Century Literature" gives a superficial summary which might prove useful for the beginning reader in this field.

Gnarowski, Michael. A CONCISE BIBLIOGRAPHY OF ENGLISH-CANADIAN LITERATURE. Toronto: McClelland & Stewart, 1973.

An alphabetical author listing with primary works and selected criticism. Approximately thirty nineteenth-century writers represented.

Haight, Willet R. CANADIAN CATALOGUE OF BOOKS, 1791-1897. London: H. Pordes, 1958.

A wide-ranging, though not comprehensive, list, arranged alphabetically by author.

4

Horning, Lewis E., and Lawrence J. Burpee. A BIBLIOGRAPHY OF CANA-
DIAN FICTION (ENGLISH). Toronto: Briggs, 1904. (Victoria University
Library Publications, no. 2.)

> Arranged alphabetically by author, with short biographical notes
> and lists of primary works.

James, Charles C. A BIBLIOGRAPHY OF CANADIAN POETRY (ENGLISH).
Toronto: Briggs, 1899. (Victoria University Library Publications, no. 1.)

> Four short sections: anonymous works, anthologies, articles on
> Canadian poets in magazines, and pen-names.

JOURNAL OF CANADIAN FICTION. Fredericton, N. B., Spring 1972--.
Quarterly.

> Contains an annual bibliography of primary and secondary litera-
> ture, classified and annotated. Also contains lists of theses, com-
> pleted and in progress.

JOURNAL OF COMMONWEALTH LITERATURE. London: Heinemann, 1965--.
Annual, 1965-66; semiannual, 1967--.

> Since 1972 the journal has contained an annual bibliography of
> critical materials about Canadian literature.

Lochhead, Douglas G. BIBLIOGRAPHY OF CANADIAN BIBLIOGRAPHIES.
2nd rev. and enl. ed. Toronto: University of Toronto Press, 1972.

> A new edition of the bibliography first compiled by Raymond
> Tanghe, this incorporates his work and adds many new items.
> Indicates whether the title is available in book, MS., or micro-
> form; new alphabetical arrangement with expanded bilingual sub-
> ject-compiler index. Excludes bibliographies in monographs, peri-
> odicals, and theses.

MLA INTERNATIONAL BIBLIOGRAPHY OF BOOKS AND ARTICLES ON THE
MODERN LANGUAGES AND LITERATURES. New York: Modern Language
Association of America, 1919--. Annual.

> This valuable bibliography of current criticism contains a small
> section on Canadian literature under "English Language and Litera-
> ture" in sub-section II: "Australia, Canada...."

Moyles, R. G., and Catherine Siemens. ENGLISH-CANADIAN LITERATURE:
A STUDENT GUIDE AND ANNOTATED BIBLIOGRAPHY. Edmonton: Athabascan
Publishing Co., 1972.

> A comprehensive student guide listing major reference sources needed
> for conducting undergraduate and graduate research into Canadian
> literature.

Peel, Bruce B. BIBLIOGRAPHY OF THE PRAIRIE PROVINCES TO 1953.
Toronto: University of Toronto Press, 1956. Supplement, 1963. 2nd ed.,
incorporating both first ed. and supplement, 1973.

> Includes approximately 3,000 books and pamphlets relating to the
> Prairies, arranged chronologically.

Rhodenizer, Vernon B[lair]. CANADIAN LITERATURE IN ENGLISH. Montreal: Quality Press, 1965.

> A bio-bibliographical survey from the earliest years to 1960. It
> comprises twenty subject chapters within which authors are treated
> chronologically. See Lois M. Thierman's INDEX TO VERNON
> BLAIR RHODENIZER'S CANADIAN LITERATURE IN ENGLISH
> (Edmonton: La Survivance Press, n.d.).

Tremaine, Marie. A BIBLIOGRAPHY OF CANADIAN IMPRINTS 1751-1800.
Toronto: University of Toronto Press, 1952.

> Quasi-facsimile title-pages; locations; lists of newspapers and print-
> ing offices; indexed.

Watters, Reginald E[yre]. A CHECKLIST OF CANADIAN LITERATURE AND
BACKGROUND MATERIALS, 1628-1960. 2nd ed. rev. and enl. Toronto:
University of Toronto Press, 1972.

> Part I is "a comprehensive list of books which constitute Canadian
> Literature written in English." Part II lists important critical ma-
> terials and location. This is indeed a "comprehensive" but by no
> means complete listing of Canadian books.

Watters, Reginald E[yre], and Inglis Bell. ON CANADIAN LITERATURE,
1806-1960. A CHECKLIST OF ARTICLES, BOOKS AND THESES ON EN-
GLISH-CANADIAN LITERATURE, ITS AUTHORS, AND LANGUAGE. Toronto:
University of Toronto Press, 1966.

> Part I deals with such subjects as poetry, fiction, literary criticism,
> and folklore. Part II lists criticism of individual authors. An
> indispensable tool.

B. BIOGRAPHICAL REFERENCES

Brown, George W. DICTIONARY OF CANADIAN BIOGRAPHY. 3 vols.
Toronto: University of Toronto Press, 1966- .

> A continuing project with volumes I (1000-1700), II (1701-1740),
> and X (1871-1880) completed to date.

MacMurchy, Archibald. HANDBOOK OF CANADIAN LITERATURE (ENGLISH).
Toronto: Briggs, 1906.

Biographical and bibliographical accounts of approximately 140 authors, all of whom wrote before 1900.

Matthews, William. CANADIAN DIARIES AND AUTOBIOGRAPHIES. Berkeley: University of California Press, 1950.

A bibliography covering both French and English Canada and including both published and unpublished documents. Alphabetical listing by author; 1276 entries. Indexed.

Morgan, Henry James. BIBLIOTHECA CANADENSIS; OR, A MANUAL OF CANADIAN LITERATURE. Ottawa: Desbarats, 1867. Reprint ed. Detroit: Gale Research Co., 1968.

Alphabetical list of authors; brief biographies; list of works, criticism, and press notices. Covers the period from the fall of Quebec to 1867.

Percival, W. P. LEADING CANADIAN POETS. Toronto: Ryerson, 1948.

Biographical essays, about six pages each, dealing with twenty-nine Canadian poets, half of them belonging to the nineteenth century: Carman, Crawford, Drummond, Katherine Hale, Pauline Johnson, Lampman, Lighthall, MacMechan, Mair, C.G.D. Roberts, Sangster, D. C. Scott, F. G. Scott, and Wetherald.

Roberts, Charles G. D., and Arthur L. Tunnell. A STANDARD DICTIONARY OF CANADIAN BIOGRAPHY. 2 vols. Toronto: Trans-Canada Press, 1934.

Long biographical sketches with good bibliographies.

Sylvestre, Guy, Brandon Conron, and Carl F. Klinck. CANADIAN WRITERS/ ECRIVANS CANADIENS: A BIOGRAPHICAL DICTIONARY. Rev. and enl. ed. Toronto: Ryerson, 1966.

Alphabetically arranged with chronological table of publication dates. Good coverage of nineteenth-century authors.

Wallace, W. Stewart. THE MACMILLAN DICTIONARY OF CANADIAN BIOGRAPHY. 3rd ed. 2 vols. London: Macmillan, 1963.

Useful and widely-used reference work.

_____. A DICTIONARY OF NORTH AMERICAN AUTHORS DECEASED BEFORE 1950. Toronto: Ryerson, 1951.

A quick guide to vital statistics; useful list of reference sources.

C. INDEXES TO SERIAL PUBLICATIONS

Brown, Mary Markham. AN INDEX TO THE "LITERARY GARLAND" (MON-TREAL, 1838-1851). Toronto: Bibliographical Society of Canada, 1962.

The "Literary Garland" was the first literary magazine in Canada to survive for more than three years and provides, according to the indexer, a "rich and convenient record of English-Canadian writing from 1838-1851." A frequent contributor was Susanna Moodie. Index arranged alphabetically by author.

CANADIAN PERIODICAL INDEX/INDEX DE PERIODIQUES CANADIENS. Ottawa: Canadian Library Association, 1938--.

This is an index to articles in periodicals, indexed under author-of-articles and subject. Since 1960 the journal has been published monthly with annual cumulations; from 1948-1963 it appeared under the title CANADIAN INDEX TO PERIODICALS AND DOCUMEN-TARY FILMS. Only occasionally useful for students of nineteenth-century Canadian literature.

Firth, Edith G. EARLY TORONTO NEWSPAPERS 1793-1867: A CATALOGUE OF NEWSPAPERS PUBLISHED IN THE TOWN OF YORK AND THE CITY OF TORONTO FROM THE BEGINNING TO CONFEDERATION. Introduction by Henry C. Campbell. Toronto: Baxter Publishing Co., in cooperation with the Toronto Public Library, 1961.

Arranged chronologically with index and descriptive notes.

Goggio, Emilio, Beatrice Corrigan, and Jack H. Parker. A BIBLIOGRAPHY OF CANADIAN PERIODICALS (ENGLISH AND FRENCH FROM COLONIAL TIMES TO 1950) IN CANADIAN LIBRARIES. Toronto: University of Toronto, 1955.

A selected checklist of periodicals chiefly concerned with the humanities and fine arts. Every item included has been seen by the bibliographers. See Tod and Cordingley, below.

Harper, J. Russell. HISTORICAL DIRECTORY OF NEW BRUNSWICK NEWS-PAPERS AND PERIODICALS. Foreword by Desmond Pacey. Fredericton: University of New Brunswick, 1961.

The preface states that "every known New Brunswick newspaper and all periodicals of literary, historical, religious, educational or scientific nature have been included." Arranged by place of location, with library locations.

Poole, William Frederick, and William I. Fletcher. POOLE'S INDEX TO PERIODICAL LITERATURE, 1802-1906. 6 vols. Boston: Houghton Mifflin, 1893-1908.

"An alphabetical index to subjects and not to authors except when

writers are treated as subjects" (which is often). Very good index
to early Canadian writers who wrote for foreign magazines, which
a majority of them did. It also indexes CANADIAN MONTHLY
(1872-81), NEW DOMINION MONTHLY (1867-79), and CANA-
DIAN MAGAZINE (1893-1906).

Tod, Dorothea Douglas, and Audrey Cordingley. A BIBLIOGRAPHY OF CANA-
DIAN LITERARY PERIODICALS 1789-1900. Ottawa: The Royal Society, 1932.

> By no means complete; no locations. See Goggio, et al., above,
> for a more up-to-date bibliography of these periodicals.

D.   INDEXES TO THESES

Canada. National Library. CANADIAN THESES: A LIST OF THESES AC-
CEPTED BY CANADIAN UNIVERSITIES. Ottawa: Queen's Printer, 1952--.
Annual.

> The preface to the 1960/61 list states that the 1952 issue is out of
> print and there are "no immediate plans for compiling lists for the
> intervening years between 1952 and 1960/61." Arranged according
> to the Dewey Decimal Classification system. See Canadian Litera-
> ture section C810, C840, within which the universities are arranged
> alphabetically. Includes both M.A. and Ph.D. theses. Alphabeti-
> cal author index.

Canada. National Library. CANADIAN THESES ON MICROFILM: CATA-
LOGUE-PRICE LIST, NOS. 1-2450. Ottawa, 1969.

> Kept up to date by supplements. A selection of Canadian theses
> on microfilm arranged by order number.

Canada. Public Archives. CANADIAN GRADUATE THESES IN THE HUMAN-
ITIES AND SOCIAL SCIENCES, 1921-46. Ottawa: King's Printer, 1951.

> See Canadian Literature section. Theses listed alphabetically by
> university and author. Supplies a brief note for each.

CANADIAN LITERATURE. Vancouver: University of British Columbia. Summer 1959--. Quarterly.

> The annual supplement (in the Winter issue up to 1966; in the
> Spring issue up to 1972) provides a checklist of critical studies
> which includes recent theses. Annual list of theses (completed and
> in progress) now carried by THE JOURNAL OF CANADIAN FIC-
> TION.

CANADIANA. Ottawa: The National Library, 1951--. Monthly.

> Annual cumulations. Section III lists theses on microfilm.

Mills, Judy, and Irene Dombra. UNIVERSITY OF TORONTO DOCTORAL
THESES, 1867-1967. Toronto: University of Toronto Press, 1968.

> Only a few on Canadian literature.

E. INDEX TO MICROMATERIALS

Canada. Public Archives. CATALOGUE OF PAMPHLETS IN THE PUBLIC
ARCHIVES OF CANADA, 1493-1877. Index by Magdalen Casey. Ottawa:
King's Printer, 1931.

> Many of these items are now on microfiche. These are chiefly of
> historical interest, but for the student of Canadian literature there
> are such oddities as: No. 531, McFINGAL; A MODERN EPIC
> POEM OR THE TOWN MEETING.

Canadian Library Association. CANADIAN NEWSPAPERS ON MICROFILM.
Compiled by the Microfilm Committee of the CLA under the supervision of
Sheila A. Egoff. Ottawa: Canadian Library Association, 1959.

> Part I, revised in 1970, is a cumulative catalogue of microfilms
> of the CLA. Part II lists other Canadian newspapers on microfilm
> (i.e., filmed by other than the CLA). Listings are by province with
> detailed information for each entry. See also Helen Elliot's FATE,
> HOPE AND EDITORIALS: CONTEMPORARY ACCOUNTS AND
> OPINIONS IN THE NEWSPAPERS, 1862-1873 (Ottawa: Canadian
> Library Association, 1967). This booklet provides brief introduc-
> tions to the newspapers by offering samplings of their editorials.

CANADIANA. Ottawa: The National Library, 1951--. Monthly. Annual
cumulations. Section III deals with microfilms.

F. RESEARCH CATALOGUES: CANADIAN AND
FOREIGN LIBRARIES

Before consulting any of the specialized catalogues listed below, the researcher
should first of all consult the following general guide to research resources in
Canada:

> Downs, Robert B. RESOURCES OF CANADIAN ACADEMIC AND
> RESEARCH LIBRARIES. Ottawa: Association of Universities and
> Colleges of Canada, 1967.

>> A study of the resources of those libraries, touching on
>> accessibility, services, student-faculty views, and so forth.
>> Of special interest is Section 12, "Some Special Collec-
>> tions in Canadian Libraries," pp. 225-267. This is an
>> alphabetical series of notes on the principal holdings of
>> individual libraries.

Beals, Helen D. A CATALOGUE OF THE ERIC R. DENNIS COLLECTION OF CANADIANA IN THE LIBRARY OF ACADIA UNIVERSITY. Wolfville, N.S.: Acadia University, 1938.

    Special emphasis on Maritime Canadiana.

Canada. Public Archives. UNION LIST OF MANUSCRIPTS IN CANADIAN REPOSITORIES. Directed by W. Kaye Lamb; ed. Robert S. Gordon. Ottawa: Public Archives, 1968.

    "A comprehensive list of all significant manuscripts and records in Canadian archival institutions"; 11,170 entries. Entered under names of individuals or institutions; details of possessions. Indexes.

Harlowe, Dorothy. A CATALOGUE OF CANADIAN MANUSCRIPTS COLLECT-ED BY LORNE PIERCE AND PRESENTED TO QUEEN'S UNIVERSITY. Toronto: Ryerson, 1946.

    Part I: Bliss Carman. Part II: Other Canadian authors, notably Marjorie Pickthall, Wilfred Campbell, and Charles G. D. Roberts.

Harvard University Library. CANADIAN HISTORY AND LITERATURE: WIDENER LIBRARY SHELFLIST, 20. Cambridge, Mass.: Harvard University Press, 1968.

    Contains 10,212 titles. The Library has an excellent Bliss Carman collection and a fine representation of other authors.

Lande, Lawrence M. THE LAWRENCE LANDE COLLECTION OF CANADIANA IN THE REDPATH LIBRARY OF McGILL UNIVERSITY: A BIBLIOGRAPHY. Montreal: Lawrence M. Lande Foundation, 1965.

    "Includes books, pamphlets, broadsides, maps, manuscripts, and letters relating to Canada, mainly before Confederation." It also includes material on Western Canada up to this century. More than 2000 titles. Nearly 200 facsimiles of titlepages and contents. Bibliographic index; index to government documents; title and sub-ject index.

New Brunswick University Library. A CATALOGUE OF THE RUFUS HATHA-WAY COLLECTION OF CANADIAN LITERATURE. Fredericton: University of New Brunswick, 1935.

Porteus, Janet. CANADIANA, 1698-1900, IN THE POSSESSION OF THE DOUGLAS LIBRARY, QUEEN'S UNIVERSITY. Kingston, 1932.

    A fine collection of early material.

Staton, Frances M., and Marie Tremaine. A BIBLIOGRAPHY OF CANADIANA: BEING ITEMS IN THE PUBLIC LIBRARY OF TORONTO RELATING TO THE EARLY HISTORY AND DEVELOPMENT OF CANADA. Toronto: The Public Library, 1934. First supplement by Gertrude M. Boyle, 1959.

One of our finest collections of Canadiana, the bibliography lists 4646 items published between 1534 and 1867. Arranged chronologically, with author-title-subject index. Supplement includes recent acquisitions and a large collection of Newfoundlandiana. Many items from this catalogue are being placed on microfiche.

G. MISCELLANEOUS REFERENCES

This brief section includes reference guides or general studies for some additional areas of research related to the study of Canadian literature.

ENGLISH-LANGUAGE DICTIONARIES

A DICTIONARY OF CANADIANISMS ON HISTORICAL PRINCIPLES. Toronto: W. J. Gage, 1967.

"Every term entered is supported by dated evidence from printed sources." Includes etymology and scope of the term in time and space, plus explanatory notes on contentious issues of usage and origin. Bibliography of sources, pp. 882-927.

LANGUAGE AND LINGUISTICS

Avis, Walter S. A BIBLIOGRAPHY OF WRITINGS ON CANADIAN ENGLISH (1857-1965). Toronto: W. J. Gage, 1965.

Linguistic and dialect studies; entries arranged alphabetically by author.

Hamilton, Robert M. CANADIAN QUOTATIONS AND PHRASES: LITERARY AND HISTORICAL. Introduction by Bruce Hutchison. Toronto: McClelland & Stewart, 1952.

"A guide to what Canadians have said in the past about themselves or things Canadian, or from a Canadian point of view." Arranged alphabetically by subject. Author index.

FOLKLORE

Haywood, Charles. A BIBLIOGRAPHY OF NORTH AMERICAN FOLKLORE AND FOLKSONG. 2nd ed., rev. New York: Dover Publications, 1961.

An "attempt" at a thorough bibliography of American folklore which defines "folklore" to include such works as travel books, biographies, and social and cultural

histories. See section on "Canada," Volume I, pp. 421-
28. Author-title-subject index.

HISTORY

Creighton, Donald. DOMINION OF THE NORTH. Rev. ed.
Toronto: Macmillan, 1957.

One historian's view of Canada and its emergence from
colonial status. Probably the most useful one-volume
paperback history because it includes a selected reading
list and index.

Wrong, G. M., and H. H. Langton. REVIEW OF HISTORICAL
PUBLICATIONS RELATING TO CANADA. 22 vols. Toronto:
Briggs, Morang, and University of Toronto Press, 1897-1918.

An excellent index to many books and articles written
during those years. Long reviews and short notes, with
bibliographical citations. Also includes reviews of literary works.

INFORMATION ABOUT CANADA

Campbell, H. C. HOW TO FIND OUT ABOUT CANADA. Oxford: Pergamon Press, 1967.

A paperback guide to the major official and unofficial
sources of information about Canada, mostly in published
works of reference. The compilers direct the reader's
attention to the major sources of information and tell
him how to use them. There are fifteen sections, some
of which are "General Guides to Canadian Achievement," "Canadian Thinkers and Religious Writers,"
"Canadian Art," "Literature," and "History."

Chapter 2

LITERARY HISTORIES AND CRITICISM

Chapter 2
LITERARY HISTORIES AND CRITICISM

The following material is divided into three sections: full-length studies, critical articles, and theses. In the first of these I have attempted to be as comprehensive as possible, listing every literary history and general study which
remains extant. For the last two sections, however, I have been selective,
listing only those articles and theses which make new contributions, add new
insights to the scholarship listed in the first section, or take issue with ideas
proposed by previous scholars. In the final two subsections I have annotated
only those entries whose titles do not reveal the nature of their subjects.

A. FULL-LENGTH STUDIES

Baker, Ray Palmer. A HISTORY OF ENGLISH-CANADIAN LITERATURE TO
THE CONFEDERATION: ITS RELATION TO THE LITERATURE OF GREAT
BRITAIN AND THE UNITED STATES. Cambridge, Mass.: Harvard University
Press, 1920. Reprint ed. New York: Russell & Russell, 1968.

> A comprehensive and scholarly work; one of the best of the early
> literary histories. Bibliography.

Bourinot, John George. THE INTELLECTUAL DEVELOPMENT OF THE CANA-
DIAN PEOPLE. Toronto: Hunter & Rose, 1881.

> A cursory survey of the state of intellectualism, education, jour-
> nalism, and native literature by a man who was personally involved.

Brown, E. K. ON CANADIAN POETRY. Toronto: Ryerson, 1943. Rev. ed.
1944.

> Brown attempts to answer three questions: What are the peculiar
> difficulties which have weighed upon Canadian writers? What
> Canadian poets remain alive and, in some degree at least, forma-
> tive? How have the masters of our poetry achieved their success
> and what are the kinds of success they have achieved? They are
> answered in three essays: "The Problem of a Canadian Literature,"
> "The Development of Poetry in Canada," and "The Masters," all
> of which concentrate on nineteenth-century poetry (two of the

three masters being Archibald Lampman and D. C. Scott). Bibliographical notes appended.

Collin, W. E. THE WHITE SAVANNAHS. Toronto: Macmillan, 1936.

A series of essays dealing, somewhat mythopoeically, with such writers as Archibald Lampman, Marjorie Pickthall, and Marie Le Franc.

Deacon, William Arthur. THE FOUR JAMESES. Ottawa: Graphic Publishers, 1927. Rev. ed. Toronto: Ryerson, 1953.

A somewhat tongue-in-cheek study of four nineteenth-century Canadian "monarchs of the quill": James Gay, James McIntyre, John McCrea, and James D. Gillis, who resemble William McGonigall and are rescued for a similar amusing reading experience.

_____. POTEEN: A POT-POURRI OF CANADIAN ESSAYS. Ottawa: Graphic Publishers, 1926.

Has a long section (pp. 141-233) on Canadian Literature which is interesting in terms of its book list, its guide to the best anthologies, and the first histories of Canadian literature. Not critical or definitive, merely engaging.

Edwards, Murray D. A STAGE IN OUR PAST: ENGLISH-CANADIAN THEATRE IN EASTERN CANADA FROM THE 1790's TO 1914. Toronto: University of Toronto Press, 1968.

The only full-length study of the subject, emphasizing Canadian-written and Canadian-produced drama. Appendices reproduce C. P. Walker's notebook (Walker was the manager of the Winnipeg Opera House and the Walker Theatre, 1897-1911) and a list of the prominent touring companies in Eastern Canada, 1880-1914. Excellent bibliography; indexed.

Eggleston, Wilfrid. THE FRONTIER AND CANADIAN LETTERS. Toronto: Ryerson, 1957.

The book constitutes what the author himself calls a "reconnaissance" of the "main events of Canadian letters in the frontier days." Its chief weakness is that it lacks specific reference to the literature itself, preferring to deal in philosophic generalizations. No bibliography.

Graham, Franklin. HISTRIONIC MONTREAL: ANNALS OF THE MONTREAL STAGE WITH BIOGRAPHICAL AND CRITICAL NOTICES OF THE PLAYS AND PLAYERS OF A CENTURY. 2nd ed. Montreal: Lovell, 1902. Reprint ed. New York: Benjamin Blom, 1969.

A chronological account of the plays performed in Montreal between 1786 and 1886 with biographical sketches of the actors who performed them. Illustrated and indexed.

Klinck, Carl F., general ed. LITERARY HISTORY OF CANADA: CANADIAN LITERATURE IN ENGLISH. Toronto: University of Toronto Press, 1965.

A collection of essays by thirty-five notable scholars tracing the "emergence and realization of a tradition in English-Canadian literature." The most authoritative literary history to date. Bibliographical notes, pp. 853-57. Author-title index.

Logan, J. D., and Donald G. French. HIGHWAYS OF CANADIAN LITERATURE: A SYNOPTIC INTRODUCTION TO THE LITERARY HISTORY OF CANADA (ENGLISH) FROM 1760 TO 1924. Toronto: McClelland & Stewart, 1924.

Still a valuable tool, one which marked the way for later literary historians.

McCourt, Edward A. THE CANADIAN WEST IN FICTION. Toronto: Ryerson, 1949. Rev. and enl. ed. 1970.

Only two chapters devoted to pre-twentieth-century literature, but they provide an adequate introduction to the early western novelists.

MacMechan, Archibald. HEAD-WATERS OF CANADIAN LITERATURE. Toronto: McClelland & Stewart, 1924. Reprint ed. Toronto: Canadiana House, 1968.

A somewhat uneven piece of work, offering a few worthwhile critical insights into the early literature of Canada.

Matthews, John Pengwerne. TRADITION IN EXILE: A COMPARATIVE STUDY OF SOCIAL INFLUENCES ON THE DEVELOPMENT OF AUSTRALIAN AND CANADIAN POETRY IN THE NINETEENTH CENTURY. Toronto: University of Toronto Press, 1962.

An excellent comparative study of the early poetry of two nations "sprung from common roots" and "responding to identical influences."

O'Hagan, Thomas. CANADIAN ESSAYS: CRITICAL AND HISTORICAL. Toronto: Briggs, 1901.

Only two literary essays: "Canadian Poets and Poetry" and "Canadian Women Writers," pp. 11-103. More historical than critical.

Pacey, Desmond. CREATIVE WRITING IN CANADA: A SHORT HISTORY OF ENGLISH-CANADIAN LITERATURE. 2nd ed., rev. and enl. Toronto: Ryerson, 1961. Paperback ed., 1967.

Chapters II and III deal with pre-1900 literature. Wide coverage; an in-depth critical approach with good bibliography.

_____. TEN CANADIAN POETS: A GROUP OF BIOGRAPHICAL AND CRITICAL ESSAYS. Toronto: Ryerson, 1958. Paperback ed. 1966.

The five pre-twentieth-century poets examined are Sangster, Roberts, Carman, Lampman, and D. C. Scott. A good bibliography. Justifiably accepted as the standard critical work for the authors treated.

Percival, W. P. LEADING CANADIAN POETS. Toronto: Ryerson, 1948.

Introductory essays dealing with twenty-nine Canadian poets, half of them belonging to the nineteenth century.

Pierce, Lorne [Albert]. AN OUTLINE OF CANADIAN LITERATURE (FRENCH AND ENGLISH). Montreal: Louis Carrier & Co., 1927.

The first to place "both English and French authors side by side." Brief introductory chapters, followed by author sketches.

Rashley, R. E. POETRY IN CANADA: THE FIRST THREE STEPS. Toronto: Ryerson, 1958.

An extremely useful introduction to the beginning and development of English-Canadian poetry. Index.

Rhodenizer, V[ernon] B[lair]. A HANDBOOK TO CANADIAN LITERATURE. Ottawa: Graphic Publishers, 1930.

A competent critical survey of the "outstanding" Canadian writers to William Henry Drummond, with a strongly patriotic slant.

Stevenson, Lionel. APPRAISALS OF CANADIAN LITERATURE. Toronto: Macmillan, 1926.

A thematic-source study of Canadian literature, offering one of the first lengthy manifestos for a national literature.

Stevenson, O. J. A PEOPLE'S BEST. Toronto: Musson, 1927.

Thirty-one sketches of well-known Canadian artists and writers, including Roberts, Parker, Lampman, Johnson, and D. C. Scott. Largely biographical and only minimally informative.

Story, Norah. OXFORD COMPANION TO CANADIAN HISTORY AND LITERATURE. Toronto: Oxford University Press, 1967. Supplement 1972.

Like the other Oxford Companions, a useful collection of notabilia and trivia pertaining to the two disciplines mentioned in the title.

Waterston, Elizabeth. SURVEY: A SHORT HISTORY OF CANADIAN LITERATURE. Toronto: Methuen, 1973.

Chapters 1-6 deal with the early literature, introducing it through its similarity of themes and preoccupations. A pleasantly readable history, with ample reference notes.

B. CRITICAL ARTICLES

Bailey, A. G. "Literature and Nationalism After Confederation." UNIVERSITY OF TORONTO QUARTERLY, 25 (July 1956), 409-24.

An interesting, but unconvincing argument that a definite "nationalist fervour" is evident in a great deal of nineteenth-century Canadian literature.

_____. "Creative Moments in the Culture of the Maritime Provinces." DALHOUSIE REVIEW, 29 (1949-50), 231-44.

An attempt to explain the social and intellectual climate which bred such writers as Haliburton and Roberts.

Bissell, Claude T. "Literary Taste in Central Canada During the Late Nineteenth Century." CANADIAN HISTORICAL ASSOCIATION REVIEW, 31 (September 1950), 237-51.

_____. "A Common Ancestry: Literature in Australia and Canada." UNIVERSITY OF TORONTO QUARTERLY, 25 (January 1956), 131-42.

Booth, Michael R. "The Actor's Eye: Impressions of Nineteenth-Century Canada." CANADIAN LITERATURE, 13 (Summer 1962), 15-24.

A brief, but interesting account of several actors' views of Canada as they toured it.

_____. "Pioneer Entertainment: Theatrical Taste in the Early Canadian West." CANADIAN LITERATURE, 4 (Spring 1960), 52-58.

With reference only to the theatres in Victoria and Barkerville, B. C.

Burpee, L[awrence] J. "Canadian Novelists." SEWANEE REVIEW, 11 (October 1903), 385-411.

An historical review of the early English-Canadian novelists, describing some little-known works, with full bibliographical information in the footnotes.

Collin, W. E. "On Canadian Poetry--The Stream and the Masters." UNIVERSITY OF TORONTO QUARTERLY, 13 (January 1944), 221-28.

A long review of E. K. Brown's ON CANADIAN POETRY (1943) with some original critical insights of his own.

Daniells, Roy. "High Colonialism in Canada." CANADIAN LITERATURE, 40 (Spring 1969), 5-16.

A new, more positive approach to the matter of Canada's colonial literature and its emphasis on relationships with the mother country.

Djwa, Sandra [Ann]. "Canadian Poetry and the Computer." CANADIAN LITERATURE, 46 (Autumn 1970), 43-54.

An article detailing the results of submitting several early writers (e.g., Roberts) to a computer analysis which indentified key words and contingent thematic patterns.

Egoff, Sheila A. "Canadian Historical Fiction for Children." CANADIAN LITERATURE, 27 (Winter 1966), 44-52.

Edwards, Mary Jane. "Essentially Canadian." CANADIAN LITERATURE, 52 (Spring 1972), 8-23.

An attempt to show that literature of "English-French relations in Canada" did not begin with Hugh MacLennan but with the first novel about Canada (Frances Brooke's EMILY MONTAGUE) and was a popular theme with several other early writers.

Hodgson, Maurice. "Initiation and Quest: Early Canadian Journals." CANADIAN LITERATURE, 38 (Autumn 1968), 29-40.

The journals specifically referred to are Samuel Hearne's A JOURNEY TO THE NORTHERN OCEAN and John Jewitt's NARRATION OF THE ADVENTURES OF JOHN JEWITT.

Logan, J. D. "Re-views of the Literary History of Canada." CANADIAN MAGAZINE, 48 (December 1916), 3-9, 125-32, 219-25, 373-78.

One of the first attempts at a critical and philosophical appreciation of Canadian literature divided into four parts: (1) "The significance of Nova Scotia in the Literary History of Canada," (2) "Canadian Fictionists and other creative prose writers," (3) "The second renaissance of Canadian nativistic poetry," (4) "Canadian poets and poetesses as lyrists of romantic love."

McCourt, E[dward] A. "The Canadian Historical Novel." DALHOUSIE REVIEW, 26 (April 1946), 30-36.

A survey.

Muddiman, Bernard. "The Immigrant Element in Canadian Literature." QUEEN'S QUARTERLY, 20 (April 1913), 404-15.

Not so much a study of the "immigrant element" in Canadian literature as a survey of literature written by immigrants.

Newton, Norman. "Classical Canadian Poetry and the Public Muse." CANADIAN LITERATURE, 51 (Winter 1972), 39-54.

An excellent essay accounting for the mediocrity of nineteenth-century Canadian poetry in terms of the artist's relationship to society.

Poirier, Michel. "The Animal Story in Canadian Literature: E. Thompson Seton and Charles G. D. Roberts." QUEEN'S QUARTERLY, 34 (January 1927), 298-312; 34 (April 1927), 398-419.

A comprehensive look at the basis of the animal story in literature and then at the contributions of Seton and Roberts to that genre.

Povey, John. "Poor Waifs upon Creation's Skirts." DALHOUSIE REVIEW, 47 (Summer 1967), 213-21.

Nineteenth-century poets' reactions to the "Red Indian" compared with similar reactions to the natives of Africa and Australia.

Pratt, E. J. "Canadian Poetry Past and Present." UNIVERSITY OF TORONTO QUARTERLY, 8 (October 1938), 1-10.

An interesting essay mainly in praise of the Confederation poets by Canada's best poet.

Pritchard, Allan. "From the Uncouth Shores: Seventeenth-Century Literature in Newfoundland." CANADIAN LITERATURE, XIV (Autumn 1962), 5-20.

Smith, A[rthur] J[ames] M[arshall]. "Canadian Anthologies, New and Old." UNIVERSITY OF TORONTO QUARTERLY, 11 (July 1942), 457-74.

_____. "The Canadian Poet: Part I, To Confederation." CANADIAN LITERATURE, 37 (Summer 1968), 6-14.

_____. "The Canadian Poet: Part II, After Confederation." CANADIAN LITERATURE, 38 (Autumn 1968), 41-49.

_____. "Colonialism and Nationalism in Canadian Poetry Before Confederation." PROCEEDINGS OF THE CANADIAN HISTORICAL ASSOCIATION (1944), 74-85.

_____. " 'Our Poets'--A Sketch of Canadian Poetry in the Nineteenth Century." UNIVERSITY OF TORONTO QUARTERLY, 12 (October 1942), 75-94.

Tait, Michael. "Playwrights in a Vacuum: English-Canadian Drama in the Nineteenth Century." CANADIAN LITERATURE, 16 (Spring 1963), 3-18.

An examination of the dramatic works of Heavysege, Mair, and Wilfred Campbell which were never performed but do "show a degree of skill, poetic if not dramatic in isolated sections."

Thomas, Clara. "Happily Ever After: Canadian Women in Fiction and Fact." CANADIAN LITERATURE, 34 (Autumn 1967), 43-53.

> A cursory look at such women writers as Sara Jeannette Duncan, C. P. Traill, Susanna Moodie, Anna Jameson, and at the women in the novels of Grove and Margaret Laurence.

Watt, Frank W. "The Growth of Proletarian Literature in Canada, 1872-1902." DALHOUSIE REVIEW, 40 (Summer 1960), 157-73.

> An examination of proletarian literature which largely appeared serially in such journals as the ONTARIO WORKMAN and LABOR ADVOCATE.

C. SELECTED THESES

Asher, Stanley A. "Playwriting in Canada: An Historical Survey." University of Montreal, 1962.

Ballstadt, Carl. "The Quest for Canadian Identity in Pre-Confederation English-Canadian Literature." University of Western Ontario, 1959.

Barnett, Elizabeth S. "The Memoirs of Pioneer Women Writers in Ontario." McGill University, 1934.

Beyea, G[eorge] P. "The Canadian Novel Prior to Confederation." University of New Brunswick, 1950.

> Extensive studies of such writers as Frances Brooke, Julia Hart, Walter Bates, John Richardson, Rosanna Leprohon, and the Strickland sisters, with a final chapter on some very minor novelists such as Mary Bennett, John Laskey, and others.

Brierley, James G. "A Study of Literature in English Produced in the Province of Quebec Prior to Confederation." McGill University, 1927.

Cogswell, Frederick W. "The Canadian Novel from Confederation to World War I." University of New Brunswick, 1950.

> Concentrates on Gilbert Parker, Sara Jeannette Duncan, Susan Frances Harrison, Robert Barr, and Norman Duncan.

Conroy, Patricia. "A History of the Theatre in Montreal Prior to Confederation." McGill University, 1936.

Dalton, Sister Mary Katherine. "Poetry of the Confederation." University of British Columbia, 1964.

Djwa, Sandra Ann. "Metaphor, World View and Continuity of Canadian Poetry: A Study of the Major English-Canadian Poets with a Computer Concordance to Metaphor." University of British Columbia, 1968.

Edwards, Mary Jane. "Fiction and Montreal, 1769-1885." University of Toronto, 1969.

Gammon, Donald B. "The Concept of Nature in Nineteenth-Century Canadian Poetry, with Special Reference to Goldsmith, Sangster and Roberts." University of New Brunswick, 1948.

Greer, Reginald Thomas. "Influence of Canadian Literature upon the Growth of Canadian Nationality to Confederation." Ottawa University, 1937.

Hall, Chipman. "A Survey of the Indian's Role in English-Canadian Literature to 1900." Dalhousie University, 1969.

Hayne, David M. "The Historical Novel and French Canada." Ottawa University, 1945.

Keller, Ella Lorraine. "The Development of the Canadian Short Story." University of Saskatchewan, 1950.

Klinck, Carl F. "Formative Influences upon the '1860 Group' of Canadian Poets." Columbia University, 1929.

Lawler, James. "Wordsworth's Influence on Major Early Canadian Poets." University of Montreal, 1963.

Leechman, Douglas. "The 'Red Indian' of Literature: A Study in the Perpetuation of Error." Ottawa University, 1941.

McDougall, Robert L. "A Study of Canadian Periodical Literature of the 19th Century." University of Toronto, 1950.

McDowell, M. "A History of Canadian Children's Literature to 1900, together with a check list." University of New Brunswick, 1957.

MacKie, Richard George. "Three Seventeenth Century Newfoundland Propagandists." University of New Brunswick, 1968.

McRae, C. Fred. "The Victorian Age in Canadian Poetry." University of Toronto, 1953.

Maybee, Janet. "A Calendar of Theatre Performances in Halifax 1850-1880."

Dalhousie University, 1965.

Oland, Sidney. "Materials for a History of the Theatre in Early Halifax." Dalhousie University, 1967.

Rogers, Amos Robert. "American Recognition of Canadian Authors Writing in English, 1890-1960." University of Michigan, 1964.

Watt, Frank W. "Radicalism in English-Canadian Literature Since Confederation." University of Toronto, 1957.

Chapter 3

ANTHOLOGIES

Chapter 3

ANTHOLOGIES

Anthologies not only provide the student of literature with convenient surveys of long periods of literary production but, more importantly, with indications of the literary tastes of previous generations of readers and of the changes, from one generation to another, in those tastes. It is for this reason, therefore, that the anthologies of Canadian literature listed below are arranged chronologically. The annotations may offer some indication of their scope, but the reader is also encouraged to look at A. J. M. Smith's article, "Canadian Anthologies, New and Old," UNIVERSITY OF TORONTO QUARTERLY, 11 (July 1942), 457-74, in which many of these books are expertly analyzed.

Dewart, Edward Hartley. SELECTIONS FROM CANADIAN POETS; WITH OCCASIONAL CRITICAL AND BIOGRAPHICAL NOTES, AND AN INTRODUCTORY ESSAY ON CANADIAN POETRY. Montreal: John Lovell, 1864. Reprint ed. with introduction by Douglas Lochhead. Toronto: University of Toronto Press, 1973.

> This first anthology of Canadian poetry, designed to rescue "from oblivion some of the floating pieces of Canadian authorship worthy of preservation in a more permanent form," contains approximately 175 poems by almost fifty writers. Included are such poets as Sangster, Reade, McLachlan, Leprohon, Dewart, McGee, Heavysege, and Moodie. Its basis of selection is literary rather than nationalistic, but its chief value, as A. J. M. Smith observes, is its introduction, where one finds such statements as this: "There is a large class of persons who could scarcely conceive it possible that a Canadian Lyric might have as deep and true feeling as those they have most observed; or that a Canadian poet might be as highly gifted as some of the favourite names who are crowned with wreaths of unfading fame. And yet such things are not altogether inconceivable."

Lighthall, William Douw. SONGS OF THE GREAT DOMINION: VOICES FROM THE FORESTS AND WATERS, THE SETTLEMENTS AND CITIES OF CANADA. London: Walter Scott, 1889. Reprint ed. in facsimile. Toronto: Coles Publishing Co., 1971.

> Contains 163 poems by fifty-six authors; is very strongly patriotic,

with statements such as this: "Canada, Eldest Daughter of the
Empire, is the Empire's completest type! She is the full-grown of
the family,--the one first to come of age and gone out into life
as a nation; and she has in her young hands the solution of all
those questions which must interest every true Briton, proud and
careful of the acquisitions of British discovery and conquest."
But, in spite of the fact that a great deal of the poetry reflects
that bias, Lighthall's anthology is the best of all the early anthologies.

Wetherell, J. E. LATER CANADIAN POEMS. Toronto: Copp Clark Co.,
1893.

A collection of poems written between 1880 and 1893 including
the young and popular writers such as George Frederick Cameron,
Wilfred Campbell, Bliss Carman, Archibald Lampman, Duncan
Campbell Scott, and Frederick George Scott.

Roberts, William Carman, Theodore Roberts, and Elizabeth Roberts MacDonald.
NORTHLAND LYRICS. SELECTED AND ARRANGED WITH A PROLOGUE BY
CHARLES G. D. ROBERTS AND AN EPILOGUE BY BLISS CARMAN. Boston:
Small, Maynard, 1899.

A small collection of poems from that poetic family, exhibiting
greater nepotism than poetic ability.

Rand, Theodore H. A TREASURY OF CANADIAN VERSE. Toronto: Briggs,
1900. 2nd ed. Toronto: Henry Frowde, 1904.

Approximately 350 poems by 135 poets, many of them justifiably
forgotten. The selection is marked by a disturbing unevenness,
and a majority of the poems are of poorer quality than those
chosen by Lighthall.

Hardy, E. A. SELECTIONS FROM THE CANADIAN POETS. Toronto: Morang,
1909. Reprint ed. Toronto: Macmillan, 1925.

An example of the "school anthology"; a poor selection, made all
the poorer by the omission of Bliss Carman and G. D. Roberts
(whose publishing rights were withheld).

Burpee, Lawrence J. A CENTURY OF CANADIAN SONNETS. Toronto:
Musson, 1910.

Approximately 100 sonnets by some sixty poets, most of whom do
little credit to the sonnet tradition.

Whyte-Edgar, Mrs. C. M. A WREATH OF CANADIAN SONG. Toronto:
Briggs, 1910.

An attempt to "resurrect" some of the early Canadian poets and
poetasters, such as Arthur Weir and Nicholas Flood Davin.

Campbell, [William] Wilfred. THE OXFORD BOOK OF CANADIAN VERSE. Toronto: Oxford University Press, [1913].

> This is interesting only as an example of Campbell's poor taste in poetry, and offers no sense of the development of Canadian poetry. In 1960 this recognized fault was rectified in A. J. M. Smith's new version of THE OXFORD BOOK OF CANADIAN VERSE.

Garvin, John W. CANADIAN POETS. Toronto: McClelland & Stewart, 1916. Rev. ed. 1926.

> A representative collection of seventy-five poets, chiefly of the nineteenth century, including a number of minor poets not represented elsewhere. Biographical sketches and photos of the poets included.

Watson, Albert Durrant, and Lorne Albert Pierce. OUR CANADIAN LITERATURE: REPRESENTATIVE PROSE AND VERSE. Toronto: Ryerson, 1922. Rev. and enl. by Lorne Pierce and Bliss Carman, 1935; further rev. and enl. by V. B. Rhodenizer, 1954.

> A very popular anthology; useful for authors no longer included in modern anthologies and for the change in taste between 1922 and 1954. Author and title index.

Broadus, Edmund Kemper, and Eleanor Broadus. A BOOK OF CANADIAN PROSE AND POETRY. Toronto: Macmillan, 1923.

> The editors describe the book as "a representative selection of Canadian poems which reflect the love of country or of empire; which relate to Canadian history; or which depict or are inspired by the Canadian landscape." In spite of such a proscriptive basis, however, the anthology is a good one, especially in its choice of prose. It anthologizes for the first time excerpts from the works of Gilbert Parker, William Kirby, Susanna Moodie, Joseph Howe, Thomas D'Arcy McGee, and others.

Caswell, Edward S. CANADIAN SINGERS AND THEIR SONGS: A COLLECTION OF PORTRAITS, AUTOGRAPH POEMS AND BRIEF BIOGRAPHIES. Toronto: McClelland & Stewart, 1925.

> One hundred and four poets included; an interesting collection of photographs and poor holographs.

Stephen, A. M. THE GOLDEN TREASURY OF CANADIAN VERSE. Toronto: Dent, 1928.

> An example of what school-children were reading; even in 1928 the bulk of the popular poetry was nineteenth century.

Gustafson, Ralph. ANTHOLOGY OF CANADIAN POETRY (ENGLISH). Harmondsworth, England: Penguin, 1942. Rev. ed. 1967.

The 1942 edition is very lean, with very little "colonial" poetry, although the later Confederation poets are well represented. The revised edition, in keeping with a renewed interest in early Canadian literature, includes selections from such early writers as Heavysege, McLachlan, Sangster, and Mair.

Smith, A[rthur] J[ames] M[arshall]. THE BOOK OF CANADIAN POETRY: A CRITICAL AND HISTORICAL ANTHOLOGY. Toronto: W. J. Gage, 1943. 3rd ed., rev. and enl., 1957.

This vies with Klinck and Watters, below, as the best-designed anthology to date; arranged chronologically, and divided into periods which define the historical development of Canadian Literature. Good bibliography.

Maxwell, L. M. B. THE RIVER ST. JOHN AND ITS POETS. N.p.: Privately printed, 1945.

A collection of regional writers, including Odell, Hogg, Roberts, and Carman. Of only passing interest.

Lande, Lawrence M. OLD LAMPS AGLOW: AN APPRECIATION OF EARLY CANADIAN POETRY. Montreal: Privately printed, 1957.

A random personal selection of some early and little-known Canadian poets, offering extracts from one or two poems by each, with facsimile title-pages of their works.

Bourinot, Arthur S. AT THE MERMAID INN: BEING SELECTIONS FROM ESSAYS ON LIFE AND LITERATURE WHICH APPEARED IN THE TORONTO 'GLOBE' 1892-1893. Ottawa: Privately printed, 1958.

The title of this book is the title of a column written for the GLOBE by Archibald Lampman, Wilfred Campbell and Duncan Campbell Scott touching on a diversity of topics associated with poetry, the arts and nationalism.

Ross, Malcolm M. POETS OF THE CONFEDERATION. Toronto: McClelland & Stewart, 1960.

An excellent collection of the poetry of Charles G. D. Roberts, Bliss Carman, Archibald Lampman, and Duncan Campbell Scott. Its title, however, is somewhat misleading, for while these poets are the best of that time they are by no means the only poets worth anthologizing. Selections from the works of Wilfred Campbell, Crawford, Mair, Cameron, and other minor poets would have enhanced the anthology and given a more balanced picture of the literary production of the period.

Moir, John S. RHYMES OF REBELLION: BEING A SELECTION OF CONTEMPORARY VERSES ABOUT THE "RECENT UNPLEASANTNESS" IN UPPER CANADA, 1837. Toronto: Ryerson, 1965.

Collected from newspapers of the day.

Smith, A[rthur] J[ames] M[arshall]. THE BOOK OF CANADIAN PROSE. VOL.
I: EARLY BEGINNINGS TO CONFEDERATION. Toronto: W. J. Gage,
1965.

Includes excerpts from the writings of fifteen Canadian authors,
with a nice balance of explorers, politicians, and belletristic
writers. An excellent anthology with a good introduction.

Gnarowski, Michael. THREE EARLY POEMS FROM LOWER CANADA. Montreal: Lawrence M. Lande Foundation, 1969.

Included are Thomas Cary, "Abram's Plains" (1789); J. Mackay,
"Quebec Hill" (1797); Cornwall Bayley, "Canada" (1805).

Sinclair, David. NINETEENTH-CENTURY NARRATIVE POEMS. Toronto:
McClelland & Stewart, 1972.

The only anthology devoted to a reprinting of some fine long dis-
cursive poems by Goldsmith, Howe, Sangster, Kirby, McLachlan,
and Crawford, poems which, perhaps more than any of the shorter
lyrics, create a large mythopoeic vision of the Canadian landscape.
Many of the poems will be new to most readers, having been
buried in a single publication now unattainable. An excellent
introduction precedes the poetry.

Edwards, Mary Jane, et al. THE EVOLUTION OF CANADIAN LITERATURE
IN ENGLISH: THE BEGINNINGS TO 1867. Toronto: Holt, Rinehart &
Winston, 1973.

_____. THE EVOLUTION OF CANADIAN LITERATURE IN ENGLISH: 1867-
1914. Toronto: Holt, Rinehart & Winston, 1973.

Two excellent anthologies (in a series of four), with choice selections from thirty-two authors. Long introduction with briefer introductions for each author and with bibliographies. The two together offer the beginning reader the most comprehensive and representative introduction to the early literature of Canada.

Klinck, Carl F., and R[eginald] E[yre] Watters. CANADIAN ANTHOLOGY.
3rd ed., rev. and enl. Toronto: W. J. Gage, 1974.

For a general, yet comprehensive survey of English-Canadian literature from the Colonial period up to the 1960s this anthology provides the best approach. Arranged chronologically, the first three
sections deal with pre-1900 writing, offering 125 well-chosen pieces
of prose and poetry by thirty-five authors. A seventy-five page
bibliography lists both primary and secondary materials for all the
authors included.

McLay, Catherine M. CANADIAN LITERATURE: THE BEGINNINGS TO THE 20th CENTURY. Toronto: McClelland & Stewart, 1974.

Another excellent anthology with fine introduction, judicial choice of authors, and good biographical introductions for each.

Lochhead, Douglas and Raymond Souster. 100 POEMS OF NINETEENTH CENTURY CANADA. Toronto: Macmillan, 1974.

Among the thirty-four poets included in this new anthology are the major Canadian Confederation writers (Roberts, Carman, Lampman and Scott), but its chief value lies in its inclusion of several minor writers such as Evan MacColl, Goldwin Smith, John Reade, Grant Allen and S.M. Bayliss. Contains a good introduction with biographical notes appended. An excellent paperback anthology.

Chapter 4

MAJOR AUTHORS

Chapter 4
MAJOR AUTHORS

I have, perhaps presumptuously, based my choice of "major" authors on my own reading of Canadian literature and also (less presumptuously) on the critical judgment of the compilers of THE LITERARY HISTORY OF CANADA. Thus chosen, there are twelve writers whose works can be considered "major" contributions to the literary history of Canada.

For each I have offered an introductory evaluation which, in part, justifies that writer's inclusion in this chapter, but which is intended primarily to provide some indication of the kind and quality of writing produced. For each author, the arrangement of titles will be as follows:

> Bibliographies and Manuscripts
>
> Collected Works
>
> Biographies, Letters, and Autobiographies
>
> Primary Works
>> Poetry
>> Fiction
>> Drama
>> Other Prose
>
> Criticism

The primary works will be listed chronologically and the criticism alphabetically by author. I have attempted to be as comprehensive as possible, omitting from the criticism only those articles (and there are few of them) which take but passing notice of the author. Where any primary work is omitted, the reader is alerted to the omission and the reasons for it.

CAMPBELL, WILLIAM WILFRED (1858-1918)

Campbell is generally grouped with the so-called "Confederation" poets (Carman, Lampman, Roberts, and Scott) who, in the last decades of the nineteenth century, lifted Canadian poetry to its highest peak of development. By and large, however, he is considered to be the least accomplished of that group: he does not rate a place in Malcolm Ross's anthology, POETS OF THE CONFEDERATION (Toronto, 1960), and he is labelled "minor" (inferior, by implication, to Isabella Valancy Crawford) in Carl F. Klinck's LITERARY HISTORY OF CANADA (Toronto, 1968). On the basis on his "nature" poetry alone, such an assessment is indeed justified; but in terms of his total contribution to Canadian literature, he deserves to be included in this "major" category. A great deal of his poetry, and THE DREAD VOYAGE in particular, provides a more provocative reading experience than any other poetry of the period and has not yet received adequate critical attention.

MANUSCRIPTS

Harlowe, Dorothy. A CATALOGUE OF CANADIAN MANUSCRIPTS COLLECTED BY LORNE PIERCE AND PRESENTED TO QUEEN'S UNIVERSITY. Toronto: Ryerson, 1946.

> Relevant material in Part II, pp. 92-99.

COLLECTED WORKS

THE POEMS OF WILFRED CAMPBELL. Toronto: Briggs, 1905.

THE POETICAL WORKS OF WILFRED CAMPBELL. Ed. with "memoir" by W. J. Vykes. Toronto: Hodder & Stoughton, 1923.

POETRY

SNOWFLAKES AND SUNBEAMS. St. Stephen, N.B.: St. Croix Courier Press, 1888.

LAKE LYRICS AND OTHER POEMS. St. John, N.B.: Macmillan, 1889.

THE DREAD VOYAGE AND OTHER POEMS. Toronto: Briggs, 1893.

BEYOND THE HILLS OF DREAM. Boston: Houghton Mifflin, 1899. Reprint ed. Toronto: Morang, 1900.

SAGAS OF VASTER BRITAIN. POEMS OF THE RACE, THE EMPIRE, AND THE DIVINITY OF MAN. Toronto: Musson; London: Hodder & Stoughton, 1914.

FICTION—NOVELS

IAN OF THE ORCADES; OR, THE ARMOURER OF GIRNIGOE. Edinburgh: Oliphant, Anderson & Ferrier, 1906.

A BEAUTIFUL REBEL. A ROMANCE OF UPPER CANADA IN 1812. Toronto: Westminster; London: Hodder & Stoughton, 1909.

DRAMA

MORDRED AND HILDEBRAND: A BOOK OF TRAGEDIES. Ottawa: Durie, 1895.

POETICAL TRAGEDIES. Toronto: Briggs, 1908.
    Contains "Mordred," "Dulac," "Morning," and "Hildebrand."

OTHER PROSE

"Life and Letters." A column in THE EVENING JOURNAL (Ottawa), each Saturday, August 22, 1903 - June 24, 1905.

CANADA. Painted by T. Mower Martin; described by Campbell. London: A. C. Black, 1907.

THE BEAUTY, HISTORY, ROMANCE, AND MYSTERY OF THE CANADIAN LAKE REGION. Toronto: Musson, 1910. Rev. ed. 1914.

THE SCOTSMAN IN CANADA. Vol. I. Toronto: Musson, [1911].

AT THE MERMAID INN, CONDUCTED BY A. LAMPMAN, W. W. CAMPBELL, AND DUNCAN C. SCOTT. Ed. A. S. Bourinot. Ottawa: Bourinot, 1958.
    Essays from the Toronto GLOBE, 1892-93.

CRITICISM

Allison, W. T. "William Wilfred Campbell." CANADIAN BOOKMAN, 1 (April 1919), 65-66.

Barnett, E[lizabeth] S. "The Poetry of William Wilfred Campbell." CANADIAN BOOKMAN, 17 (August 1935), 93-94.

Burpee, L[awrence] J. "Canadian Poet: W. W. Campbell." SEWANEE REVIEW, 8 (October 1900), 425-36.

Graham, Jean. "Canadian Celebrities. 66: Mr. Wilfred Campbell." CANADIAN MAGAZINE, 26 (December 1905), 109-11.

Klinck, Carl F. "William Wilfred Campbell: Poet of Lakes." CANADIAN BOOKMAN, 21 (August 1939), 34-37.

_____. WILFRED CAMPBELL: A STUDY IN LATE VICTORIAN PROVINCIALISM. Toronto: Ryerson, 1942.

Knister, Raymond. "The Poetical Works of Wilfred Campbell." QUEEN'S QUARTERLY, 31 (May 1924), 435-49.

Mackay, L. A. "W. W. Campbell." CANADIAN FORUM, 14 (October 1933), 66-67.

Miller, Judith. "Towards a Canadian Aesthetic: Descriptive Colour in the Landscape Poetry of Duncan Campbell Scott, Archibald Lampman, and William Wilfred Campbell." Thesis, University of Waterloo, 1970.

Muddiman, Bernard. "William Wilfred Campbell." QUEEN'S QUARTERLY, 27 (October 1919), 201-10.

Ower, John. "Portraits of the Landscape as Poet: Canadian Nature as Aesthetic Symbol in Three Confederation Writers." JOURNAL OF CANADIAN STUDIES, 6 (February 1971), 27-32.

Scott, Colin A. "William Wilfred Campbell." CANADIAN MAGAZINE, 2 (January 1894), 270-74.

Stevenson, O. J. "Who's Who in Canadian Literature: William Wilfred Campbell." CANADIAN BOOKMAN, 9 (March 1927), 67-71.

Sykes, W. J. "Wilfred Campbell." In LEADING CANADIAN POETS, pp.37-44. Ed. W. P. Percival. Toronto: Ryerson, 1948.

Campbell, William Wilfred

Tait, Michael. "Playwrights in a Vacuum: English-Canadian Drama in the Nineteenth Century." CANADIAN LITERATURE, 16 (Spring 1963), 3-18.

Tucker, J. A. "The Poems of William Wilfred Campbell." UNIVERSITY OF TORONTO QUARTERLY, 1 (May 1895), 140-45.

CARMAN, BLISS (1861-1929)

Bliss Carman, cousin to Charles G. D. Roberts and descendant of Daniel Bliss, the grandfather of Ralph Waldo Emerson, was born in Fredericton, New Brunswick. After studying at Harvard, where he met Richard Hovey (they later collaborated in writing the "Vagabondia" series), he settled in New York and spent the rest of his life in the United States, returning to Canada frequently for visits and lecture tours. Carman's poetry was strongly influenced by the 'transcendentalist' writers and by the 'unitrinian' philosophy formulated during his acquaintance with Mary Perry King. Among his vast corpus, chiefly lyrics and ballads, there are many trite and childish poems; on the other hand, there are many which, in their evocation of mood, are among the finest lyrics written. "Low Tide on Grand Pré" is a memorable example.

BIBLIOGRAPHIES AND MANUSCRIPTS

Harlowe, Dorothy. A CATALOGUE OF CANADIAN MANUSCRIPTS COLLECTED BY LORNE PIERCE AND PRESENTED TO QUEEN'S UNIVERSITY. Toronto: Ryerson, 1946.

> Part I is devoted entirely to listing the extensive collection of Carman MSS. at Queen's.

Morse, William Inglis. BLISS CARMAN: BIBLIOGRAPHY, LETTERS, FUGITIVE VERSES, AND OTHER DATA. Windham, Conn.: Hawthorn House, 1941.

Sherman, F. F. A CHECK LIST OF FIRST EDITIONS OF THE WORKS OF BLISS CARMAN. New York: Privately printed, 1913. Updated version by R. H. Hathaway published in BLISS CARMAN, pp. 171-84, by Odell Shepard (Toronto: McClelland & Stewart, 1923).

Stephens, Donald. "Letters and Manuscripts of Bliss Carman." In BLISS CARMAN, pp. 138-39. New York: Twayne Publishers, 1966.

COLLECTED WORKS

POEMS. 2 vols. London: Murray, 1904.

BLISS CARMAN'S POEMS. Toronto: McClelland & Stewart, 1931.

THE SELECTED POEMS OF BLISS CARMAN. Ed. with introduction by Lorne Pierce. Toronto: McClelland & Stewart, 1954.

POETRY

FLOWER OF THE ROSE. By Louis Norman [pseud.] New York: Primrose Bindery, 1892.

LOW TIDE ON GRAND PRÉ. Toronto: Copp Clark, [1889].
> This was an unauthorized edition in the "Canadian Series of Booklets" and the author's name is misspelled "Carmen." The title poem was originally published in THE ATLANTIC MONTHLY, 1887. The first authorized edition, more extensive than this, was published by Charles L. Webster (New York, 1893).

ST. KAVIN. A BALLAD. Cambridge, Mass.: Wilson, 1894.

SONGS FROM VAGABONDIA (with Richard Hovey). Boston: Copeland & Day, 1894. Reprint ed. New York: Johnson Reprint Corp., 1969.

AT MICHAELMAS. A LYRIC. Wolfville, N. S.: Acadian Press, 1895.

BEHIND THE ARRAS. A BOOK OF THE UNSEEN. Boston: Lamson, Wolffe, 1895.

A SEAMARK. A THRENODY FOR ROBERT LOUIS STEVENSON. Boston: Lamson, Wolffe, 1895.

MORE SONGS FROM VAGABONDIA (with Richard Hovey). Boston: Lamson, Wolffe, 1896.

BALLADS OF LOST HAVEN. A BOOK OF THE SEA. Boston: Lamson, Wolffe, 1897.

THE GIRL IN THE POSTER. For a design by Miss Ethel Reed. Springfield, Mass.: Wayside Press, 1897.

BY THE AURELIAN WALL, AND OTHER ELEGIES. Boston: Lamson, Wolffe, 1898.

CORYDON. A TRILOGY IN COMMEMORATION OF MATTHEW ARNOLD. Fredericton, N. B.: MacNutt, 1898.

THE GREEN BOOK OF THE BARDS. Cambridge, Mass.: Harvard University Press, 1898.

LAST SONGS FROM VAGABONDIA (with Richard Hovey). Boston: Small, Maynard, 1900.

CHRISTMAS EVE AT ST. KAVIN'S. New York: Kimball, 1901.

BALLADS AND LYRICS. London: A. H. Bullen, 1902.

FROM THE BOOK OF MYTHS. "Pipes of Pan," no. 1. Boston: L. C. Page, 1902.

ODE ON THE CORONATION OF KING EDWARD. Boston: L. C. Page, 1902.

SAPPHO. LYRICS. New York: Privately printed, 1902.

FROM THE GREEN BOOK OF THE BARDS. "Pipes of Pan," no. 2. Boston: L. C. Page, 1903.

A VISION OF SAPPHO. New York: Privately printed, 1903.

THE WORD AT ST. KAVIN'S. Nelson, N.H.: Monadock Press, 1903.

SAPPHO: ONE HUNDRED LYRICS. Introduction by Charles G. D. Roberts. Boston: L. C. Page, 1904.

SONGS OF THE SEA CHILDREN. "Pipes of Pan," no. 3. Boston: L. C. Page, 1904.

SONGS FROM A NORTHERN GARDEN. "Pipes of Pan," no. 4. Boston: L. C. Page, 1904.

FROM THE BOOK OF VALENTINES. "Pipes of Pan," no. 5. Boston: L. C. Page, 1905.

THE PIPES OF PAN: DEFINITIVE EDITION. Boston: L. C. Page, 1906.

Brings together the five books in the "Pipes of Pan" Series.

THE PRINCESS OF THE TOWER, THE WISE MEN FROM THE EAST, AND TO THE WINGED VICTORY. New York: Village Press, 1906.

THE GATE OF PEACE. New York: Village Press, 1907.
> Nearly all copies of this edition were destroyed by fire and the poem was reprinted in 1909 by John Hershaw of New York.

THE PATH TO SANKOTY. Siasconset, Mass.: The Figt Shop, 1908.

THE ROUGH RIDER AND OTHER POEMS. New York: Mitchell Kennerley, 1909.

A PAINTER'S HOLIDAY, AND OTHER POEMS. New York: F. F. Sherman, 1911.

SONGS FROM VAGABONDIA, MORE SONGS FROM VAGABONDIA, LAST SONGS FROM VAGABONDIA. 3 vols. in 1. Boston: Small Maynard, 1911.
> An omnibus edition of the "Vagabondia" series.

ECHOES FROM VAGABONDIA. Boston: Small, Maynard, 1912.

DAUGHTERS OF DAWN: A LYRICAL PAGEANT (with Mary Perry King). New York: Mitchell Kennerley, 1914.

EARTH'S DEITIES, AND OTHER RHYTHMIC MASQUES (with Mary Perry King). New York: Mitchell Kennerley, 1914.

APRIL AIRS. A BOOK OF NEW ENGLAND LYRICS. Boston: Small, Maynard, 1916.

FOUR SONNETS. Boston: Small, Maynard, 1916.

THE MAN OF THE MARNE, AND OTHER POEMS (with Mary Perry King). New Canaan, Conn.: Ponus Press, 1918.

LATER POEMS. Appreciation by R. H. Hathaway. Toronto: McClelland & Stewart, 1921.

BALLADS AND LYRICS. Toronto: McClelland & Stewart, 1923.

FAR HORIZONS. Toronto: McClelland & Stewart, 1925.

SANCTUARY. SUNSHINE HOUSE SONNETS. New York: Dodd, Mead, 1929.

WILD GARDEN. New York: Dodd, Mead, 1929.

THE MUSIC OF EARTH. Foreword and notes by Lorne Pierce. Toronto: Ryerson, 1931.

YOUTH IN THE AIR. A POEM. Palo Alto, Calif.: Yerba Buena Press, 1932.

TO A CHICKADEE. Palo Alto, Calif.: Yerba Buena Press, 1933.

For a detailed list of published broadsheets see NATIONAL UNION CATALOG: PRE-1956 IMPRINTS (Library of Congress) under "Carman" and "A Check List of First Editions of the Works of Bliss Carman," compiled by F. F. Sherman, in BLISS CARMAN, pp. 171-84, by Odell Shepard (Toronto: McClelland & Stewart, 1923).

FICTION

THE VENGEANCE OF NOEL BRASSARD; A TALE OF THE ACADIAN EXPULSION. Cambridge, Mass.: Harvard University Press, [1899].

OTHER PROSE

THE FRIENDSHIP OF ART. Boston: L. C. Page, 1904.
    Essays.

THE POETRY OF LIFE. Boston: L. C. Page, 1905.
    Essays.

THE MAKING OF PERSONALITY (with Mary Perry King). Boston: L. C. Page, 1908.
    Essays.

ADDRESS TO THE GRADUATING CLASS 1911 OF THE UNITRINIAN SCHOOL OF PERSONAL HARMONIZING. New York: Tabord Press, 1911.

JAMES WHITCOMB RILEY. AN ESSAY BY BLISS CARMAN AND SOME LETTERS TO HIM FROM JAMES WHITCOMB RILEY. New York: Smith, [1917].

TALKS ON POETRY AND LIFE. Toronto: Ryerson, 1926.
    Five lectures given at the University of Toronto in December, 1925.

MISCELLANEOUS

BLISS CARMAN'S SCRAPBOOK. A TABLE OF CONTENTS. Ed. Lorne Pierce.
Toronto: Ryerson, 1931.

CRITICISM

Archer, William. "Bliss Carman." In POETS OF THE YOUNGER GENERA-
TION, pp. 66-82. London: Lane, 1902.

Brown, Harry W. "Bliss Carman's Latest Book of Poems." CANADIAN MAGA-
ZINE, 6 (March 1896), 477-81.

Cappon, James. "Bliss Carman's Beginnings." QUEEN'S QUARTERLY, 36
(October 1929), 637-65.

_____. BLISS CARMAN AND THE LITERARY CURRENTS AND INFLUENCES
OF HIS TIME. Toronto: Ryerson, 1930.

Douglas, R. W. "Canada's Poet Laureate: Bliss Carman." BRITISH COLUMBIA
MONTHLY, 19 (July and August, 1922), 4-6, 12, 3-4, 14-16.

Edgar, Pelham. "Bliss Carman." In LEADING CANADIAN POETS, pp. 45-50.
Ed. W. P. Percival. Toronto: Ryerson, 1948.

Gary, C. "The Mystery of Bliss Carman's Ashes." MACLEAN'S MAGAZINE,
August 1, 1951, p. 50.

Gundy, H. P. "The Bliss Carman Centenary." DOUGLAS LIBRARY NOTES
[Queen's University], 10 (Summer 1961), 1-16.

_____. "Bliss Carman's Comic Muse." DOUGLAS LIBRARY NOTES, 20
(Winter 1972), 8-18.

Hathaway, R. H. "Bliss Carman: An Appreciation." CANADIAN MAGAZINE,
56 (April 1921), 521-36.

_____. "Bliss Carman's First Editions." CANADIAN BOOKMAN, 6 (January
1924), 8-9.

_____. "Bliss Carman's Rare Editions." CANADIAN BOOKMAN, 1 (October
1919), 16-17.

_____. "The Poetry of Bliss Carman." SEWANEE REVIEW, 33 (October 1925), 467-83.

_____. "Who's Who in Canadian Literature: Bliss Carman." CANADIAN BOOKMAN, 8 (October 1926), 299-302.

_____. "Vale! Bliss Carman." CANADIAN BOOKMAN, 11 (July 1929), 155-59.

Hind, C. Louis. "Bliss Carman." In MORE AUTHORS AND I, pp. 65-70. New York: Dodd, Mead, 1922.

Lee, H. D. C. BLISS CARMAN: A STUDY IN CANADIAN POETRY. Buxton, England: Herald Printing, 1912.

McCracken, M. S. "Bliss Carman: His Status in the Annals of Canadian Literature." Thesis, Ottawa University, 1936.

MacDonald, Allan H. RICHARD HOVEY: MAN AND CRAFTSMAN. Durham, N.C.: Duke University Press, 1957.

MacFarland, Kenneth. "The Poetry of Bliss Carman." LITERARY MISCELLANY, 2 (Summer 1909), 35-39.

Mackay, L. A. "Bliss Carman." CANADIAN FORUM, 13 (February 1933), 182-83. Reprinted in MASKS OF POETRY, pp. 55-59, edited by A.J.M. Smith (Toronto: McClelland & Stewart, 1962).

McPherson, Hugo. "The Literary Reputation of Bliss Carman: A Study in the Development of Canadian Taste in Poetry." Thesis, University of Western Ontario, 1950.

Marshall, J. "Pipes of Pan." QUEEN'S QUARTERLY, 11 (October 1903), 203-8.

Martin, Mary C. "The Early Development of Bliss Carman." Thesis, University of New Brunswick, 1957.

Massey, Vincent. "Roberts, Carman, Sherman: Canadian Poets." CANADIAN AUTHOR AND BOOKMAN, 23 (Fall 1947), 29-32.

Miller, Muriel. BLISS CARMAN: A PORTRAIT. Toronto: Ryerson, 1935.

Muddiman, Bernard. "A Vignette in Canadian Literature." CANADIAN MAG-AZINE, 40 (March 1913), 451-58.

Pacey, Desmond. "Bliss Carman: A Reappraisal." NORTHERN REVIEW, 3 (February–March 1950), 2–10.

_____. "Bliss Carman." In TEN CANADIAN POETS, pp. 59–113. Toronto: Ryerson, 1958.

_____. "Garland for Bliss Carman." ATLANTIC ADVOCATE, 51 (April 1961), 17, 19–20.

Pierce, Lorne [Albert]. "Bliss Carman." In THREE FREDERICTON POETS, pp. 18–24. Toronto: Ryerson, 1933.

Rittenhouse, Jessie B. "Bliss Carman." In YOUNGER AMERICAN POETS, pp. 46–74. Boston: Little, Brown, 1904.

Roberts, Charles G. D. "Mr. Bliss Carman's Poems." THE CHAP-BOOK, 1 (June 15, 1894), 53–57.

_____. "Bliss Carman." DALHOUSIE REVIEW, 9 (January 1930), 409–17.

_____. "More Reminiscences of Bliss Carman." DALHOUSIE REVIEW, 10 (April 1930), 1–9.

_____. "Some Reminiscences of Bliss Carman in New York." CANADIAN POETRY, 5 (December 1940), 5–10.

Roberts, Lloyd. "Bliss Carman: A Memory." CANADIAN BOOKMAN, 21 (April 1939), 42–46.

Rogers, A[mos] R[obert]. "American Recognition of Bliss Carman and Sir Charles G. D. Roberts." HUMANITIES ASSOCIATION BULLETIN, 22, no. 2 (Spring 1971), 19–24.

Ross, Malcolm M. "A Symbolic Approach to Carman." CANADIAN BOOKMAN, 14 (December 1932), 140–44.

_____. "Carman by the Sea." DALHOUSIE REVIEW, 27 (October 1947), 294–98.

Shepard, Odell. BLISS CARMAN. Toronto: McClelland & Stewart, 1923.

Sorfleet, John Robert. "Bliss Carman's Major Years: A Chronological Study of his Work in Relation to his Thought." Thesis, University of Manitoba, 1971.

Stephens, Donald. "The Influence of English Poets upon the Poetry of Bliss Carman." Thesis, University of New Brunswick, 1955.

_____. "A Maritime Myth." CANADIAN LITERATURE, 9 (Summer 1961), 38-48.

_____. BLISS CARMAN. New York: Twayne Publishers, 1966.

Van Patten, Nathan. "Bliss Carman and the Bibliophile." QUEEN'S QUAR-TERLY, 33 (November 1925), 202-5.

Waldron, Gordon. "Canadian Poetry: A Criticism." CANADIAN MAGAZINE, 8 (December 1896), 101-8.

White, Greenough. "A Pair of Canadian Poets." SEWANEE REVIEW, 7 (January 1899), 48-52.

The other poet is Charles G. D. Roberts.

CRAWFORD, ISABELLA VALANCY (1850-1887)

A poet largely ignored until the 1950's, Crawford has now become the subject of renewed interest among Canadian scholars. Her poetry, once considered "overwrought" and highly romantic, is now seen to be, in mythopoeic terms, an intense and personal interpretation of the Canadian pioneer scene through the employment of a unique symbolic style.

MANUSCRIPTS

Harlowe, Dorothy. A CATALOGUE OF MANUSCRIPTS COLLECTED BY LORNE PIERCE AND PRESENTED TO QUEEN'S UNIVERSITY. Toronto: Ryerson, 1946.

> Pages 100-04 list the manuscripts--prose, poetry, and letters-- which make up the bulk of the Crawford corpus and which remain unpublished.

POETRY

OLD SPOOKES' PASS, MALCOLM'S KATIE, AND OTHER POEMS. Toronto: James Bain, 1884.

THE COLLECTED POEMS OF ISABELLA VALANCY CRAWFORD. Ed. by J. W. Garvin. Introduction by Ethelwyn Wetherald. Toronto: Briggs, 1905. Reprint ed. with introduction by James Reaney. Toronto: University of Toronto Press, 1973.

For a list of Crawford's poems published in newspapers and other serial publications see ISABELLA VALANCY CRAWFORD, by Katherine Hale (Toronto, 1923), pp. 114-17.

CRITICISM

Bessai, Frank. "The Ambivalence of Love in the Poetry of Isabella Valancy

Crawford, Isabella Valancy

Crawford." QUEEN'S QUARTERLY, 77 (Autumn 1970), 404-18.

Burpee, L[awrence] J. "Isabella Valancy Crawford." POET-LORE, 12 (October 1901), 575-86.

Hale, Katherine. ISABELLA VALANCY CRAWFORD. Toronto: Ryerson, 1923.

Hathaway, E. J. "Isabella Valancy Crawford." CANADIAN MAGAZINE, 5 (October 1895), 569-72.

Livesay, Dorothy. "The Native People in our Canadian Literature." ENGLISH QUARTERLY, 4 (Spring 1971), 21-32.

_____. "The Hunters Twain: An Examination of the Narrative Background to Isabella Valancy Crawford's Poems, 'The Dark Stag,' 'The Lily Bed' and 'The Canoe.' " CANADIAN LITERATURE, 55 (Winter 1973), 75-98.

_____. "Tennyson's Daughter or Wilderness Child? The Factual and the Literary Background of Isabella Valancy Crawford." JOURNAL OF CANADIAN FICTION, 2 (Summer 1973), 161-67.

MacGillivray, Richard. "Theme and Imagery in the Poetry of Isabella Valancy Crawford." Thesis, University of New Brunswick, 1963.

McManus, Emily. "With the Canadian Poets. III: Isabella Valancy Crawford." THE PRESBYTERIAN, January 1, 1907, pp. 135-36.

Martin, Mary F. "The Short Life of Isabella Valancy Crawford." DALHOUSIE REVIEW, 52 (Fall 1972), 391-400.

O'Brien, Sister Patricia. "Isabella Valancy Crawford." In PETERBOROUGH: LAND OF SHINING WATERS, pp. 379-83. Toronto: Ryerson, 1967.

Ower, John. "Isabella Valancy Crawford: 'The Canoe.' " CANADIAN LITERATURE, 34 (Autumn 1967), 54-62.

Pomeroy, E[lsie] M. "Isabella Valancy Crawford." CANADIAN POETRY MAGAZINE, 7 (June 1944), 36-38.

Reaney, James. "Isabella Valancy Crawford." In OUR LIVING TRADITION, pp. 268-86. Ed. R. L. McDougall. Toronto: University of Toronto Press, 1959.

Yeoman, Ann. "Towards a Native Mythology: The Poetry of Isabella Valancy Crawford." CANADIAN LITERATURE, 52 (Spring 1972), 39-47.

DUNCAN, SARA JEANNETTE (MRS. COTES) (1861-1922)

Born in Brantford, Ontario, Sara Jeannette Duncan became a newspaper journalist, a successful occupation (with the Toronto GLOBE, THE WEEK, and the
Washington POST) which offered her an opportunity to see the world. Her
travels, in turn, provided the material for a dozen novels and some travel books.
Like Gilbert Parker, she left Canada to live in India and England and so achieved
an international literary popularity. Also like Parker, she used a Daisy Miller
theme, but there the comparison ends. Parker's treatment is superficial; Duncan's,
like that of James, is witty, penetrating, humorous, and eminently entertaining.
In AN AMERICAN GIRL IN LONDON and COUSIN CINDERELLA: A CANA-
DIAN GIRL IN LONDON, she explores the problem of the colonial confronting
old-world social values; in THOSE DELIGHTFUL AMERICANS a young Englishwoman, on a visit to the United States, confronts the new-world values. Few
Canadian women writers have skill equal to that of Duncan; her work deserves
better recognition.

FICTION

AN AMERICAN GIRL IN LONDON. London: Chatto & Windus, 1890.

THE SIMPLE ADVENTURES OF MEMSAHIB. New York: Appleton, 1893.

THE DAUGHTER OF TODAY. New York: Appleton, 1894.

THE STORY OF SONNY SAHIB. London: Macmillan, 1894.

VERNON'S AUNT, BEING THE ORIENTAL EXPERIENCES OF MISS LAVINIA
MOFFATT. London: Chatto & Windus, 1894.

HIS HONOUR AND A LADY. New York: Appleton; Toronto: Rose, 1896.

HILDA, A STORY OF CALCUTTA. New York: Stokes, 1898.

A VOYAGE OF CONSOLATION. London: Methuen, 1899.

> Sequel to AN AMERICAN GIRL IN LONDON.

THE PATH OF A STAR. London: Methuen; Toronto: W. J. Gage, 1899.

THOSE DELIGHTFUL AMERICANS. New York: Appleton, 1902.

THE POOL IN THE DESERT. New York: Appleton, 1903.

> Four novelettes: "The Pool in the Desert," "A Mother in India," "An Impossible Ideal" and "The Hesitation of Miss Anderson."

THE IMPERIALIST. Toronto: Copp Clark, 1904. Ed. with introduction by Claude Bissell. Toronto: McClelland & Stewart, 1961.

SET IN AUTHORITY. New York: Doubleday, 1906.

COUSIN CINDERELLA: A CANADIAN GIRL IN LONDON. New York and Toronto: Macmillan, 1908.

THE BURNT OFFERING. London: Methuen, 1909; New York: J. Lane, 1910.

THE CONSORT. London: Stanley Paul, 1912.

HIS ROYAL HAPPINESS. New York: Appleton, 1914.

THE GOLD CURE. London: Hutchinson, 1922.

TITLE CLEAR. London: Hutchinson, 1922.

OTHER PROSE

A SOCIAL DEPARTURE: HOW ORTHODOCIA AND I WENT ROUND THE WORLD BY OURSELVES. New York: Appleton, 1890.

ON THE OTHER SIDE OF THE LATCH. London: Methuen, 1901. Published as THE CROW'S NEST. New York: Dodd, Mead, 1901.

> Essays.

CRITICISM

Bissell, Claude T. "Introduction" to THE IMPERIALIST. Toronto: McClelland & Stewart, 1961.

Burness, Jean F. "Sara Jeannette Duncan: A Neglected Canadian." ON-
TARIO LIBRARY REVIEW, 45 (August 1961), 205-6.

Cogswell, Frederick W. "The Canadian Novel from Confederation on to World
War I." Thesis, University of New Brunswick, 1950.

Donaldson, F. "Mrs. Everard Cotes." BOOKMAN (London), 14 (June 1898),
65-67.

Goodwin, Rae E. "The Early Journalism of Sara Jeannette Duncan, with a
Chapter of Biography." Thesis, University of Toronto, 1964.

MacMurchy, M. "Mrs. Everard Cotes." BOOKMAN (London), 48 (May 1915),
39-40.

Ross, M. E. "Sara Jeannette Duncan: Personal Glimpses." CANADIAN
LITERATURE, 27 (Winter 1966), 15-19.

GORDON, CHARLES WILLIAM (RALPH CONNOR)

(1860-1937)

There is nothing of the schizophrenic in the Charles Gordon-Ralph Connor dual-
ity: as the former he was a staunch Presbyterian, a campaigner for social jus-
tice, an able preacher, and a strong supporter of the labour movement. As the
latter, the novelist, he was much the same: his novels, clearly on the side of
Good, depict hard-working, Christian manual-labourers emerging victorious from
clashes with unbelievers, scorners, and devious men. Such a summary may make
the novels sound dull, shallow, and inartistic. On the contrary, Connor was
an excellent storyteller, with a penchant for fast action (including violence),
an eye for regional colour, a vivid recollection of his youth, and an ear for
humorous anecdote.

Gordon was born in Glengarry County, Ontario, the setting for his best-loved
work, GLENGARRY SCHOOL DAYS; he served as Presbyterian minister in Banff,
Alberta, and Winnipeg, Manitoba, areas which also provide the background for
other novels. Edward McCourt, in THE CANADIAN WEST IN FICTION, esti-
mates that more than five million copies of Connor's books were sold, making
him one of Canada's best-selling novelists. Only Connor's fictional work is
listed below; for a list of his religious writings see A CHECKLIST OF CANA-
DIAN LITERATURE AND BACKGROUND MATERIALS, by Reginald E. Watters
(Toronto, 1972), p. 788.

AUTOBIOGRAPHY

POSTSCRIPT TO ADVENTURE. New York: Farrar, Straus, 1938.

FICTION—ALL UNDER THE PSEUDONYM "RALPH CONNOR"

BEYOND THE MARSHES. Toronto: Westminster, 1897. Reprint ed. New
York: Revell, 1900.

> Short story.

BLACK ROCK. A TALE OF THE SELKIRKS. Toronto: Westminster; New York:
Revell, 1898.

A collection of sketches which Connor had written for the Presbyterian magazine, THE WESTMINSTER, 1897. Several subsequent editions were issued.

GWEN'S CANYON. Toronto: Westminster, 1898.

Short story, subsequently included in THE SKY PILOT.

THE SKY PILOT. A TALE OF THE FOOTHILLS. Toronto: Westminster; New York: Revell, 1899. Reprint ed. with introduction by Robin W. Winks. Lexington: University of Kentucky Press, 1970.

MICHAEL McGRATH, POSTMASTER. London: Sharp, 1900.

Short story.

THE MAN FROM GLENGARRY. A TALE OF THE OTTAWA. Toronto: Westminster; New York: Revell, 1901. Reprint ed. with introduction by S. R. Beharriell. Toronto: McClelland & Stewart, 1960.

GLENGARRY SCHOOL DAYS. A STORY OF EARLY DAYS IN GLENGARRY. Toronto: Westminster; New York: Revell, 1902. Published as GLENGARRY DAYS. London: Hodder & Stoughton, 1902. Several subsequent editions.

BREAKING THE RECORD. Toronto and New York: Revell, 1904.

Short story.

GWEN, AN IDYLL OF THE CANYON. New York: Revell, 1904.

A reprinting of Chapters 9-13 of THE SKY PILOT.

THE PROSPECTOR. A TALE OF CROW'S NEST PASS. Toronto: Westminster; New York: Revell, 1904.

THE SWAN CREEK BLIZZARD. New York: Revell, 1904.

Short story.

THE PILOT AT SWAN CREEK. London: Hodder & Stoughton, 1905.

Short story.

THE DOCTOR. A TALE OF THE ROCKIES. Toronto: Westminster, 1906. Published as THE DOCTOR OF CROW'S NEST. London: Hodder & Stoughton, 1909.

THE FOREIGNER. A TALE OF SASKATCHEWAN. Toronto: Westminster; New York: Doran, 1909. Published as THE SETTLER. London: Hodder & Stoughton, 1909.

CORPORAL CAMERON OF THE NORTH WEST MOUNTED POLICE. A TALE OF THE McLEOD TRAIL. Toronto: Westminster; London and New York: Hodder & Stoughton, 1912.

THE PATROL OF THE SUNDANCE TRAIL. Toronto: Westminster; New York: Doran; London: Hodder & Stoughton, 1914.

THE MAJOR. Toronto: McClelland & Stewart; New York: Doran; London: Hodder & Stoughton, 1917.

THE SKY PILOT IN NO MAN'S LAND. Toronto: McClelland & Stewart; New York: Doran, 1919.

TO HIM THAT HATH. A NOVEL OF THE WEST TODAY. Toronto: McClelland & Stewart; New York: Doran, 1921.

THE GASPARDS OF PINE CROFT. A ROMANCE OF THE WINDERMERE. Toronto: McClelland & Stewart; New York: Doran; London: Hodder & Stoughton, 1923.

TREADING THE WINEPRESS. Toronto: McClelland & Stewart; London: Hodder & Stoughton, 1925.

THE FRIENDLY FOUR, AND OTHER STORIES. New York: Doran; London: Hodder & Stoughton, 1926.

THE RUNNER. A ROMANCE OF THE NIAGARAS. Toronto: Doubleday, Doran & Gundy, 1929; London: Hodder & Stoughton, 1930.

THE ROCK AND THE RIVER. A ROMANCE OF QUEBEC. Toronto: McClelland & Stewart; New York: Dodd, Mead, 1931; London: Lane, 1932.

THE ARM OF GOLD. Toronto: McClelland & Stewart; New York: Dodd, Mead, 1932; London: Lane, 1933.

THE GIRL FROM GLENGARRY. Toronto: McClelland & Stewart; New York: Dodd, Mead, 1933. Published as THE GLENGARRY GIRL. London: Lane, 1934.

TORCHES THROUGH THE BUSH. A TALE OF GLENGARRY. Toronto: McClelland & Stewart; New York: Dodd, Mead, 1934; London: Lane, 1935.

THE REBEL LOYALIST. Toronto: McClelland & Stewart; New York: Dodd, Mead, 1935; London: Lane, 1936.

THE GAY CRUSADER. A ROMANCE OF QUEBEC. Toronto: McClelland & Stewart; New York: Dodd, Mead, 1936.

HE DWELT AMONG US. New York: Revell; London: Hodder & Stoughton, 1936.

CRITICISM

Adams, Harris L. "The Career of 'Ralph Connor.' " MacLEAN'S MAGAZINE, 25 (April 1913), 109-13.

Carpenter, David C. "Alberta in Fiction." Thesis, University of Alberta, 1973.

Doran, George H. "A Modern Apostle." In CHRONICLES OF BARABBAS, 1884-1934, pp. 200-06. Toronto: McLeod, 1935.

French, Donald G. "Who's Who in Canadian Literature: Ralph Connor." CANADIAN BOOKMAN, 12 (April 1930), 77-79.

LeClerc, Cyprian. "Ralph Connor: Canadian Novelist." Thesis, University of Montreal, 1962.

McCourt, Edward. "Sky Pilot." In THE CANADIAN WEST IN FICTION, pp. 24-41. Toronto: Ryerson, 1949.

Paterson, Beth. "Ralph Connor and His Million-Dollar Sermons." MacLEAN'S MAGAZINE, 26 (November 15, 1953), 56-60.

Thompson, J. Lee and John H. Thompson. "Ralph Connor and the Canadian Identity." QUEEN'S QUARTERLY, 79 (Summer 1972), 159-70.

Watt, Frank W. "Western Myth, the World of Ralph Connor." CANADIAN LITERATURE, 1 (Summer 1959), 26-36.

HALIBURTON, THOMAS CHANDLER (1796-1861)

"Sam Slick" is probably the most universally-known fictional character in Canadian literature. His creator, T. C. Haliburton, was labelled by Artemus Ward "the father of American humor." The Clockmaker series alone went through some seventy editions, mainly in the United States and Great Britain. Haliburton was the first Canadian (and indeed the first colonial) to be honored by Oxford University for his literary achievement.

No attempt is made here to list all the various editions of each work, although certain bibliographical peculiarities are mentioned. All first editions are cited, and some good modern editions are noted. For a more detailed bibliographical listing, see the bibliographies appended to Ray Palmer Baker's edition of SAM SLICK (Toronto, 1923), listed under Prose, below, and V.L.O. Chittick's THOMAS CHANDLER HALIBURTON (New York, 1924), included in the Criticism section, below.

BIBLIOGRAPHY

O'Brien, Arthur Henry. "Haliburton ('Sam Slick') a Sketch and Bibliography." ROYAL SOCIETY OF CANADA TRANSACTIONS, 3rd ser., 3 (1909), Section II, 53-66. Reprint ed. Montreal: Gazette, 1909.

CORRESPONDENCE

Bond, W. H. "The Correspondence of Thomas Chandler Haliburton and Richard Bentley." In THE CANADIAN COLLECTION AT HARVARD UNIVERSITY, pp. 48-105. Ed. W. I. Morse. Bulletin IV (1947).

PROSE

A GENERAL DESCRIPTION OF NOVA SCOTIA. Published anonymously. Halifax: Royal Acadian School, 1823. Rev. ed. 1825.

The authorship has been disputed but was authoritatively assigned to

Haliburton by V. L. O. Chittick in THOMAS CHANDLER HALI-
BURTON, Chapter IV.

AN HISTORICAL AND STATISTICAL ACCOUNT OF NOVA SCOTIA. 2 vols.
Halifax: Joseph Howe, 1829.

THE CLOCKMAKER; OR, THE SAYINGS AND DOINGS OF SAMUEL SLICK
OF SLICKSVILLE. Published anonymously. First Series. Halifax: Joseph
Howe, 1836. Reprint ed., paperback, with introduction by R. L. McDougall.
Toronto: McClelland & Stewart, 1958.

> Chapters 1-21 were published serially in Joseph Howe's NOVA-
> SCOTIAN in 1835 and 1836. These proved so popular that in
> 1836 the series was discontinued; the first chapters plus eleven
> others were then published in book form. An unauthorized second
> edition was published in 1837 by Richard Bentley of London.

Second Series. London: Richard Bentley, 1838.

Third Series. London: Richard Bentley, 1840.

Combined edition. London: Richard Bentley, 1849.

> The best modern combined edition is SAM SLICK (Toronto: Mc-
> Clelland & Stewart, 1923), edited by Ray Palmer Baker (see main
> entry, below).

THE BUBBLES OF CANADA. London: Richard Bentley, 1839.

A REPLY TO THE REPORT OF THE EARL OF DURHAM. Published under the
pseudonym "The Colonist." London: Richard Bentley, 1839.

THE LETTER-BAG OF THE GREAT WESTERN; OR, LIFE IN A STEAMER.
London: Richard Bentley, 1840.

THE ATTACHE; OR, SAM SLICK IN ENGLAND. First Series. 2 vols. London: Richard Bentley, 1843. Second Series. 2 vols. London: Richard Bentley, 1844.

THE OLD JUDGE; OR, LIFE IN A COLONY. 2 vols. London: Henry Colburn,
1849.

> The best selections from this edition have been reprinted in paper-
> back as THE OLD JUDGE, edited by Reginald Eyre Watters (Toronto:
> Clarke Irwin, 1968).

RULE AND MISRULE OF THE ENGLISH IN AMERICA. 2 vols. London: Henry
Colburn, 1851.

TRAITS OF AMERICAN HUMOR, BY NATIVE AUTHORS. Ed. by the author of
"Sam Slick." 3 vols. London: Colburn & Co., 1852.

SAM SLICK'S WISE SAWS AND MODERN INSTANCES; OR, WHAT HE SAID, DID, OR INVENTED. 2 vols. London: Hurst & Blackett, 1853.

THE AMERICANS AT HOME; OR, BYEWAYS, BACKWOODS, AND PRAIRIES. 3 vols. London: Hurst & Blackett, 1854.

NATURE AND HUMAN NATURE. 2 vols. London: Hurst & Blackett, 1855.

AN ADDRESS ON THE PRESENT CONDITION, RESOURCES, AND PROSPECTS OF BRITISH NORTH AMERICA. London: Hurst & Blackett, 1857.

THE SEASON-TICKET. London: Richard Bentley, 1860.

FRAGMENTS FROM SAM SLICK. Selected and arranged by Lawrence J. Burpee. Toronto: Musson, 1909.

SAM SLICK. Ed. with critical estimate by Ray Palmer Baker. Toronto: McClelland & Stewart, 1923.

> An anthology including all the Clockmaker and Attache series, plus five other pieces of Haliburton writing.

SELECTIONS FROM SAM SLICK. Ed. Paul A. W. Wallace. Toronto: Ryerson, 1923.

SAM SLICK IN PICTURES. THE BEST OF THE HUMOUR OF THOMAS CHANDLER HALIBURTON. Illustrated by C. W. Jefferys, R.C.A. Ed. with introduction by Lorne Pierce. Toronto: Ryerson, 1956.

THE SAM SLICK ANTHOLOGY. Ed. with introduction by Reginald Eyre Watters; text modernized by Walter S. Avis. Toronto: Clarke, Irwin, 1969.

CRITICISM

Anon. "Sam Slick: Mark Twain's Inspiration?" TWAINIAN, 16 (March-April, May-June, 1957), 3-4, 4.

Avis, Walter S. "The Speech of Sam Slick." Thesis, Queen's University, 1950.

Baker, Ray Palmer. "Haliburton and the Loyalist Tradition in the Development of American Humor." In A HISTORY OF ENGLISH-CANADIAN LITERATURE TO THE CONFEDERATION, pp. 68-97. Cambridge, Mass.: Harvard University Press, 1920.

Belanger, Reynald. "Canadian Humorists: Leacock, Haliburton, Earle Birney, W. O. Mitchell." Thesis, Laval University, 1967.

Bengtsson, Elna. THE LANGUAGE AND VOCABULARY OF SAM SLICK. Upsala: Lundequistoka Bokhandeln, 1956.

Bissell, Claude T. "Haliburton, Leacock and the American Humourous Tradition." CANADIAN LITERATURE, 39 (Winter 1969), 5–19.

Bourinot, John George. "Thomas Chandler Haliburton." In BUILDERS OF NOVA SCOTIA, pp. 62–5. Toronto: Copp Clark, 1900.

Calnek, W. A., and A. W. Savary. "Thomas Chandler Haliburton." In HISTORY OF THE COUNTY OF ANNAPOLIS, pp. 418–26. Toronto: Briggs, 1897.

Chisholm, M. P. F. "Sam Slick and Catholic Disabilities in Nova Scotia." CATHOLIC WORLD, 64 (January 1897), 459–65.

Chittick, V. L. O. "Books and Music in Haliburton." DALHOUSIE REVIEW, 38 (Summer 1958), 207–21.

_____. "The Gen-u-ine Yankee." In MASKS OF FICTION, pp. 53–80. Ed. A. J. M. Smith. Toronto: McClelland & Stewart, 1961. Reprinted from THOMAS CHANDLER HALIBURTON (New York, 1924), below.

_____. "Haliburton as Member of Parliament." UNIVERSITY OF TORONTO QUARTERLY, 33 (October 1963), 78–88.

_____. "Haliburton on Men and Things." DALHOUSIE REVIEW, 38 (Spring 1958), 55–64.

_____. "Haliburton Postscript I: Ring-Tailed Yankee." DALHOUSIE REVIEW, 37 (Spring 1957), 19–36.

_____. "Haliburton's 'Wise Saws' and Homily Imagery." DALHOUSIE REVIEW, 38 (Autumn 1958), 358–62.

_____. "The Hybrid Comic: Origins of Sam Slick." CANADIAN LITERATURE, 14 (Autumn 1962), 35–42.

_____. "Many-Sided Haliburton." DALHOUSIE REVIEW, 41 (Summer 1961), 194–207.

_____. "The Persuasiveness of Sam Slick." DALHOUSIE REVIEW, 33 (Summer

1953), 88-101.

_____. THOMAS CHANDLER HALIBURTON: A STUDY IN PROVINCIAL TORYISM. New York: Columbia University Press, 1924.

Crofton, F. Blake. HALIBURTON, THE MAN AND THE THINKER. Winslow, N.S.: Anslow, 1889.

_____. "Thomas Chandler Haliburton." ATLANTIC MONTHLY, 69 (March 1892), 355-63.

Fenety, G. E. LIFE AND TIMES OF THE HON. JOSEPH HOWE. St. John, N.B.: Carter, 1896.

Fredericks, Carrie MacMillan. "The Development of Sam Slick: Twenty Years of Change in a Character, 1835-1855." Thesis, Dalhousie University, 1970.

Frye, Northrop. "Haliburton: Mask and Ego." ALPHABET, 5 (December 1962), 58-63.

Harding, L. A. A. "Compassionate Humour in Haliburton." DALHOUSIE REVIEW, 49 (Summer 1969), 223-28.

_____. "Folk Language in Haliburton's Humour." CANADIAN LITERATURE, 24 (Spring 1965), 47-51.

_____. "Yankee at the Court of Judge Haliburton." CANADIAN LITERATURE, 39 (Winter 1969), 62-73.

Harvey, Daniel Cobb. "The Centenary of Sam Slick." DALHOUSIE REVIEW, 16 (January 1937), 420-40.

Liljegren, S. B. CANADIAN HISTORY AND THOMAS CHANDLER HALIBURTON: SOME NOTES ON SAM SLICK. Upsala: Lundequistsoka Bokhandeln, 1969.

Logan, J. D. SCOTT AND HALIBURTON. Halifax, N.S.: Allen, 1921.

_____. THOMAS CHANDLER HALIBURTON. Toronto: Ryerson, [1923?].

_____. "Why Haliburton Has No Successor: An Essay in the Psychology of Creative Satiric Humor." CANADIAN MAGAZINE, 57 (September 1921), 362-68.

MacDonald, Adrian. "Thomas Chandler Haliburton." In CANADIAN PORTRAITS, pp. 52-63. Toronto: Ryerson, 1925.

McDougall, Robert L. "Thomas Chandler Haliburton." In OUR LIVING TRADI-TION, SECOND AND THIRD SERIES, pp. 3-30. Toronto: University of Toronto Press, 1959.

MacMechan, Archibald. "Who's Who in Canadian Literature: Thomas Chandler Haliburton." CANADIAN BOOKMAN, 8 (January 1926), 8-9.

Mahon, A. Wylie, "Sam Slick's Letters." CANADIAN MAGAZINE, 44 (No-vember 1914), 75-79.

Phelps, Arthur L. "Thomas Chandler Haliburton." In CANADIAN WRITERS, pp. 19-27. Toronto: McClelland & Stewart, 1951.

Rimmington, Gerald T. "The Geography of Haliburton's Nova Scotia." DAL-HOUSIE REVIEW, 48 (Winter 1968), 488-99.

Ross, Effie May. "Thomas Chandler Haliburton: Sam Slick, the Founder of American Humor." AMERICANA, 16 (January 1922), 62-70.

Stuart-Stubbs, Basil. "On the Authorship of 'A General Description of Nova Scotia, 1823.'" PAPERS OF THE BIBLIOGRAPHY SOCIETY OF CANADA, 4 (1965), 14-18.

Thompson, David Glen. "Thomas Chandler Haliburton and the Failure of Cana-dian Humour." Thesis, University of Manitoba, 1956.

Trent, William P. "A Retrospect of American Humor." CENTURY MAGAZINE, n.s. 41 (November 1921), 45-64.

Van Tongerloo, R. R. "Thomas Chandler Haliburton: Satirical Humorist." Thesis, University of Manitoba, 1967.

Wilson, Milton. "Haliburton's Tales." THE ENGLISH QUARTERLY, 6 (Winter 1973), 327-44

Wood, Ruth K. "The Creator of the First Yankee in Literature." BOOKMAN (New York), 41 (April 1915), 152-60.

LAMPMAN, ARCHIBALD (1861-1899)

In a brief poetic career, Keatsian in many ways, Lampman produced some of the best and most typical poetry of the Confederation era. Strongly influenced by the English Romantic tradition, he nevertheless brought a considerable independence of insight to bear on the Canadian scene and his poetry is marked by a quality which, all critics agree, is peculiarly "Canadian." The large body of critical work devoted to such a brief career is itself testimony to the esteem in which Lampman is still held.

POETRY

AMONG THE MILLET AND OTHER POEMS. Ottawa: Durie, 1888.

LYRICS OF EARTH. Boston: Copeland & Day, 1895.

ALCYONE. Ottawa: Ogilvy, 1899.

THE POEMS OF ARCHIBALD LAMPMAN. Ed. with "memoir" by Duncan Campbell Scott. Toronto: Morang, 1900. Holiday ed. 2 vols. Toronto: Morang, 1901.

LYRICS OF EARTH: SONNETS AND BALLADS. Introduction by Duncan Campbell Scott. Toronto: Musson, 1925.

AT THE LONG SAULT AND OTHER NEW POEMS. Ed. with introduction by E. K. Brown. Foreword by D. C. Scott. Toronto: Ryerson, 1943.

SELECTED POEMS OF ARCHIBALD LAMPMAN. Chosen with a "memoir" by Duncan Campbell Scott. Toronto: Ryerson, 1947.

THE CITY AT THE END OF THINGS. Rev. ed. Ottawa: The Golden Dog, 1972.

   Originally published in ALCYONE.

PROSE

"Two Canadian Poets: A Lecture, 1891." In MASKS OF POETRY. Ed. A. J. M. Smith. Toronto: McClelland & Stewart, 1962. Reprinted from UNIVERSITY OF TORONTO QUARTERLY, 13 (July 1944), 406-23.

AT THE MERMAID INN, CONDUCTED BY A. LAMPMAN, W. W. CAMPBELL AND DUNCAN C. SCOTT. Ed. A. S. Bourinot. Ottawa: Bourinot, 1958.

Essays from the Toronto GLOBE, 1892-93.

"The Character and Poetry of Keats." Prefatory note by E. K. Brown. UNIVERSITY OF TORONTO QUARTERLY, 15 (July 1946), 356-72.

CRITICISM

Beattie, Munro. "Archibald Lampman." In OUR LIVING TRADITION, FIRST SERIES, pp. 6-88. Ed. Claude T. Bissell. Toronto: University of Toronto Press, 1957.

Bedwell, William Thomas. "Archibald Lampman and the Origin of Canadian Nature Poetry." Thesis, University of Manitoba, 1962.

Bissell, Claude T. "Literary Taste in Central Canada During the Late Nineteenth Century." CANADIAN HISTORICAL ASSOCIATION REVIEW, 31 (September 1950), 237-51.

Brennan, M. W. "The Prosody of Archibald Lampman." Thesis, Queen's University, 1931.

Brown, E. K. "Archibald Lampman." In ON CANADIAN POETRY, pp. 88-118. Rev. ed. Toronto: Ryerson, 1944.

Burton, Jean. "Archibald Lampman's Poetry of Release." WILLISON'S MONTHLY, 3 (April 1928), 425-27.

Campbell, Brian R. "Motion in the Poems of Archibald Lampman." Thesis, University of Alberta, 1971.

Coblentz, Stanton A. "Archibald Lampman: Canadian Poet of Nature." ARIZONA QUARTERLY, 17 (1961), 344-51.

Collin, W. E. "Natural Landscape." In THE WHITE SAVANNAHS, pp. 3-40. Toronto: McClelland & Stewart, 1936.

Connor, Carl Y. ARCHIBALD LAMPMAN, CANADIAN POET OF NATURE. Montreal: Carrier, 1929.

Davies, Barrie. "The Alien Mind: A Study of the Poetry of Archibald Lampman." Thesis, University of New Brunswick, 1970.

_____. "Answering Harmonies." HUMANITIES ASSOCIATION BULLETIN, 23, no. 2 (Spring 1972), 57-68.

_____. "Lampman and Religion." CANADIAN LITERATURE, 56 (Spring 1973), 40-60.

_____. "A Lampman Manuscript." JOURNAL OF CANADIAN FICTION, 1 (Spring 1972), 55-58.

_____. "Lampman: Radical Poet of Nature." THE ENGLISH QUARTERLY, 4 (Spring 1971), 33-43.

Djwa, Sandra [Ann]. "Lampman's Fleeting Vision." CANADIAN LITERATURE, 56 (Spring 1973), 22-39.

Gnarowski, Michael, ed. ARCHIBALD LAMPMAN. "Critical Views on Canadian Writers." Toronto: Ryerson, 1970.

To avoid unnecessary duplication of titles, the essays included in Gnarowski are listed below in chronological order, citing their original source of publication.

Machar, Agnes Maule [Fidelis]. "Some Recent Canadian Poems." THE WEEK, 6 (March 1889), 251-52.

Barry, L. E. F. "Prominent Canadian: Archibald Lampman." THE WEEK, 8 (April 1891), 298-300.

Stringer, Arthur. "A Glance at Lampman." CANADIAN MAGAZINE, 2 (April 1894), 545-48.

Crawford, A. W. "Archibald Lampman." ACTA VICTORIANA, 17 (December 1894), 77-81.

Marshall, John. "Archibald Lampman." QUEEN'S QUARTERLY, 9 (July 1901), 63-79.

Untermeyer, Louis. "Archibald Lampman and the Sonnet." POET LORE, 20 (November 1909), 432-37.

Burpee, Lawrence J. "Archibald Lampman." In LITTLE BOOK OF CANADIAN ESSAYS. Toronto: Musson, 1909, pp. 30-42.

Muddiman, Bernard. "Archibald Lampman." QUEEN'S QUARTERLY, 22 (January 1915), 233-43.

Unwin, G. H. "The Poetry of Archibald Lampman." UNIVERSITY MAGAZINE, 16 (February 1917), 55-73.

Knister, Raymond. "The Poetry of Archibald Lampman." DALHOUSIE REVIEW, 7 (October 1927), 348-61.

Kennedy, Leo. "Canadian Writers of the Past: Archibald Lampman." CANADIAN FORUM, 13 (May 1933), 301-3.

Collin, W. E. "Archibald Lampman." UNIVERSITY OF TORONTO QUARTERLY, 4 (October 1934), 103-20.

Gustafson, Ralph. "Among the Millet." NORTHERN REVIEW, 1 (February-March 1947), 26-34.

Scott, Duncan Campbell. "Copy of Letter to Ralph Gustafson." THE FIDDLEHEAD, 41 (Summer 1959), 12-14.

Sutherland, John. "Edgar Allan Poe in Canada." NORTHERN REVIEW, 4 (February-March 1951), 22-37.

Pacey, Desmond. "A Reading of Lampman's 'Heat.' " CULTURE, 14 (September 1953), 292-97.

Dudek, Louis. "The Significance of Lampman." CULTURE, 18 (September 1957), 277-90.

Watt, F[rank] W. "The Masks of Archibald Lampman." UNIVERSITY OF TORONTO QUARTERLY, 27 (January 1958), 169-84.

Guthrie, Norman G. THE POETRY OF ARCHIBALD LAMPMAN. Toronto: Musson, 1927.

Howells, W[illiam] D[ean]. "Editor's Study." HARPER'S MAGAZINE, 78 (April 1889), 821-23.

Jobin, M. "Archibald Lampman." Thesis, McGill University, 1971.

Logan, J. D. "Literary Group of '61." CANADIAN MAGAZINE, 37 (October 1911), 555-63.

MacDonald, Adrian. "Archibald Lampman." In CANADIAN PORTRAITS, pp. 220-30. Toronto: Ryerson, 1925.

MacDonald, E[lizabeth] R[oberts]. "A Little Talk About Lampman." CANADIAN MAGAZINE, 52 (April 1919), 1012-16.

Miller, Judith. "Towards a Canadian Aesthetic: Descriptive Colour in the Landscape Poetry of Duncan Campbell Scott, Archibald Lampman, and William Wilfred Campbell." Thesis, University of Waterloo, 1970.

Nesbitt, Bruce. "A Gift of Love: Lampman and Life." CANADIAN LITERATURE, 50 (Autumn 1971), 35-40.

_____. "Matthew Arnold in Canada: A Dialogue Begun?" CULTURE, 28 (March 1967), 53-54.

Pacey, Desmond. "Archibald Lampman." In TEN CANADIAN POETS, pp. 114-40. Toronto: Ryerson, 1958.

Phelps, Arthur L. "Archibald Lampman." In CANADIAN WRITERS, pp. 51-59. Toronto: McClelland & Stewart, 1952.

Scott, Duncan Campbell. "Archibald Lampman." In LEADING CANADIAN POETS, pp. 98-106. Ed. W. P. Percival. Toronto: Ryerson, 1948.

Voorhis, Ernest. "The Ancestry of Archibald Lampman, Poet." TRANSACTIONS OF THE ROYAL SOCIETY OF CANADA, 3rd ser., 15 (1921), 103-21.

MOODIE, SUSANNA (1803-1885)

When the Strickland family, a middle-class English family, lost its fortune in 1818, five of the sisters (Eliza, Agnes, Jane, Catherine, and Susanna) took up writing to supplement their income. Thus, when Susanna emigrated with her husband (William Dunbar Moodie) to Canada in 1832, she had already published some second-rate fiction and poetry. Life on an Ontario homestead so shocked her genteel sensibility, however, that she ceased writing and only resumed in 1838. When she did it was to produce a different kind of work, markedly affected by her six years in the Canadian bush. Her ROUGHING IT IN THE BUSH, implicitly depicting the love-hate relationship between the emigrant and the new land, is in fact a "touchstone" in Canadian literary history. Her contributions to THE LITERARY GARLAND and her editorship of THE VICTORIA MAGAZINE are characteristic of her later attempts to encourage the "life of letters" in Canada.

POETRY

ENTHUSIASM AND OTHER POEMS. London: Smith & Elder, 1831.

PROSE

SPARTACUS, A ROMAN STORY. Published anonymously. London: Newman, 1822.

> Attributed to Moodie by the BRITISH MUSEUM CATALOGUE and Reginald E. Watters in A CHECKLIST OF CANADIAN LITERATURE AND BACKGROUND MATERIALS (Toronto, 1972).

THE HISTORY OF MARY PRINCE, A WEST INDIAN SLAVE. Published anonymously. London: Maunder, 1831.

> Attributed to Moodie by Carl Ballstadt in CANADIAN NOTES AND QUERIES, November, 1971.

NEGRO SLAVERY DESCRIBED BY A NEGRO. BEING THE NARRATIVE OF

ASTON WARNER, A NATIVE OF ST. VINCENTS. Published anonymously. London: Maunder, 1831.

Attributed to Moodie by Ballstadt (see previous item).

PROFESSION AND PRINCIPLE. TALES. Published anonymously. London: Dean, 1833.

Not provably Moodie's, but attributed to her by Watters (see SPARTACUS, A ROMAN STORY, above).

ROWLAND MASSINGHAM, THE BOY THAT WOULD BE HIS OWN MASTER. Published anonymously. London: Dean, 1837.

Not provably Moodie's, but attributed to her by Watters (see SPARTACUS, A ROMAN STORY, above).

THE VICTORIA MAGAZINE, 1847-1848. Ed. by Susanna and J. W. D. Moodie. Facsimile reprint with introduction by William H. New. Vancouver: University of British Columbia Library, 1968.

The Moodies not only edited this magazine but wrote ninety per-cent of the articles as well.

ROUGHING IT IN THE BUSH; OR, LIFE IN CANADA. 2 vols. London: Richard Bentley, 1852. Reprint ed. with introduction by Carl F. Klinck. Toronto: McClelland & Stewart, 1962.

LIFE IN THE CLEARINGS VERSUS THE BUSH. London: Richard Bentley, 1853. Ed. with introduction by R. L. McDougall. Toronto: Macmillan, 1959.

THE SOLDIER'S ORPHAN; OR, HUGH LATIMER. London: Dean, 1853.

Not provably Moodie's, but attributed to her by Watters (see SPARTACUS, A ROMAN STORY, above) and BRITISH MUSEUM CATALOGUE.

MARK HURDLESTONE, THE GOLD WORSHIPPER. 2 vols. London: Richard Bentley, 1853.

FLORA LYNDSAY; OR, PASSAGES IN AN EVENTFUL LIFE. 2 vols. London: Richard Bentley, 1854.

MATRIMONIAL SPECULATIONS. London: Richard Bentley, 1854.

GEOFFREY MONCTON; OR, THE FAITHLESS GUARDIAN. New York: De-Witt, 1855. Reprinted as THE MONCTONS. 2 vols. London: Richard Bent-ley, 1856.

THE WORLD BEFORE THEM. 3 vols. London: Richard Bentley, 1868.

GEORGE LEATRIM; OR, THE MOTHER'S TEST. Edinburgh: Hamilton, 1875.

Not provably Moodie's but attributed to her by Watters (see SPARTACUS, A ROMAN STORY, above) and the BRITISH MUSEUM CATALOGUE.

CRITICISM

Ballstadt, Carl. "The Literary History of the Strickland Family." Thesis, University of London, 1965.

_____. "Susanna Moodie and the English Sketch." CANADIAN LITERATURE, 51 (Winter 1972), 32-38.

Davies, Robertson. AT MY HEART'S CORE. Toronto: Clarke, Irwin, 1950.

A dramatized character study of Mrs. Moodie.

Gairdner, William D. "Traill and Moodie: The Two Realities." JOURNAL OF CANADIAN FICTION, 1, no. 2 (Spring 1972), 35-42

Guttenberg, A[ntoine] Ch[arles] v[on]. "Susanna Moodie." In EARLY CANADIAN ART AND LITERATURE, pp. 99-119. Liechtenstein: Europe Printing Establishment, 1969.

Griffith, Louise A. "Susanna Moodie, a Biography." Thesis, University of Toronto, 1949.

Hume, Blanche. "Grandmothers of Canadian Literature." WILLISON'S MONTHLY, 3 (May 1928), 474-77.

_____. THE STRICKLAND SISTERS. Toronto: Ryerson, 1928.

Klinck, Carl F. "A Gentlewoman of Upper Canada." CANADIAN LITERATURE, 1 (Summer 1959), 75-77.

_____. "Introduction" to ROUGHING IT IN THE BUSH. Toronto: McClelland & Stewart, 1962.

Lande, Lawrence M. "The Strickland Sisters." In OLD LAMPS AGLOW, pp. 301-7. Montreal: Privately printed, 1957.

McCourt, Edward A. "Roughing it with the Moodies." QUEEN'S QUARTERLY, 52 (February 1945), 77-89. Reprinted in MASKS OF FICTION, pp. 81-92.

Ed. A. J. M. Smith. Toronto: McClelland & Stewart, 1961.

MacDonald, R. D. "Design and Purpose." CANADIAN LITERATURE, 51 (Winter 1972), 20-31.

Examines ROUGHING IT IN THE BUSH as a work of art.

McDougall, Robert L. "Introduction" to LIFE IN THE CLEARINGS. Toronto: Macmillan, 1959.

Morris, Audrey Y. GENTLE PIONEERS: FIVE NINETEENTH-CENTURY CANA-DIANS. Toronto & London: Hodder & Stoughton, 1968.

The pioneers are Susanna Moodie, Samuel Strickland, John Moodie, Catherine Parr Traill, and Thomas Traill.

Needler, G. H. OTONABEE PIONEERS: THE STORY OF THE STEWARTS, THE STRICKLANDS, THE TRAILLS AND THE MOODIES. Toronto: Burns & MacEachern, 1953.

Park, Sheila A. "Susanna Moodie and the 'Literary Garland.'" Thesis, Carleton University, 1965.

Contains an excellent bibliography of Moodie's contributions to THE LITERARY GARLAND.

Partridge, F. G. "The Stewarts and the Stricklands, the Moodies and the Traills." ONTARIO LIBRARY REVIEW, 40 (August 1956), 179-81.

Scott, Lloyd M. "The English Gentlefolk in the Backwoods of Canada." DALHOUSIE REVIEW, 39 (Spring 1959), 56-69.

Thomas, Clara. "The Strickland Sisters." In THE CLEAR SPIRIT: TWENTY CANADIAN WOMEN AND THEIR TIMES, pp. 42-73. Ed. Mary Q. Innis. Toronto: University of Toronto Press, 1966.

_____. "Happily Ever After: Canadian Women in Fiction and Fact." CA-NADIAN LITERATURE, 34 (Autumn 1967), 43-53.

_____. "Journeys to Freedom." CANADIAN LITERATURE, 51 (Winter 1972), 11-19.

Weaver, Emily. "Mrs. Traill and Mrs. Moodie, Pioneers in Literature." CANADIAN MAGAZINE, 48 (March 1917), 473-76.

RICHARDSON, JOHN (1796-1852)

John Richardson, born at Queenston, Upper Canada, the son of an army surgeon, was just sixteen when the War of 1812 was declared between the United States and Great Britain. Canada being the battlefield, he enlisted immediately, fought in several major campaigns with the armies of Brock and Tecumseh and was, for a year, a prisoner of war. These experiences provided the material for his best literary works, TECUMSEH, WAR OF 1812, and WACOUSTA (although the actual setting for the last is the Pontiac conspiracy of 1763). Richardson spent much of his life in England, then returned to Canada in 1838. However, failing to find an appreciative audience for his work, he became an early emigre to the United States, where he successfully completed several new novels but died penniless. In Canadian literary history he stands as Canada's first major novelist.

BIBLIOGRAPHY

Morley, William F. E. "A Bibliographical Study of John Richardson." PAPERS OF THE BIBLIOGRAPHICAL SOCIETY OF CANADA, 4 (1965), 21-88.

> This bibliography, a model for bibliographers of Canadian authors, is quite detailed, offering quasi-facsimile titlepages with collation for every Richardson item known to exist, and two which may be ghosts. Amply annotated, it is a basic resource for every serious student of Richardson.

POETRY

TECUMSEH; OR, THE WARRIOR OF THE WEST. A POEM IN FOUR CANTOS. London: R. Glynn, 1828.

KENSINGTON GARDENS IN 1830. A SATIRICAL TRIFLE. London: Marsh & Miller, 1830. Reprint ed. with introduction by Carl F. Klinck. Toronto: Bibliographical Society of Canada, 1957.

> "A verse satire on fashionable moustaches and beards" (LITERARY HISTORY OF CANADA).

FICTION

ECARTE; OR, THE SALONS OF PARIS. 3 vols. London: Colburn, 1829.

WACOUSTA; OR, THE PROPHECY. A TALE OF THE CANADAS. 3 vols. London: Cadell, 1832. First Canadian edition. Montreal: Lovell, 1886. Modern paperback ed. Toronto: McClelland & Stewart, 1967.

THE CANADIAN BROTHERS; OR, THE PROPHECY FULFILLED. A TALE OF THE LATE AMERICAN WAR. 2 vols. Montreal: A. H. Armour, 1840. Reprinted as MATILDA MONTGOMERIE. New York: DeWitt & Davenport, 1851.

THE MONK KNIGHT OF ST. JOHN. A TALE OF THE CRUSADES. New York: DeWitt, 1850.

HARDSCRABBLE; OR, THE FALL OF CHICAGO. A TALE OF INDIAN WAR- FARE. New York: DeWitt, [1851].

> See Morley's "A Bibliographical Study," above, for a discussion of the dating of this novel.

WESTBROOK, THE OUTLAW; OR, THE AVENGING WOLF. Printed in THE SUNDAY MERCURY (New York), September 4 - October 26, 1851. Reprint ed. with introduction by David R. Beasley. Montreal: Grant Woolmer Books, 1973.

WAU-NAN-GEE; OR, THE MASSACRE AT CHICAGO. New York: H. Long, 1852.

OTHER PROSE

WAR OF 1812. Brockville, Ont.: Privately printed, 1842. Reprint ed. with biography and bibliography by A. C. Casselman. Toronto: Historical Publishing Co., 1902.

> This eye-witness account of the War first appeared in THE NEW ERA (Vol. 2, nos. 1-15, 1842), a magazine produced by Richard- son in Brockville.

EIGHT YEARS IN CANADA. Montreal: H. H. Cunningham, 1847.

THE GUARDS IN CANADA; OR, THE POINT OF HONOR. Montreal: H. H. Cunningham, 1848.

> A sequel to EIGHT YEARS IN CANADA.

TECUMSEH AND RICHARDSON: THE STORY OF A TRIP TO WALPOLE ISLAND AND PORT SARNIA. Ed. with introduction and biography by A. H. V. Colquohoun. Toronto: Ontario Book Co., 1924.

"A Trip to Walpole Island and Port Sarnia" first appeared in THE LITERARY GARLAND (Vol. 7, no. 1, January 1849) and is reprinted in THE EVOLUTION OF CANADIAN LITERATURE IN ENGLISH: BEGINNINGS TO 1867, pp. 148-62. Edited by Mary Jane Edwards (Toronto: Holt, Rinehart & Winston, 1973).

CRITICISM

Baker, Ray Palmer. "John Richardson and the Historical Romance." In A HISTORY OF ENGLISH-CANADIAN LITERATURE TO THE CONFEDERATION. pp. 125-39. Cambridge, Mass.: Harvard University Press, 1920.

Burwash, I[da]. "John Richardson, 1796-1852, Young Volunteer of 1812." CANADIAN MAGAZINE, 39 (July 1912), 218-25.

Carstairs, J. S. "Richardson's War of 1812." CANADIAN MAGAZINE, 29 (May 1901), 72-74.

Greig, Peter E. "Major John Richardson (1796-1852): Two Manuscripts." CANADIAN NOTES & QUERIES, 9 (1972), 10-11.

Klinck, Carl F. "Early Creative Literature of Western Ontario." ONTARIO HISTORY, 45, no. 4 (Autumn 1953, 155-63.

_____. "Introduction" to WACOUSTA. Toronto: McClelland & Stewart, 1967.

_____. "Major Richardson's 'Kensington Gardens in 1830.'" ONTARIO HISTORY, 45, no. 3 (Summer 1956), 101-10.

_____. "A Note on 'A Canadian Campaign' by Major John Richardson." PAPERS OF THE BIBLIOGRAPHICAL SOCIETY OF CANADA, 5 (1966), 93-94.

Lande, Lawrence M. "Major John Richardson." In OLD LAMPS AGLOW, pp. 228-40. Montreal: Privately printed, 1957.

Pacey, Desmond. "A Colonial Romantic, Major John Richardson, Soldier and Novelist." CANADIAN LITERATURE, 2 (Autumn 1959), 20-31; 3 (Winter 1960), 47-56. Reprinted in ESSAYS IN CANADIAN CRITICISM 1938-1968, pp. 151-71. Toronto: Ryerson, 1969.

_____. "A Note on Major John Richardson." CANADIAN LITERATURE, 39

(Winter 1969), 103-4.

Riddell, W[illiam] R. JOHN RICHARDSON. Toronto: Ryerson, [1926].

ROBERTS, CHARLES GEORGE DOUGLAS (1860-1943)

If there is one writer, more than any other, who deserves to be called the "father of Canadian literature," it is Roberts. His ORION (1890) signified a new beginning in Canadian poetry; his novels and short stories received international acclaim; and his contribution to the modern animal story, in a critical sense, places him in a prominent position in world literary history. More important, however, is that to his fellow poets (Carman, Lampman, and Scott) he was a source of inspiration and confidence and thus contributed to making the post-Confederation era one of the richest in Canadian literary history.

COLLECTED WORKS

POEMS. New York: Silver, Burdett, 1901. Reprint ed. Toronto: Copp Clark, 1903. Rev. ed. Toronto: Copp Clark, 1907.

> "Of all my verse written before the end of 1898 this collection contains everything I care to preserve."

SELECTED POEMS. Toronto: Ryerson, 1936.

THE SELECTED POEMS. Ed. with introduction by Desmond Pacey. Toronto: Ryerson, 1955.

SELECTED POETRY AND CRITICAL PROSE. Ed. with introduction by W. J. Keith. Toronto: University of Toronto Press, 1974.

POETRY

ORION, AND OTHER POEMS. Philadelphia: J. B. Lippincott, 1880.

LATER POEMS. Fredericton, N.B.: Privately printed, 1881.

LATER POEMS. Fredericton, N.B.: Privately printed, 1882.

This and the above are two different collections, both small pamphlets containing a total of three poems.

IN DIVERS TONES. Boston: D. Lothrop; Montreal: Dawson, 1886.

AUTOCHTHON. Windsor, N.S.: Privately printed, 1889. Reprinted in SONGS OF THE COMMON DAY (1893).

AVE: AN ODE FOR THE CENTENARY OF THE BIRTH OF PERCY BYSSHE SHELLEY, AUGUST 4, 1792. Toronto: Williamson, 1892. Reprinted in SONGS OF THE COMMON DAY (1893).

SONGS OF THE COMMON DAY. London: Longmans; Toronto: Briggs, 1893.

THE BOOK OF THE NATIVE. Boston: Lamson, Wolffe; Toronto: Copp Clark, 1896.

NEW YORK NOCTURNES AND OTHER POEMS. Boston: Lamson, Wolffe, 1898.

THE BOOK OF THE ROSE. Boston: L. C. Page; Toronto: Copp Clark, 1903.

NEW POEMS. London: Constable, 1919.

THE SWEET O'THE YEAR AND OTHER POEMS. Toronto: Ryerson, 1925.

BE QUIET. UNSAID: TWO UNPUBLISHED POEMS. Toronto: Privately printed, 1929.

THE ICEBERG AND OTHER POEMS. Toronto: Ryerson, 1934.

TWILIGHT OVER SHAUGAMAUK AND THREE OTHER POEMS. Toronto: Ryerson, 1937.

CANADA SPEAKS OF BRITAIN. Toronto: Ryerson, 1941.

FICTION

THE RAID FROM BEAUSEJOUR, AND HOW THE CARTER BOYS LIFTED THE MORTGAGE: TWO STORIES OF ACADIE. New York: Hunt & Eaton, 1894. THE RAID FROM BEAUSEJOUR republished as THE YOUNG ACADIAN. Boston: L. C. Page, 1907.

REUBE DARE'S SHAD BOAT: A TALE OF THE TIDE COUNTRY. New York: Hunt & Eaton, 1895. Republished as THE CRUSE OF THE YACHT 'DIDO.' Boston: L. C. Page; Toronto: Copp Clark, 1906.

Boy's story.

THE FORGE IN THE FOREST. Boston: Lamson, Wolffe, 1896; Toronto: Briggs, 1897.

Novel.

EARTH'S ENIGMAS. Boston: Lamson, Wolffe, 1896. Rev. ed. Boston: L. C. Page; Toronto: Copp Clark, 1903.

Animal stories.

AROUND THE CAMP FIRE. New York: Crowell; Toronto: Briggs, 1896.

Short stories.

A SISTER TO EVANGELINE. Boston: Lamson, Wolffe, 1898; Toronto: Morang, 1899. Republished as LOVERS IN ACADIE. London & Toronto: Dent, 1924.

Novel.

BY THE MARSHES OF MINAS. Boston: Silver, Burdett; Toronto: Briggs, 1900.

Short stories.

THE HEART OF THE ANCIENT WOOD. New York: Silver, Burdett, 1900; Toronto: Copp Clark, 1901. Reprint ed. New York: A. Wessels, 1906.

Novel.

THE KINDRED OF THE WILD. Boston: L. C. Page; Toronto: Copp Clark, 1902.

Animal stories. The following stories from this book were published separately by L. C. Page in 1905: "The Haunters of the Pine Gloom," "Lord of the Air," "The Watchers of the Camp-Fire," and "The King of the Mamozekel."

BARBARA LADD. Boston: L. C. Page; Toronto: Copp Clark, 1902.

Novel.

THE PRISONER OF MADEMOISELLE. Boston: L. C. Page; Toronto: Copp Clark, 1904.

Novel.

THE WATCHERS OF THE TRAILS. Boston: L. C. Page, 1904.

> Animal stories. Two stories from this book, "The Little People of the Sycamore" and "The Return of the Trails," were published by L. C. Page under separate covers in 1906.

RED FOX. Boston: L. C. Page, 1905. Reprint ed. New York: McGraw, 1948.

> Full-length animal story.

THE HEART THAT KNOWS. Boston: L. C. Page; Toronto: Copp Clark, 1906.

> Novel.

THE HAUNTERS OF THE SILENCES. Boston: L. C. Page; Montreal: Montreal News Co., 1904.

> Animal stories.

IN THE DEEP OF THE SNOW. New York: Crowell; Toronto: Musson, 1907. Reprinted in THE BACKWOODSMEN (1909).

> Novelette.

THE HOUSE IN THE WATER. Boston: L. C. Page; Toronto: Ward, Lock, 1908.

> Short stories.

RED OXEN OF BONVAL. New York: Dodd, Mead, 1908.

> Novelette.

THE BACKWOODSMEN. New York: Macmillan, 1909. Reprint ed. 1922.

> Short stories.

KINGS IN EXILE. London & Toronto: Ward, Lock, 1909. New York: Macmillan, 1910.

> Animal stories.

NEIGHBOURS UNKNOWN. London & Toronto: Ward, Lock, 1910; New York: Macmillan, 1911.

> Animal stories.

MORE KINDRED OF THE WILD. London & Toronto: Ward, Lock, 1911.

> Animal stories.

BABES OF THE WILD. New York: Cassell, 1912. Reprint ed. Toronto: Dent, 1924. Republished as CHILDREN OF THE WILD. New York: Macmillan, 1913. Reprint eds. 1925, 1929.

Animal stories.

THE FEET OF THE FURITIVE. London & Toronto: Ward, Lock, 1912; New York: Macmillan, 1913.

Animal stories.

A BALKAN PRINCE. London: Everett, 1913.

Novel.

HOOF AND CLAW. London & Toronto: Ward, Lock, 1913; New York: Macmillan, 1914.

Animal stories.

THE SECRET TRAILS. London & Toronto: Ward, Lock; New York: Macmillan, 1914.

Animal stories.

THE LEDGE ON BALD FACE. London & Toronto: Ward, Lock, 1918. Republished as HIM: THE STORY OF THE BACKWOODS POLICE DOG. New York: Macmillan, 1919.

Animal stories.

IN THE MORNING OF TIME. London: Hutchinson, 1919. Reprint ed. New York: Frederick A. Stokes, 1922. Rev. ed. Toronto: Dent, 1923.

Quasi-historical treatise.

SOME ANIMAL STORIES. London & Toronto: Dent; New York: Dutton, 1921.

WISDOM OF THE WILDERNESS. London & Toronto: Dent, 1922; New York: Macmillan, 1923.

Animal stories.

MORE ANIMAL STORIES. London & Toronto: Dent; New York: Dutton, 1922.

THEY WHO WALK IN THE WILD. New York: Macmillan, 1924. Also published as THEY THAT WALK IN THE WILD. London & Toronto: Dent, 1924.

Animal stories.

EYES OF THE WILDERNESS. London: Dent; New York & Toronto: Macmillan,

Roberts, Charles George Douglas

1933.

   Short stories.

FURTHER ANIMAL STORIES. London & Toronto: Dent: New York: Dutton, 1936.

THIRTEEN BEARS. Ed. Ethel H. Bennett. Toronto: Ryerson, 1935.

   Selected prose.

FOREST FOLK. Ed. Ethel H. Bennett. Toronto: Ryerson, 1949.

   Selected prose.

THE LAST BARRIER AND OTHER STORIES. Ed. Alec Lucas. Toronto: Mc-Clelland & Stewart, 1958.

KING OF THE BEASTS AND OTHER STORIES. Ed. Joseph Gold. Toronto: Ryerson, 1967.

3. Other Prose

"New Brunswick." In PICTURESQUE CANADA. Ed. G. M. Grant. Toronto: Belden Brothers, 1884.

"Introduction" to POEMS OF WILD LIFE. Ed. Charles G. D. Roberts. Toronto: W. J. Gage, 1888.

"Introduction" to HALIBURTON, THE MAN AND THE WRITER, by F. Blake Crofton. Windsor, N.S.: Haliburton Club, 1889.

Translation of THE CANADIANS OF OLD by Phillipe de Gaspe. New York: Appleton, 1890. Reprinted as CAMERON OF LOCHIEL. Boston: L. C. Page, 1905.

THE CANADIAN GUIDE BOOK. THE TOURIST'S AND SPORTSMAN'S GUIDE TO EASTERN CANADA AND NEWFOUNDLAND. New York: Appleton, 1891.

"Mr. Bliss Carman's Poems." THE CHAP-BOOK, 1 (June 1894), 53.

THE LAND OF EVANGELINE AND THE GATEWAY THITHER. Kentville, N.S.: Dominion Atlantic Railway, [1895].

   Travel guide.

A HISTORY OF CANADA. Boston: Lamson, Wolffe; Toronto: Morang, 1897.
School text.

"Introduction" to WALDEN, by Henry David Thoreau. New York: Crowell, 1899.

"The Pastoral Elegy." Ed. Charles G. D. Roberts. In ALASTOR AND ADON-AIS, by Percy Bysshe Shelley. Boston: Silver, Burdett, 1902.

DISCOVERIES AND EXPLORATIONS. Vol. XIV of NINETEENTH-CENTURY SERIES: THE STORY OF HUMAN PROGRESS AND EVENTS OF THE CENTURY. London: Chambers, 1902.

"Introduction" to SAPPHO: ONE HUNDRED LYRICS, by Bliss Carman. Boston: L. C. Page, 1904.

"Bliss Carman." DALHOUSIE REVIEW, 9 (January 1930), 409-17.

"Introduction" to VERSES BY THE SEA, by E. J. Pratt. Toronto: Macmillan, 1930.

"More Reminiscences of Bliss Carman." DALHOUSIE REVIEW, 10 (April 1930), 1-9.

"Foreword" to THE COMPLETE POEMS OF FRANCIS SHERMAN. Toronto: Ryerson, 1935.

"Some Reminiscences of Bliss Carman in New York." CANADIAN POETRY, 5 (December 1940), 5-10.

"Introduction" to FLYING COLOURS. Ed. Charles G. D. Roberts. Toronto: Ryerson, 1942.
A collection of patriotic verse.

ECHOES FROM OLD ACADIA. Toronto: Canadiana House, 1968. Reprinted from CANADIAN LEAVES. Ed. G. M. Fairchild. New York: Thompson, 1887.

CRITICISM

Anon. "The Animal Story." EDINBURGH REVIEW, 214 (July 1911), 94-118.

Archer, William. "Charles G. D. Roberts." In POETS OF THE YOUNGER GENERATION, pp. 299-315. London: Lane, 1902.

Roberts, Charles George Douglas

Boucher, Brother Laurent. "Sources of Inspiration in Charles G. D. Roberts' Poetry of Nature." Thesis, Laval University, 1966.

Campbell, John Hugh. "The Prose of Sir Charles G. D. Roberts." Thesis, University of New Brunswick, 1963.

Cappon, James. CHARLES G. D. ROBERTS. Toronto: Ryerson, 1925.

_____. ROBERTS AND THE INFLUENCES OF HIS TIME. Toronto: Briggs, 1905.

Carman, Bliss. "Charles G. D. Roberts." THE CHAP-BOOK, 2 (January 1895), 163-71.

De Mille, A. B. "Canadian Celebrities: The Roberts Family." CANADIAN MAGAZINE, 15 (September 1900), 426-30.

Edgar, Pelham. "Sir Charles G. D. Roberts and His Times." UNIVERSITY OF TORONTO QUARTERLY, 13 (October 1943), 117-26.

Forbes, Elizabeth. "The Development of Style and Thought in Charles G. D. Roberts' Poetry to 1897." Thesis, University of New Brunswick, 1953.

Gammon, Donald B. "The Concept of Nature in Nineteenth Century Poetry, with Special Reference to Goldsmith, Sangster and Roberts." Thesis, University of New Brunswick, 1948.

Gold, Joseph. "The Precious Speck of Life." CANADIAN LITERATURE, 26 (Autumn 1965), 22-32.

Hawkins, E. F. "The Literary Career of Roberts." In LITTLE PILGRIMAGES AMONG THE MEN WHO HAVE WRITTEN FAMOUS BOOKS, pp. 229-315. Boston: L. C. Page, 1902.

Henry, Lorne J. "Sir Charles G. D. Roberts (1860-1943)." In CANADIANS: A BOOK OF BIOGRAPHIES, pp. 69-75. London: Longmans, 1950.

Keith, W. J. CHARLES G. D. ROBERTS. Toronto: Copp Clark, 1969.
    The best full-length critical study of Roberts' work.

Lampman, Archibald. "Two Canadian Poets: A Lecture, 1891." UNIVERSITY OF TORONTO QUARTERLY, 13 (July 1944), 406-23. Reprinted in MASKS OF POETRY, pp. 26-44. Toronto: McClelland & Stewart, 1962.

Livesay, Dorothy. "Open Letter to Sir Charles G. D. Roberts." CANADIAN BOOKMAN, 21 (April 1931), 34-35.

Magee, William H. "The Animal Story: A Challenge in Technique." DAL-HOUSIE REVIEW, 44 (Summer 1964), 156-64.

Marquis, T. G. "Roberts." CANADIAN MAGAZINE, 1 (September 1893), 572-75.

Matthews, Robin. "Charles G. D. Roberts and the Destruction of the Canadian Imagination." JOURNAL OF CANADIAN FICTION, 1 (Winter 1972), 47-56.

Muddiman, Bernard. "A Vignette in Canadian Literature." CANADIAN MAG-AZINE, 40 (March 1913), 451-58.

Pacey, Desmond. "Sir Charles G. D. Roberts." In OUR LIVING TRADITION, FOURTH SERIES, pp. 31-56. Ed. R. L. McDougall. Toronto: University of Toronto Press, 1962.

_____. "Sir Charles G. D. Roberts." In TEN CANADIAN POETS, pp. 34-58. Toronto: Ryerson, 1958.

Pierce, Lorne [Albert]. "Charles G. D. Roberts." In THREE FREDERICTON POETS, pp. 11-17. Toronto: Ryerson, 1933.

Poirier, Michel. "The Animal Story in Canadian Literature: E. Thompson Seton and Charles G. D. Roberts." QUEEN'S QUARTERLY, 34 (January-March 1927), 298-312; (April-June 1927), 398-419.

Polk, James. "Lives of the Hunted." CANADIAN LITERATURE, 53 (Summer 1972), 51-59.

Pomeroy, Elsie M. SIR CHARLES G. D. ROBERTS: A BIOGRAPHY. Toronto: Ryerson, 1943.

Rittenhouse, Jessie B. "Evolution in the Poetry of Roberts." In YOUNGER AMERICAN POETS, pp. 132-50. Boston: Little, Brown, 1904.

Rogers, A[mos] R[obert]. "American Recognition of Bliss Carman and Sir Charles G. D. Roberts." HUMANITIES ASSOCIATION BULLETIN, 22, no. 2 (Spring 1971), 19-24.

Stephen, A. M. "The Poetry of Charles G. D. Roberts." QUEEN'S QUAR-TERLY, 36 (Winter 1929), 48-64.

Stevenson, O. J. "New Visions and New Ventures." In A PEOPLE'S BEST, pp. 85-94. Toronto: Musson, 1927.

Stringer, Arthur. "Eminent Canadians in New York: The Father of Canadian Poetry." NATIONAL MONTHLY OF CANADA, 4 (February 1904), 61-64.

White, Greenough. "A Pair of Canadian Poets." SEWANEE REVIEW, 7 (January 1899), 48-52.

The other poet is Bliss Carman.

SCOTT, DUNCAN CAMPBELL (1862-1947)

Like the other major Confederation poets (Carman, Roberts, and Lampman), Scott is basically a descriptive-nature poet, whose work (like theirs) is grounded in a vague sort of transcendentalism. His unique contribution consists of a small number of "northern wilderness" and "Indian" poems (his best work). As head of the Department of Indian Affairs he knew both of these subjects well; in such poems as "The Forsaken" and "On the Way to the Mission" he captures the combined sorrow and beauty of the northern way of life.

COLLECTED WORKS

POEMS. Toronto: McClelland & Stewart, 1935.

THE CIRCLE OF AFFECTION. Toronto: McClelland & Stewart, 1947.

  Short stories, poems, and essays.

SELECTED POEMS. With "memoir" by E. K. Brown. Toronto: Ryerson, 1951.

SELECTED STORIES OF DUNCAN CAMPBELL SCOTT. Ed. with introduction by Glenn Clever. Ottawa: University of Ottawa Press, 1973.

CORRESPONDENCE

SOME LETTERS OF DUNCAN CAMPBELL SCOTT, ARCHIBALD LAMPMAN AND OTHERS. Ed. A. S. Bourinot. Ottawa: Bourinot, 1960.

MORE LETTERS OF DUNCAN CAMPBELL SCOTT. Ed. A. S. Bourinot. Ottawa: Bourinot, 1960.

POETRY

THE MAGIC HOUSE AND OTHER POEMS. Ottawa: J. Durie; London: Methuen, 1893.

LABOR AND THE ANGEL. Boston: Copeland & Day, 1898.

NEW WORLD LYRICS AND BALLADS. Toronto: Morang, 1905.

VIA BOREALIS. Toronto: W. Tyrell, 1906.

LINES IN MEMORY OF EDMUND MORRIS. N.p.: Privately printed, 1915.

LUNDY'S LANE AND OTHER POEMS. Toronto: McClelland & Stewart; New York: Doran, 1916.

TO THE CANADIAN MOTHERS AND THREE OTHER POEMS. N.p.: Mortimer, 1917.

BEAUTY AND LIFE. Toronto: McClelland & Stewart, 1921.

THE GREEN CLOISTER. Toronto: McClelland & Stewart, 1935.

FICTION

IN THE VILLAGE OF VIGER. Boston: Copeland & Day, 1896. Reprint ed. Toronto: Ryerson, 1945. Reprint ed. with introduction by Raymond Knister. Toronto: McClelland & Stewart, 1973.

    Short stories.

THE WITCHING OF ELSPIE. New York: Doran; Toronto: McClelland & Stewart, 1923.

    Stories.

DRAMA

PIERRE: A PLAY IN ONE ACT. In CANADIAN PLAYS FROM HART HOUSE THEATRE, vol. 1, pp. 51-76. Ed. Vincent Massey. Toronto: Macmillan, 1926.

OTHER PROSE

AT THE MERMAID INN, CONDUCTED BY A. LAMPMAN, W. W. CAMPBELL
AND DUNCAN C. SCOTT. Ed. A. S. Bourinot. Ottawa: Bourinot, 1958.

Essays from the Toronto GLOBE, 1892-93.

POETRY AND PROGRESS. Toronto: Canadiana House, 1968. Reprinted from
PROCEEDINGS AND TRANSACTIONS OF THE ROYAL SOCIETY OF CANADA,
3rd ser., 16 (1922), xlvii-lxvii.

JOHN GRAVES SIMCOE. Toronto: Morang, 1905. Reprint ed. Toronto:
Oxford University Press, 1926.

Biography.

THE ADMINISTRATION OF INDIAN AFFAIRS IN CANADA. Toronto: Canadian Institute of International Affairs, 1931.

WALTER J. PHILLIPS. Toronto: Ryerson, 1947.

Biography.

CRITICISM

Archer, William. "Duncan Campbell Scott." In POETS OF THE YOUNGER
GENERATION, pp. 385-95. London: Lane, 1902.

Brodie, Allan D[ouglas]. "Canadian Short Story Writers." CANADIAN MAG-
AZINE, 4 (February, 1895), 334-44.

Brown, E. K. "Duncan Campbell Scott." In ON CANADIAN POETRY,
pp. 118-43. Rev. ed. Toronto: Ryerson, 1944.

_____. "Duncan Campbell Scott, An Individual Poet." MANITOBA ARTS
REVIEW, 2 (Spring 1941), 51-54.

Burrell, Martin. "Canadian Poet." In BETWIXT HEAVEN AND CHARING
CROSS, pp. 253-61. Toronto: Macmillan, 1928.

Clarke, George Herbert. "Duncan Campbell Scott, 1862-1948." PROCEED-
INGS AND TRANSACTIONS OF THE ROYAL SOCIETY OF CANADA, 3rd
ser., 42 (1958), 115-19.

Crozier, Daniel F. "Imagery and Symbolism in the Poetry of Duncan Campbell
Scott." Thesis, University of New Brunswick, 1963.

Dagg, Melvin H. "Scott and the Indians." HUMANITIES ASSOCIATION BUL-
LETIN, 23, no. 4 (Fall 1972), 3-11.

Denham, William Paul. "Music and Painting in the Poetry of Duncan Campbell
Scott." Thesis, University of Manitoba, 1964.

Dragland, Stanley Louis. "Duncan Campbell Scott." Thesis, Queen's University, 1970.

Edgar, Pelham. "Duncan Campbell Scott." DALHOUSIE REVIEW, 7 (April
1927), 38-46.

_____. "The Poetry of Duncan Campbell Scott." In LEADING CANADIAN
POETS, pp. 213-19. Ed. W. P. Percival. Toronto: Ryerson, 1948.

_____. "Travelling With a Poet." In ACROSS MY PATH, pp. 58-74.
Ed. Northrop Frye. Toronto: Ryerson, 1952.

Geddes, Gary. "Piper of Many Tunes: Duncan Campbell Scott." CANADIAN
LITERATURE, 37 (Summer 1968), 14-27.

Knister, Raymond. "Duncan Campbell Scott." WILLISON'S MONTHLY, 2
(January 1927), 295-96.

Miller, Judith. "Towards a Canadian Aesthetic: Descriptive Colour in the
Landscape Poetry of Duncan Campbell Scott, Archibald Lampman, and William
Wilfred Campbell." Thesis, University of Waterloo, 1970.

Monk, Patricia. "The Role of Prosodic and Structural Elements in the Poetry
of Duncan Campbell Scott." Thesis, Carleton University, 1971.

Muddiman, Bernard. "Duncan Campbell Scott." CANADIAN MAGAZINE,
43 (May 1914), 63-72.

Pacey, Desmond. "Duncan Campbell Scott." In TEN CANADIAN POETS,
pp. 141-64. Toronto: Ryerson, 1958.

_____. "The Poetry of Duncan Campbell Scott." CANADIAN FORUM, 28
(August 1948), 107-9. Reprinted in ESSAYS IN CANADIAN CRITICISM 1938-
1968, pp. 39-44. Toronto: Ryerson, 1969.

Patterson, E. Palmer. "The Poet and the Indian: Indian Themes in the Poetry
of Duncan Campbell Scott and John Collier." ONTARIO HISTORY, 49, no.
2 (June 1967), 69-78.

Smith, A[rthur] J[ames] M[arshall]. "Duncan Cambell Scott." In OUR LIVING TRADITION, THIRD SERIES, pp. 73-94. Ed. R. L. McDougall. Toronto: University of Toronto Press, 1959.

_____. "Duncan Campbell Scott, a Reconsideration." CANADIAN LITERATURE, 1 (Summer 1959), 13-25.

_____. "The Poetry of Duncan Campbell Scott." DALHOUSIE REVIEW, 28 (April 1948), 12-21.

Stevenson, Lionel. "Who's Who in Canadian Literature: Duncan Campbell Scott." CANADIAN BOOKMAN, 11 (March 1929), 59-62.

Sykes, W. J. "The Poetry of Duncan Campbell Scott." QUEEN'S QUARTERLY, 46 (February 1939), 51-64.

SETON, ERNEST THOMPSON (1860-1946)

When critics make a case for the realistic animal story being a peculiarly Canadian genre, the focus of attention is always on Charles G. D. Roberts and Ernest Thompson Seton. Invariably, however, Seton is relegated to a secondary role. Alec Lucas, for example, in his introduction to THE LAST BARRIER, writes: "Roberts wrote as a creative artist and Seton as a naturalist, the one dependent on his imagination and the other on his powers of observation to give his natural-history meaning, or, more briefly, for Roberts it was art first; for Seton it was science." While it is true that Seton was a scientist first and writer second, and while, perhaps, his writings may be more strictly called "biographies" than "short stories," it is nevertheless an indisputable fact that his stories are masterfully written and belong as much to the realm of entertaining fiction as to that of the naturalistic essay, a claim substantiated by Patricia Morley in her article, "Seton's Animals," cited under Criticism, below.

AUTOBIOGRAPHIES

TRAIL OF AN ARTIST-NATURALIST. New York: Scribner, 1940.

BY A THOUSAND FIRES. NATURE NOTES AND EXTRACTS FROM THE LIFE AND UNPUBLISHED JOURNALS OF ERNEST THOMPSON SETON. Ed. Julia M. Seton. New York: Doubleday, 1967.

FICTION

WILD ANIMALS I HAVE KNOWN. New York: Scribner, 1898. Modern paperback ed. with original illustrations. New York: Lancer Books, 1966.

LOBO, RAG, AND VIXEN. New York: Scribner, 1899. Stories reprinted from WILD ANIMALS I HAVE KNOWN. New York: Scribner, 1898.

THE TRAIL OF THE SANDHILL STAG. New York: Scribner, 1899.

THE BIOGRAPHY OF A GRIZZLY. New York: Century; Toronto: Copp Clark, 1900.

RAGGYLUG, THE COTTONTAIL RABBIT AND OTHER ANIMAL STORIES. London: David Nutt, 1900.

LIVES OF THE HUNTED. New York: Scribner, 1901.

KRAG AND JOHNNY BEAR. New York: Scribner, 1902. Stories reprinted from LIVES OF THE HUNTED. New York: Scribner, 1901.

TWO LITTLE SAVAGES. New York: Grosset & Dunlap, 1903.

MONARCH, THE BIG BEAR OF TALLAC. New York: Scribner, 1904.

ANIMAL HEROES; BEING THE HISTORIES OF A CAT, A DOG, A PIGEON, A LYNX, TWO WOLVES AND A REINDEER AND IN ELUCIDATION OF THE SAME OVER 200 DRAWINGS. New York: Scribner, 1905. Reprint ed. New York: Grosset & Dunlap, 1966.

WOODMYTH AND FABLE. Toronto: Briggs; London: Hodder & Stoughton, 1905.

THE NATURAL HISTORY OF THE TEN COMMANDMENTS. New York: Scribner, 1907. Reprinted as THE TEN COMMANDMENTS IN THE ANIMAL WORLD. New York: Doubleday, 1923.

THE BIOGRAPHY OF A SILVER FOX. New York: Century; Toronto: Copp Clark, 1909.

ROLF IN THE WOODS. New York: Doubleday, 1911.

WILD ANIMALS AT HOME. Toronto: Briggs, 1913.

THE SLUM CAT; SNAP; THE WINNIPEG WOLF. London: Constable, 1915.
   Short stories.

THE WHITE REINDEER; ARNAUX; THE BOY AND THE LYNX. London: Constable, 1915.

LITTLE WARHORSE: THE HISTORY OF A JACK-RABBIT AND BADLANDS BILLY. London: Constable, [1915].

WILD ANIMAL WAYS. New York: Doubleday, 1916.

THE PREACHER OF CEDAR MOUNTAIN: A TALE OF THE OPEN COUNTRY.
New York: Doubleday, 1917.

WOODLAND TALES. New York: Doubleday, 1921.

BANNERTAIL: THE STORY OF A GRAY SQUIRREL. New York: Scribner;
London: Hodder & Stoughton, 1922.

BILLY, AND OTHER STORIES FROM "WILD ANIMAL WAYS." London: Hodder
& Stoughton, 1925.

JOHNNY BEAR, AND OTHER STORIES FROM "LIVES OF THE HUNTED."
London: Hodder & Stoughton, 1925.

OLD SILVER GRIZZLE, THE BADGER, AND OTHER STORIES FROM "WILD
ANIMALS AT HOME." London: Hodder & Stoughton, 1925.

RAGGYLUG, AND OTHER STORIES FROM "WILD ANIMALS I HAVE KNOWN."
London: Hodder & Stoughton, 1925.

CHINK, A WOOLY COATED LITTLE DOG; AND OTHER STORIES FROM
"LIVES OF THE HUNTED" AND "WILD ANIMALS AT HOME." London:
Hodder & Stoughton, 1929.

FOAM RAZORBACK, AND OTHER STORIES FROM "WILD ANIMAL WAYS."
London: Hodder & Stoughton, 1929.

KATUG THE SNOW CHILD. Oxford: Blackwell, 1929.

KRAG, THE KOOTENAY RAM AND OTHER ANIMAL STORIES. London:
University of London Press, 1929.

THE CUTE COYOTE, AND OTHER ANIMAL STORIES...FROM "WILD ANIMALS
AT HOME," "WILD ANIMAL WAYS," AND "LIVES OF THE HUNTED." London: University of London Press, 1930.

JOHNNY BEAR, LOBO AND OTHER STORIES. New York: Scribner, 1935.

THE BIOGRAPHY OF AN ARCTIC FOX. New York: Appleton-Century, 1937.

GREAT HISTORIC ANIMALS: MAINLY ABOUT WOLVES. London: Methuen,
1937.

ERNEST THOMPSON SETON'S TRAIL AND CAMP-FIRE STORIES. Ed. Julia
M. Seton. New York: Appleton-Century, 1940.

SANTANA, THE HERO DOG OF FRANCE. Los Angeles: Phoenix Press, 1945.

THE BEST OF ERNEST THOMPSON SETON. Selected by W. Kay Robinson. London: Hodder & Stoughton, 1949.

OTHER PROSE

For a list of Seton's essays and other nature books see A CHECKLIST OF CA-NADIAN LITERATURE AND BACKGROUND MATERIALS, by Reginald E. Watters (Toronto, 1972), pp. 639-40 and 982.

CRITICISM

Anon. "The Animal Story." EDINBURGH REVIEW, 214 (July 1911), 94-118.

Bodsworth, C. F. "Backwoods Genius with the Magic Pen." MacLEAN'S MAGAZINE, 72 (June 6, 1959), 22.

Chapman, F. M. "Champion of E. T. Seton." SATURDAY REVIEW OF LITER-ATURE, 16 (October 2, 1937), 9.

Garst, Shannon and Warren Garst. ERNEST THOMPSON SETON, NATURALIST. New York: Messner, 1959.

Magee, William H. "The Animal Story: A Challenge in Technique." DAL-HOUSIE REVIEW, 44 (Summer 1964), 156-64.

Morley, Patricia. "Seton's Animals." JOURNAL OF CANADIAN FICTION, 2 (Summer 1973), 195-98.

Poirier, Michel. "The Animal Story in Canadian Literature: E. Thompson Seton and Charles G. D. Roberts." QUEEN'S QUARTERLY, 34 (January-March 1927), 298-312; (April-June 1927), 398-419.

Polk, James. "Lives of the Hunted." CANADIAN LITERATURE, 53 (Summer 1972), 51-59.

Read, Stanley E. "Flight to the Primitive: Ernest Thompson Seton." CANA-DIAN LITERATURE, 13 (Summer 1962), 45-57.

Chapter 5

MINOR AUTHORS

Chapter 5
MINOR AUTHORS

The number of Canadian writers whose work appeared in print at least once reaches into the several hundreds. In his HANDBOOK OF CANADIAN LITERATURE (see Chapter 1, above), Archibald MacMurchy provides brief biographies for one hundred and thirty-six writers, and Dewart, as early as 1864, found forty-eight poets worthy of inclusion in his SELECTIONS FROM CANADIAN POETS (see Chapter 3). Not all are worthy of critical attention, however, and not all are included in this bibliography.

I have chosen those writers who have appeared consistently in modern anthologies, who have received some notice in THE LITERARY HISTORY OF CANADA and a few who, though they appear in neither, have in my opinion made a distinct contribution to the progress of Canadian letters. Should any reader wish to examine the work of an omitted writer, he will find the anthologies of Dewart and Lighthall, cited in Chapter 3, and MacMurchy's HANDBOOK good places to begin.

ADAMS, LEVI (d. 1832)

Most pioneer poets took themselves quite seriously and turned out some very dull poems on the virtues of hard work and the beauties of nature. Very few felt that either the time or place lent itself to satiric treatment. Levi Adams was an exception: in THE CHARIVARI he not only left us an amusing poem (still eminently readable)--

> I like thee Canada, I like thy woods
> ....
> Thy seasons too, when Nature can imprint her
> Steps on the green--but the deuce take thy Winter.

--but also provided a picture of Canadian colonial customs and social habits. The authorship of THE CHARIVARI, published anonymously, has been established by Carl Klink's research, below.

POETRY

THE CHARIVARI; OR, CANADIAN POETICS. A TALE AFTER THE MANNER OF BEPPO. Montreal: n.p., 1824. Reprinted in full in THE EVOLUTION OF CANADIAN LITERATURE IN ENGLISH: BEGINNINGS TO 1867. Ed. Mary Jane Edwards. Toronto: Holt, Rinehart & Winston, 1973, pp. 89-134.

JEAN BAPTISTE. A POETIC OLIO IN II CANTOS. Montreal: n.p., 1825.

TALES OF CHIVALRY AND ROMANCE. Edinburgh: Robertson; London: Cradock & Joy, 1826.

CRITICISM

Edwards, Mary Jane. "Levi Adams." In THE EVOLUTION OF CANADIAN LITERATURE IN ENGLISH: BEGINNINGS TO 1867, pp. 87-89. Toronto: Holt, Rinehart & Winston, 1973.

Klinck, Carl F. "The Charivari and Levi Adams." DALHOUSIE REVIEW, 40 (Spring 1960), 34-42.

Lande, Lawrence M. "Levi Adams." In OLD LAMPS AGLOW, pp. 108-12, 130-43. Montreal: Privately printed, 1957.

BALLANTYNE, ROBERT MICHAEL (1825-1894)

Ballantyne is one of several non-native writers who wrote about Canada while
in Canada. Born in Scotland (to the family which founded the Ballantyne Press
and had disastrous business associations with Walter Scott), he apprenticed himself at sixteen to the Hudson's Bay Company and spent six years at several Canadian fur-trading posts.. His experiences provided material for several juvenile
novels and pseudo-fictitious works involving adventures among the Indians in
the wilds of Canada. These were highly popular, as were his other non-Cana-
dian novels, notably CORAL ISLAND.

Only the Canadian-based works are listed below; for a complete list of Ballantyne's work see Eric Quayle's bibliography, below. Since many of his novels,
particularly those published in later editions by Musson in Toronto, are without imprint date, I have recorded dates of first publication only.

BIBLIOGRAPHY

Quayle, Eric. R. M. BALLANTYNE: A BIBLIOGRAPHY OF FIRST EDITIONS.
London: Dawsons, 1968.

FICTION

SNOWFLAKES AND SUNBEAMS; OR, THE YOUNG FUR TRADERS. A TALE
OF THE FAR NORTH. London: Nelson, 1856. Subsequently published as
THE YOUNG FUR TRADERS.

UNGAVA: A TALE OF ESQUIMAUX-LAND. London: Nelson, 1858.

THE DOG CRUSOE: A TALE OF THE WESTERN PRAIRIES. London: Nelson,
1861.

THE GOLDEN DREAM: OR, ADVENTURES IN THE FAR WEST. London:
Shaw & Co., 1861.

AWAY IN THE WILDERNESS: OR, LIFE AMONG THE RED INDIANS AND FUR-TRADERS OF NORTH AMERICA. London: Nisbet & Co., 1863.

> This is vol. I of BALLANTYNE'S MISCELLANY, a series of eighteen novels written and priced for "the poor." For a complete list of the novels in this series see Eric Quayle, R.M. BALLANTYNE: A BIBLIOGRAPHY OF FIRST EDITIONS (cited above).

THE WILD MAN OF THE WEST: A TALE OF THE ROCKY MOUNTAINS. London: Routledge, 1863.

OVER THE ROCKY MOUNTAINS: OR, WANDERING WILL IN THE LAND OF THE RED SKINS. London: Nisbet & Co., 1869.

> Vol. VII of BALLANTYNE'S MISCELLANY.

THE PIONEERS: A TALE OF THE WESTERN WILDERNESS. London: Nisbet & Co., 1872.

> Based on the explorations of Sir Alexander MacKenzie.

TALES OF ADVENTURE BY FLOOD, FIELD, AND MOUNTAIN. London: Nisbet & Co., 1874.

THE RED MAN'S REVENGE: A TALE OF THE RED RIVER FLOOD. London: Nisbet & Co., 1880.

THE PRAIRIE CHIEF. London: Nisbet & Co., 1886.

THE BIG OTTER: A TALE OF THE GREAT NOR'WEST. London: Routledge, 1887.

THE BUFFALO RUNNERS: A TALE OF THE RED RIVER PLAINS. London: Nisbet & Co., 1891.

CRITICISM

Quayle, Eric. BALLANTYNE THE BRAVE. London: Rupert Hart-Davis, 1967.

Selby, Joan. "Ballantyne and the Fur Traders." CANADIAN LITERATURE, 18 (Autumn 1963), 40-46.

BARR, ROBERT ("LUKE SHORT") (1850-1912)

Barr is one of the "displaced" writers of the nineteenth century. Born in Scotland, he was brought to Canada as a very young boy, lived there for nearly thirty years, went to the United States where, for a few years, he pursued a career as a humorist with the Detroit FREE PRESS, and finally settled in England where he continued to write fiction and collaborated with Jerome K. Jerome to found THE IDLER (1892-1911). In the course of his career he published more than forty books and completed Stephen Crane's THE O'RUDDY. Literary historians, however, still have not decided whether Barr is to be regarded as an American, English, or Canadian writer. He is practically ignored by the historians of the former two nations and is not included in Watters' CHECKLIST OF CANADIAN LITERATURE. Frederick W. Cogswell, cited below, suggests that perhaps Canada has the best claim to Barr because his formative years were spent there and because his best novel, THE MEASURE OF THE RULE, is "Canadian." Overlooking the fact that most of his other novels are not so oriented, I have accepted Cogswell's argument and included Barr in this bibliography. Since no bibliography of his work exists, I have listed all Barr's fiction.

FICTION

STRANGE HAPPENINGS. London: W. A. Dunkerley, 1883.

IN A STEAMER CHAIR AND OTHER SHIPBOARD STORIES. New York: Stokes; London: Chatto & Windus, 1892.

FROM WHOSE BOURNE. London: Chatto & Windus, 1893; New York: Stokes, 1896.
    Three long stories.

THE FACE AND THE MASK. London: Hutchinson, 1894; New York: Stokes, 1895.

IN THE MIDST OF ALARMS. Philadelphia: J. B. Lippincott, 1893; New York: Stokes; London: Methuen, 1894.

The only Barr novel except THE MEASURE OF THE RULE which may be considered "Canadian"; a humorous account of the Fenian Raids during which Barr was a Canadian Volunteer.

A WOMAN INTERVENES. New York: Stokes; London: Chatto & Windus, 1896.

ONE DAY'S COURTSHIP, AND THE HERALDS OF FAME. New York: Stokes, [1896].

THE MUTABLE MANY. New York: Stokes, 1896; London: Methuen, 1897.

REVENGE! New York: Stokes; London: Chatto & Windus, 1896.
Short stories.

GENTLEMEN, THE KING! New York: Stokes, 1899.

TEKLA. A ROMANCE OF LOVE AND WAR. New York: Stokes; Toronto: Morang, 1898. Published as THE COUNTESS TEKLA. London: Methuen, 1899.

JENNIE BAXTER, JOURNALIST. New York: Stokes; Toronto: Copp Clark; London: Methuen, 1899.

THE STRONG ARM. New York: Stokes; Toronto: Briggs, 1899; London: Methuen, 1900.
Short stories.

THE VICTORS. A ROMANCE OF YESTERDAY MORNING AND THIS AFTERNOON. New York: Stokes, 1901; London: Methuen, 1902.

THE KING DINES. London: McClure, 1901.

A PRINCE OF GOOD FELLOWS. New York: McClure; London: Chatto & Windus, 1902.
A story of James V of Scotland.

OVER THE BORDER. New York: Stokes; London: Ibister, 1903.

THE O'RUDDY (with Stephen Crane). New York: Stokes, 1903.

A CHICAGO PRINCESS. New York: Stokes, 1904.

THE WOMAN WINS. New York: Stokes, 1904.

THE LADY ELECTRA. London: Methuen, 1904.

THE SPECULATIONS OF JOHN STEELE. New York: Stokes; London: Chatto & Windus, 1905.

THE TEMPESTUOUS PETTICOAT. London: Methuen, 1905.

THE TRIUMPHS OF EUGENE VALMONT. New York: Appleton; London: Hunt & Blackett, 1906.

THE WATERMEAD AFFAIR. Philadelphia: H. Altemus, 1906.

THE MEASURE OF THE RULE. London: Constable, 1907; New York: Appleton, 1908. Reprint ed. with introduction by Louis K. MacKendrick. Toronto: University of Toronto Press, 1973.

YOUNG LORD STRANLEIGH. London & Toronto: Ward, Lock; New York: Appleton, 1908.

CARDILLAC. Toronto: McLeod & Allan; New York: Stokes; London: Mills & Boon, 1909.

STRANLEIGH'S MILLIONS. London: Eveleigh Nash, 1909.

THE GIRL IN THE CASE: BEING THE MANOEUVRES OF THE INADVERTENT MR. PEPPERTON. London: Eveleigh Nash, 1910; Hodder & Stoughton, 1914.

THE SWORD MAKER. A ROMANCE OF LOVE AND ADVENTURE. New York: Stokes; London: Mills & Boon, 1910.

LORD STRANLEIGH, PHILANTHROPIST. London: Ward, Lock, 1911.

LADY ELEANOR, LAWBREAKER. Chicago: Rand McNally, [1911].

THE PALACE OF LOGS. London: Mills & Boon, 1912.

LORD STRANLEIGH ABROAD. London: Lock & Co., 1913.

MY ENEMY JONES. AN EXTRAVAGANZA. London: Eveleigh Nash, 1913.

A WOMAN IN A THOUSAND. London: Hodder & Stoughton, 1913.

THE HELPING HAND AND OTHER STORIES. London: Mills & Boon, 1920.

TALES OF TWO CONTINENTS. London: Mills & Boon, 1920.

CRITICISM

Allan, C. S. "A Glimpse of Robert Barr." CANADIAN MAGAZINE, 4 (April 1895), 545-50.

Brown, W. J. "Robert Barr and Literature in Canada." CANADIAN MAGA-ZINE, 15 (June 1900), 170-76.

Burpee, L[awrence] J. "Canadian Novels and Novelists." SEWANEE REVIEW, 11 (October 1903), 385-411.

C., J. A. "Canadian Celebrities: Robert Barr." CANADIAN MAGAZINE, 14 (December 1899), 181-82.

Cogswell, Frederick W. "The Canadian Novel from Confederation to World War I." Thesis, University of New Brunswick, 1950.

Full chapter devoted to Barr.

McKendrick, Tom. "Robert Barr: His Life and Work." Thesis, University of Toronto, 1906.

BROOKE (MOORE), FRANCES (1723-1789)

Frances Brooke was born and died in England; she was, and is even now, usually classified as an English, not a Canadian, writer. She lived in Canada for five years, 1763-1768, while her husband was military chaplain at Quebec, and there she wrote, or at least compiled notes for, the first novel to come out of North America, EMILY MONTAGUE (1769). It is for that reason and because the book is distinctively "Canadian" (see New, William H. "Frances Brooke's Chequered Gardens," below) that she is accorded a place, and a fairly prominent one, in Canadian literature. In England, she was, in E. P. Poole's words, "a literary lion of a minor order," and among the guests attending a gathering held to celebrate her departure to Canada were Hannah More, Miss Seward, Dr. Johnson, and James Boswell.

FICTION

THE OLD MAID. A weekly periodical edited by Frances Moore under the pseudonym "Mary Singleton, Spinster." Nos. 1-37, November 15, 1755 to July 24, 1756. A revised one-volume edition was published by Millar of London in 1764.

Translation of LETTERS FROM LADY JULIA CATESBY, TO HER FRIEND HENRIETTA CAMPLEY, by M. J. Riccoboni. London: Dodsley, 1760.

THE HISTORY OF LADY JULIA MANDEVILLE. 2 vols. London: Dodsley, 1763. Modern ed. Ed. E. Phillips Poole. London: Partridge, 1930.

THE HISTORY OF EMILY MONTAGUE. 4 vols. London: Dodsley, 1769. Modern ed. Ed. L. J. Burpee. Ottawa: Graphic Press, 1931; ed. Carl F. Klinck. Toronto: McClelland & Stewart, 1961.

Translation of MEMOIRS OF THE MARQUIS DE ST. FORLAIX, by M. Framery. 4 vols. London: Dodsley, 1770.

ALL'S RIGHT AT LAST: OR, THE HISTORY OF MISS WEST. 2 vols. London, 1774.

Not provably Brooke's, but attributed to her by Andrew Block in THE ENGLISH NOVEL 1740-1850 (London, 1961). The writing, however, is of much poorer quality than that of Brooke's other novels.

THE EXCURSION. 2 vols. London: Cadell, 1777.

THE HISTORY OF CHARLES MANDEVILLE. 2 vols. London: Lane, 1790.

ACCUSING SPIRIT: OR, DE COURCY AND EGLANTINE. 4 vols. London, 1802. Attributed to Brooke by Halkett and Laing in DICTIONARY OF ANONYMOUS AND PSEUDONYMOUS LITERATURE (New ed. Edinburgh, 1926-62).

MANNERS: A NOVEL. 3 vols. London: Baldwin, Cradock & Joy, 1818. Attributed to Brooke by Block in THE ENGLISH NOVEL 1740-1850.

A YEAR AND A DAY: A NOVEL IN TWO VOLUMES BY MADAME PANACHE. London, 1818. Attributed to Brooke by Halkett and Laing in DICTIONARY OF ANONYMOUS AND PSEUDONYMOUS LITERATURE.

DRAMA

VIRGINIA, A TRAGEDY, WITH ODES, PASTORALS AND TRANSLATIONS. London: Privately printed, 1756.

Halkett and Laing, in their DICTIONARY OF ANONYMOUS AND PSEUDONYMOUS LITERATURE, state that the real author of the play was not Brooke but Samuel Crisp. Their opinion, however, does not weigh heavily with modern bibliographers.

THE SIEGE OF SINOPE: A TRAGEDY. London: Cadell, 1781.

ROSINA: A COMIC OPERA IN TWO ACTS. London: Cadell, 1781.

MARION: A COMIC OPERA IN TWO ACTS. London: Longman, 1800.

CRITICISM

Baker, Ernest A. "Mrs. Frances Brooke." In THE HISTORY OF THE ENGLISH NOVEL, vol. V, pp. 144-46. London: Witherby, 1934.

Beyea, George P. "The Canadian Novel Prior to Confederation." Thesis, University of New Brunswick, 1950.

Blue, Charles S. "Canada's First Novelist." CANADIAN MAGAZINE, 58 (November 1921), 3-12.

Burwash, Ida. "An Old Time Novel." CANADIAN MAGAZINE, 28 (January 1907), 252-56.

Klinck, Carl F. "Introduction" to his edition of EMILY MONTAGUE. Toronto: McClelland & Stewart, 1961.

Lighthall, William Douw [Wilfrid Chateauclair]. "The First Canadian Novel." DOMINION ILLUSTRATED, 4 (January 1890), 31.

New, William H. "Frances Brooke's Chequered Gardens." CANADIAN LITERATURE, 52 (Spring 1972), 24-38.

Pacey, Desmond. "The First Canadian Novel." DALHOUSIE REVIEW, 26 (July 1946), 145-50. Reprinted in his ESSAYS IN CANADIAN CRITICISM 1938-1968. Toronto: Ryerson, 1969, pp. 30-38.

Poole, E. Phillips. "Introduction and Bibliographical Lists" in his edition of THE HISTORY OF LADY JULIA MANDEVILLE. London: Partridge, 1930, pp. 11-40.

Woodley, E. C. "The First Canadian Novel and Its Author." EDUCATIONAL RECORD, 57 (January 1914), 31-36.

BURWELL, ADAM HOOD (1790-1849)

As a poet, Adam Burwell was neither particularly prolific nor able. His "Talbot Road", however, remains one of the most representative poems of early Canada. In its depiction of the early settlers' determination to carve a new social order out of the wilderness of Canada (in theme somewhat akin to Goldsmith's "The Rising Village"), it established certain archetypal symbols (the axe-wielder, for example) which became common in later literature. For that reason Burwell has found a permanent place in Canadian anthologies and in Canadian literary history.

POETRY

SUMMER EVENING CONTEMPLATIONS. Montreal: Lovell, 1849.

THE POEMS OF ADAM HOOD BURWELL, PIONEER POET OF UPPER CANADA. Ed. Carl F. Klinck. London, Ontario: University of Western Ontario, 1963.

CRITICISM

Edwards, Mary Jane. "Adam Hood Burwell." In THE EVOLUTION OF CANADIAN LITERATURE IN ENGLISH: BEGINNINGS TO 1867, pp. 59-69. Toronto: Holt, Rinehart & Winston, 1973.

Klinck, Carl F. "Adam Hood Burwell, 1790-1849." In THE POEMS OF ADAM HOOD BURWELL, pp. iii-lx. London, Ontario: University of Western Ontario, 1963.

Lande, Lawrence M. "Adam Hood Burwell." In OLD LAMPS AGLOW, pp. 242-53. Montreal: Privately printed, 1957.

CAMERON, GEORGE FREDERICK (1854-1885)

Cameron died at the age of thirty-one, too young to have written enough to establish himself as a major Canadian poet, and his only book of poems was published posthumously. But LYRICS ON FREEDOM, LOVE AND DEATH contains evidence sufficient to indicate that Cameron could write good poetry and was devoted to his craft. The number of his poems included in anthologies (such as those of Klinck and Watters and A. J. M. Smith) supports this assertion.

POETRY

LYRICS ON FREEDOM, LOVE AND DEATH. Ed. Charles J. Cameron. Boston: Moore; Kingston, Ont.: Shannon, 1887.

LEO, THE ROYAL CADET. Kingston, Ont.: Henderson, [1889].
> Libretto for an opera.

CRITICISM

Bourinot, Arthur S. "George Frederick Cameron." CANADIAN AUTHOR AND BOOKMAN, 29 (Winter 1954), 3-5. Reprinted in his FIVE CANADIAN POETS, pp. 22-26. Montreal: Quality Press, 1956.

Burpee, Lawrence J. "George Frederick Cameron." In his A LITTLE BOOK OF CANADIAN ESSAYS, pp. 73-87. Toronto: Musson, 1909.

Dyde, S. W. "The Two Camerons." QUEEN'S REVIEW, 3 (August 1929), 196-98.

Kyte, E. C. "George Frederick Cameron." EDUCATIONAL RECORD, 63 (April-June 1947), 117-22.

Lampman, Archibald. "Two Canadian Poets: A Lecture, 1891." UNIVERSITY OF TORONTO QUARTERLY, 13 (July 1944), 406-23. Reprinted in MASKS OF POETRY, pp. 26-44. Ed. A. J. M. Smith. Toronto: McClelland & Stewart, 1962.

M., J. "Who's Who in Canadian Literature: George Frederick Cameron." CANADIAN BOOKMAN, 13 (September 1931), 179-80.

Vivien, Geoffrey. "A Forgotten Canadian Poet." CANADIAN AUTHOR AND BOOKMAN, 23 (December 1947), 57.

DE MILLE, JAMES (1833-1880)

James De Mille is another Canadian writer whose reputation rests largely on a single book: A STRANGE MANUSCRIPT FOUND IN A COPPER CYLINDER, published posthumously in 1888. It is, as Fred Cogswell asserts in LITERARY HISTORY OF CANADA (Toronto, 1968, p. 115), a very interesting work and the best produced in eastern Canada up to 1888. Yet, before this novel was published, De Mille had been extremely popular (particularly in the United States) as a writer of both juvenile and adult fiction. Boys raved over his B.O.W.C. (Brethren of the White Cross) series; adults looked forward eagerly to his romances. The boys' stories, in which humour is redemptive, are superior to the latter, the crudity and implausibility of which make them barely readable today. In the final analysis, therefore, A STRANGE MANUSCRIPT remains the single basis for according De Mille any critical attention.

BIBLIOGRAPHY AND MANUSCRIPTS

MacLeod, Douglas E. "A Critical Biography of James De Mille." Thesis, Dalhousie University, 1968.

    Contains a comprehensive list of stories published in serials (chiefly THE CHRISTIAN WATCHMAN).

The De Mille manuscript collection is housed at Dalhousie University in Halifax, Nova Scotia.

POETRY

BEHIND THE VEIL. Halifax, N.S.: T. C. Allen, 1893.

FICTION

The "B.O.W.C." Series
    THE "B.O.W.C." A BOOK FOR BOYS. Boston: Lee & Shepard,

1869.

LOST IN THE FOG. Boston: Lee & Shepard, 1871 [1870].

THE BOYS OF THE GRAND PRÉ SCHOOL. Boston: Lee & Shepard, 1871 [1870].

FIRE IN THE WOODS. Boston: Lee ·& Shepard, 1872 [1871]. Reprint ed. 1893.

PICKED UP ADRIFT. Boston: Lee & Shepard, 1872.

THE TREASURE OF THE SEAS. Boston: Lee & Shepard, [1872]. Reprint ed. 1898.

The Young Dodge Club Series

THE DODGE CLUB; OR, ITALY IN 1859. New York: Harper, 1869.

AMONG THE BRIGANDS. Boston: Lee & Shepard, 1872 [1871]. Reprint ed. 1899.

THE SEVEN HILLS. Boston: Lee & Shepard, 1873 [1872].

THE WINGED LION; OR, STORIES OF VENICE. Boston: Lee & Shepard, 1877 [1876].

JOHN WHEELER'S TWO UNCLES; OR, LAUNCHING INTO LIFE. New York: Carlton & Porter, [1860].

ANDY O'HARA; OR, THE CHILD OF PROMISE. New York: Carlton & Porter, 1861.

THE MARTYR OF THE CATACOMBS. A TALE OF ANCIENT ROME. New York: Carlton & Porter, 1865.

HELENA'S HOUSEHOLD; A TALE OF ROME IN THE FIRST CENTURY. New York: Robert Carter, 1868 [1867]. Reprinted as HELENA'S HOUSEHOLD; AN IDEAL OF ROMAN LIFE IN THE TIME OF PAUL AND NERO. New York: Ward & Drummond, 1890.

CORD AND CREESE. New York: Harper, [1869].

THE LADY OF THE ICE. New York: Appleton, 1870.

THE CRYPTOGRAM. New York: Harper, 1871 [1870].

THE AMERICAN BARON. New York: Harper, 1872.

A COMEDY OF TERRORS. Boston: J. R. Osgood, 1872.

AN OPEN QUESTION. New York: Appleton, 1873.

THE LILY, AND THE CROSS. A TALE OF ACADIA. Boston: Lee & Shepard, [1874]. Reprint ed. 1890.
   Juvenile fiction.

THE LIVING LINK. New York: Harper, 1874.

THE BABES IN THE WOODS. A TRAGIC COMEDY. A TALE OF THE ITALIAN REVOLUTION OF 1848. Boston: W. F. Gilly, 1875.

A CASTLE IN SPAIN. New York: Harper, 1883. Originally published in HARPER'S MAGAZINE, vols. 66 & 67, 1883.

OLD GARTH. A STORY OF SICILY. New York: G. Munro, 1883.

A STRANGE MANUSCRIPT FOUND IN A COPPER CYLINDER. New York: Harper; London: Chatto & Windus, 1888. Reprint ed. Toronto: Macmillan, 1910. Reprint ed. in paperback with introduction by R. E. Watters. Toronto: McClelland & Stewart, 1969.

CRITICISM

Bevan, A. R. "James De Mille and Archibald MacMechan." DALHOUSIE REVIEW, 36 (Autumn 1955), 201-15.

Burpee, L[awrence] J. "James De Mille." CANADIAN BOOKMAN, 8 (July 1926), 203-6.

_____. "Canadian Novels and Novelists." SEWANEE REVIEW, 11 (October 1903), 308-411.

Crockett, A. J. "Concerning James De Mille." In MORE STUDIES IN NOVA SCOTIAN HISTORY, pp. 120-48. Ed. George Patterson. Halifax: Imperial Publishing Co., 1941.

Douglas, R. W. "James De Mille." CANADIAN BOOKMAN, 4 (January 1922), 39-44.

Killian, Crawford. "The Cheerful Inferno of James De Mille." JOURNAL OF CANADIAN FICTION, 1, no. 3 (Summer 1972), 61-67.

MacLeod, Douglas E. "A Critical Biography of James De Mille." Thesis, Dalhousie University, 1968.

MacMechan, Archibald. "Concerning James De Mille." CANADIAN BOOK-MAN, 4 (April 1922), 125-26.

_____. "De Mille, the Man and Writer." CANADIAN MAGAZINE, 27 (September 1906), 404-16.

Woodcock, George. "De Mille and the Utopian Vision." JOURNAL OF CA-NADIAN FICTION, 2 (Summer 1973), 174-79.

DOUGALL, LILY A. (1858-1923)

Born in Montreal, educated in Scotland, Lily Dougall lived most of her life in England and wrote novels about Canada (or at least used a Canadian setting). In THE ZEIT-GEIST she summarized the tenor of her novels: "I do not believe that it belongs to the novel to teach theology; but I do believe that religious sentiments and opinions are a legitimate subject of its art, and perhaps its highest function is to promote understanding by bringing into contact minds that habitually misinterpret one another" (preface). Accordingly, in each of her eleven novels she uses the framework of the mystery novel to discuss religion (Mormon, Adventist, Mesmerism) and philosophy. Often the plot gets in the way of the idea, and most of the novels, while original in conception, fail to impress. In 1908 Dougall gave up novel-writing to devote her time to straightforward religious writing (for a list of these works, see A CHECKLIST OF CANADIAN LITERATURE AND BACKGROUND MATERIALS, 1628-1960, by Reginald E. Watters [Toronto, 1972]).

POETRY

ARCADES AMBO (with Gilbert Sheldon). Oxford: Blackwell, 1919.

FICTION

BEGGARS ALL. London: Longmans, 1891.

WHAT NECESSITY KNOWS. 3 vols. London & New York: Longmans, 1893.

THE MADONNA OF A DAY. New York: Appleton, 1895; London: Richard Bentley, 1896. Reprinted from TEMPLE BAR, Vols. 106 (1895) and 107 (1896).

THE MERMAID. New York: Appleton, 1895.

A QUESTION OF FAITH. Boston: Houghton Mifflin; London: Hutchinson, 1895.

Dougall, Lily A.

THE ZEIT-GEIST. New York: Appleton, 1895.

A DOZEN WAYS OF LOVE. London: A. & C. Black, 1897.

THE MORMON PROPHET. New York: Appleton; London: A. & C. Black, 1899.

THE EARTHLY PURGATORY. London: Hutchinson, 1904. Reprinted as THE SUMMIT HOUSE MYSTERY. New York: Funk & Wagnall's, 1905.

YOUNG LOVE. London: A. & C. Black, 1904.
    Short stories.

THE SPANISH DOWRY. London: Hutchinson; Toronto: Copp Clark, 1906.

PATHS OF THE RIGHTEOUS. London: Macmillan, 1908.

CRITICISM

MacPherson, Katherine L. "Lily Dougall and Her Work." CANADIAN MAGA-ZINE, 27 (September 1906), 478-80.

DRUMMOND, WILLIAM HENRY (1854-1907)

In the preface to his book of poems, THE HABITANT (1897), Drummond included the following reminder: "My friends: Understand that I have not written the verses as examples of 'dialect, or with any thought of ridicule." For many years (and many editions) readers accepted Drummond's word and settled back, untroubled by questions of plausibility, to enjoy the good humour of his habitant poems, written in a mixture of French and English, the non-language that was his trademark.

Born in Ireland, Drummond came to Canada in 1864. He became a physician in rural Quebec and later in Montreal. That he admired French-Canadians and loved their way of life, there is no doubt; that his poems represented their true feelings

> An' onder de flag of Angleterre, so long as that flag was fly--
> Wit deir English broder, les Canayens is satisfy leev and die

is another matter. In any event, Drummond's poetry, though widely read, was not truly representative of his own era and is now out of fashion.

POETRY

THE HABITANT AND OTHER FRENCH-CANADIAN POEMS. New York: Putnam's, 1897.

PHIL-O-RUM'S CANOE AND MADELEINE VERCHERES. New York: Putnam's, 1898.

JOHNNIE COURTEAU AND OTHER POEMS. New York: Putnam's, 1901.

THE VOYAGEUR AND OTHER POEMS. New York: Putnam's, 1901.

THE GREAT FIGHT. POEMS AND SKETCHES. New York: Putnam's, 1908.

THE POETICAL WORKS. Introduction by Louis Frechette. New York: Putnam's 1912. Published in Canada as DR. WILLIAM HENRY DRUMMOND'S COMPLETE POEMS. Toronto: McClelland & Stewart, 1926.

HABITANT POEMS. Selected with introduction by Arthur L. Phelps. Paperback ed. Toronto: McClelland & Stewart, 1959.

CRITICISM

Anon. "Two Canadian Poets: Frechette and Drummond." EDINBURGH REVIEW, 209 (April 1909), 474-99.

Bell, Merirose. "The Image of French Canada in the Poetry of William Henry Drummond, Emile Coderre, and A. M. Klein." Thesis, McGill University, 1967.

Burpee, Lawrence J. "William Henry Drummond." NATION, 84 (April 11, 1907), 334-36.

_____. "William Henry Drummond." In LEADING CANADIAN POETS, pp. 71-78. Ed. W. P. Percival. Toronto: Ryerson, 1948.

Craig, R. H. "Reminiscences of W. H. Drummond." DALHOUSIE REVIEW, 5 (July 1925), 161-69.

Drummond, Mary Harvey. "William Henry Drummond." In THE GREAT FIGHT, pp. 3-48. New York: Putnam's.

Dustan, William G. "The Interpreter of the Habitant: William Henry Drummond." Thesis, Dalhousie University, 1928.

Gibbon, John Murray. "William Henry Drummond." EDUCATIONAL RECORD, 60 (April-June 1944), 93-96.

MacDonald, John Ford. WILLIAM HENRY DRUMMOND. Toronto: Ryerson, n.d.

Mahon, A. Wylie. "The Poet of the Habitant." CANADIAN MAGAZINE, 29 (May 1907), 56-60.

O'Hagan, Thomas. "A Canadian Dialect Poet." In INTIMACIES IN CANA-DIAN LIFE AND LETTERS, pp. 83-94. Ottawa: Graphic Press, 1927.

Rashley, R. E. "W. H. Drummond and the Dilemma of Style." DALHOUSIE REVIEW, 28 (January 1949), 387-96.

Rhodenizer, V[ernon] B[lair]. "Who's Who in Canadian Literature: William Henry Drummond." CANADIAN BOOKMAN, 9 (February 1927), 35-36.

Stevenson, O. J. "Poet, Artist and Citizen." In A PEOPLE'S BEST, pp. 211-18. Toronto: Musson, 1927.

V., E.Q. "Canadian Celebrities: Dr. W. H. Drummond." CANADIAN MAGAZINE, 13 (May 1899), 62-64.

FLEMING, MAY AGNES (1840-1880)

Mrs. Fleming, a Saint John housewife turned novelist, is distinguished in the literary history of Canada by two curious facts: (1) during the eighteen-seventies, lean years for writers and non-writers alike, she is reputed to have earned as much as $10,000 a year from her novels, and (2) twenty-seven of her forty-two novels were published posthumously. Both distinctions, perhaps unequalled, attest to her industry and high popularity as a writer of readable romances; the popularity, however, was more a tribute to her facility than to her artistry. Her novels are shallow, unrealistic treatments of English high society into which, out of token respect for her native land, she introduced a few Canadian characters.

FICTION

Carleton, Cousin May [pseud.] SILVER STAR; OR, THE MYSTERY OF FONTELLE HALL. A TALE OF NEW JERSEY IN THE OLDEN TIME. New York: Brady, [1861].

SYBIL CAMPBELL; OR, THE QUEEN OF THE ISLE. New York: Beadle, 1861. Published as AN AWFUL MYSTERY (New York: Beadle, 1875) and as THE QUEEN OF THE ISLE (New York: Dillingham, 1886).

Carleton, Cousin May [pseud.] ERMINIE; OR, THE GYPSY'S VOW. A TALE OF LOVE AND VENGEANCE. New York: Brady, 1863. Published as THE GYPSY QUEEN'S VOW. New York: Beadle, 1869.

LA MASQUE; OR, THE MIDNIGHT QUEEN. New York: Brady, 1863. Published as THE MIDNIGHT QUEEN. New York: Beadle, 1876.

THE TWIN SISTERS; OR, THE WRONGED WIFE'S HATE. New York: Beadle, 1864. Published as THE RIVAL BROTHERS. New York: Beadle, 1875.

VICTORIA; OR, THE HEIRESS OF CASTLE CLIFFE. New York: Brady, [1864]. Published as UNMASKED. New York: Beadle, 1870.

Early, Miss M. A. [pseud.] EVLALIE; OR, THE WIFE'S TRAGEDY. New York: Brady, [1866].

LADY EVELYN; OR, THE LORD OF ROYAL REST. Chicago: Donohue, [1869]; New York: Street & Smith, 1899.

WHO WINS? OR, THE SECRET OF MONKSWOOD WASTE. Chicago: Donohue, [1870]; New York: Munro, 1895.

GUY EARLSCOURT'S WIFE. New York: Carleton; London: Low, 1873.

A WONDERFUL WOMAN. New York: Carleton, 1873.

A TERRIBLE SECRET. New York: Carleton; London: Low, 1874; New York: Dillingham, 1887.

THE DARK SECRET. New York: Hurst, [1875].

A MAD MARRIAGE. New York: Carleton; London: Low, 1875.

NORINE'S REVENGE, AND, SIR NOEL'S HEIR. New York: Carleton, 1875. SIR NOEL'S HEIR published separately. New York: Lupton, 1892.

KATE DANTON; OR, CAPTAIN DANTON'S DAUGHTERS. New York: Carleton; London: Low, 1876.

ONE NIGHT'S MYSTERY. New York: Carleton; London: Low, 1876.

SILENT AND TRUE; OR, A LITTLE QUEEN. New York: Carleton, 1877.

THE HEIR OF CHARLTON. New York: Carleton, 1878.

LOST FOR A WOMAN. New York: Carleton; London: Low, 1880.

CARRIED BY STORM. New York: Carleton, 1880.

A CHANGED HEART. New York: Carleton; London: Low, 1881.

FATED TO MARRY; A NIGHT OF TERROR; KATHLEEN. New York: Ogilvie, 1881.

THE THREE COUSINS; ONE SUMMER MONTH. New York: Ogilvie, 1881.

A WIFE'S TRAGEDY. New York: Carleton; Toronto: Rose Belford, 1881.

PATRICIA KEMBERLEY. Toronto: Rose Belford, 1882.

PRIDE AND PASSION. New York: Carleton, 1882; New York: Dillingham, 1888.

THE SECRET SORROW. New York: Ogilvie, 1883.

SHARING HER CRIME. New York: Carleton; London: Low, 1883.

A WRONGED WIFE. New York: Dillingham, 1883.

MAUDE PERCY'S SECRET. New York: Carleton, 1884.

THE ACTRESS' DAUGHTER. New York: Carleton; London: Low, 1886.

UNCLE FRED'S VISIT AND HOW IT ENDED. London: Mowbray, [1888].

THE VIRGINIA HEIRESS. New York: Street & Smith, 1888.

ESTELLA'S HUSBAND; OR, THRICE LOST, THRICE WON. New York: Munro, [1891].

MARRIED FOR MONEY, AND OTHER STORIES. New York: Ogilvie, 1891.

A PRETTY GOVERNESS, AND OTHER STORIES. New York: Ogilvie, 1891.

THE BARONET'S BRIDE; OR, A WOMAN'S VENGEANCE. Ed. W. J. Bennens, Jr. New York: Munro, [1892].

THE UNSEEN BRIDEGROOM; OR, WEDDED FOR A WEEK. Ed. W. J. Bennens, Jr. New York: Munro, [1892].

THE HEIRESS OF GLEN GOWER; OR, THE HIDDEN CRIME. Ed. W. J. Bennens, Jr. New York: Munro, [1892].

EDITH PERCIVAL. New York: Dillingham, 1893.

MAGDALEN'S VOW. Ed. W. J. Bennens, Jr. New York: Munro, [1893].

THE GHOST OF RIVERDALE HAL. New York: Lupton, 1895.

WEDDED FOR PIQUE. New York: Dillingham, 1897.

THE SISTERS OF TORMOOD. New York: Dillingham, 1898.

A FATEFUL ABDUCTION; OR, THE SECRET SORROW. New York: Dillingham, [1907].

SHE MIGHT HAVE DONE BETTER. Toronto: Rose Publishing Co., n.d.

Authorship attributed to Fleming by Reginald E. Watters in A CHECKLIST OF CANADIAN LITERATURE AND BACKGROUND MATERIALS, 1628-1960 (Toronto, 1972).

CRITICISM

Klinck, Carl F., et al. THE LITERARY HISTORY OF CANADA. Toronto: University of Toronto Press, 1965.

The brief reference to Mrs. Fleming on page 111 is the only critical notice which could be found.

GOLDSMITH, OLIVER (1794-1861)

Grandnephew and namesake of the author of THE DESERTED VILLAGE (1770), the Canadian Oliver (born in New Brunswick) produced one of the earliest "colonial" poems to receive any serious attention from reviewers. The derivative title of THE RISING VILLAGE, however, was unfortunate, for while it sparked recognition it also invited comparison with the acknowledged poetic masterpiece of the author's famous relative. Such a comparison revealed obvious flaws in the work of the Canadian Oliver and so disheartened him that he wrote little other poetry. The poem, however, has some redeeming features and stands as a good example of the pioneer-English attitude towards Canada.

MANUSCRIPTS

THE MANUSCRIPT BOOK OF OLIVER GOLDSMITH. With description and comments by E. Cockburn Kyte. Toronto: Bibliographical Society of Canada, 1950.

AUTOBIOGRAPHY

THE AUTOBIOGRAPHY OF OLIVER GOLDSMITH. Introduction and notes by Wilfred E. Myatt. Toronto: Ryerson, 1943.

POETRY

THE RISING VILLAGE. London: Sharp, 1825.

THE RISING VILLAGE, WITH OTHER POEMS. St. John, N.B.: M'Millan, 1834.

THE RISING VILLAGE. New ed. incorporating textual differences between the 1825 and 1834 texts. Ed. Michael Gnarowski. Montreal: Delta Canada, 1968.

CRITICISM

Gammon, Donald B. "The Concept of Nature in Nineteenth Century Canadian Poetry, with Special Reference to Goldsmith, Sangster and Roberts." Thesis, University of New Brunswick, 1948.

Lande, Lawrence M. "Oliver Goldsmith." In OLD LAMPS AGLOW, pp. 67-74. Montreal: Privately printed, 1957.

Pacey, Desmond. "The Goldsmiths and Their Villages." UNIVERSITY OF TORONTO QUARTERLY, 21 (October 1951), 27-38. Reprinted in ESSAYS IN CANADIAN CRITICISM 1938-1968, pp. 53-66. Toronto: Ryerson, 1969.

GREY, WILLIAM FRANCIS (1860-1939)

One of the best novels produced in Canada before 1900 was Grey's THE CURÉ OF ST. PHILIPPE, a realistic yet humorous portrait of French-Canadian rural life, with all its religious, racial, and political intrigues. It was, however, the only novel written by Grey, a regrettable fact considering his engaging style, his sure handling of character, his acute perception of regional life, and his quasi-satirical attitude. His other works include some published plays and a number of poems scattered throughout the pages of such journals as WESTMINSTER REVIEW, QUARTERLY REVIEW, and DUBLIN REVIEW. His one novel, however, is enough to ensure him a permanent niche in the literary history of Canada.

FICTION

THE CURÉ OF ST. PHILIPPE: A STORY OF FRENCH-CANADIAN POLITICS. London: Digby, Long, 1899. Reprint ed. with introduction by Rupert Scheider. Toronto: McClelland & Stewart, 1970.

DRAMA

SIXTEEN-NINETY: A SERIES OF HISTORICAL TABLEAUX. Ottawa: Mortimer, 1904.

FOUR PLAYS. Ottawa: Miller, 1931.

Religious festival plays.

CRITICISM

Klinck, Carl F., et al. THE LITERARY HISTORY OF CANADA. Toronto: University of Toronto Press, 1965.

The brief notice on page 326, and Scheider's introduction to the McClelland & Stewart edition of THE CURE OF ST. PHILIPPE, cited above, are the only critical appraisals of Grey's work to date.

HARRISON, SUSIE FRANCES ("SERANUS") (1859-1935)

At first glance, Mrs. Harrison may appear to be simply another one of the cultured, genteel, and talented group of Canadian women writers who made good marriages, lived restricted upper-class lives, and wrote poetry and novels in their spare time. For much of Harrison's writing, like that of Rosanna Leprohon, exhibits a technical preoccupation with romantic language and an ignorance of real life. Unlike the less able writers of this group, however, her poetry is varied in terms of subject matter and, in one novel at least, THE FOREST OF BOURG MARIE, she adopts a more realistic style and creates, in her portrayal of Magloire Caron, the Americanized habitant, a character deserving of renewed recognition.

POETRY

Seranus [pseud.], comp. THE CANADIAN BIRTHDAY BOOK. Toronto: Blackett, Robinson, 1887.

A small anthology of Canadian poems.

PINE, ROSE, AND FLEUR DE LIS. Toronto: Hart, 1891.

SONGS OF LOVE AND LABOR. Toronto: Privately printed, 1925.

LATER POEMS AND NEW VILLANELLES. Toronto: Ryerson, 1928.

FOUR BALLADS AND A PLAY. N. p.: n.pag., 1933.

FICTION

CROWDED OUT AND OTHER SKETCHES. Ottawa: "Evening Journal," 1886.

THE FOREST OF BOURG MARIE. London: Arnold; Toronto: Morang, 1898.

RINGFIELD. Toronto: Musson, [1914].

CRITICISM

Cogswell, Frederick W.   "The Canadian Novel from Confederation to World War I."   Thesis, University of New Brunswick, 1950.

Harrison is the subject of chapter V.

_____.   "THE FOREST OF BOURG MARIE: An Ancestor of MARIA CHAPDE-LAINE and TRENTE ARPENTS."   JOURNAL OF CANADIAN FICTION, 2 (Summer 1973), 199-200.

Willison, Marjory.   "Seranus."   CANADIAN BOOKMAN, 14 (July-August 1932), 80-81.

HART (BECKWITH), JULIA C. (1796-1867)

Mrs. Hart is included in this bibliography because her novel, ST. URSULA'S CONVENT (1824), was the first written by a Canadian to be published in Canada (Frances Brooke was not a Canadian and THE HISTORY OF EMILY MONTAGUE (1769) was originally published in London). Poor as the novel is, that historical fact alone has been enough to gain the author attention denied to some of her superiors.

FICTION

ST. URSULA'S CONVENT; OR, THE NUN OF CANADA. 2 vols. Kingston, Ont.: Hugh C. Thompson, 1824.

TONNEWONTE, THE ADOPTED SON OF AMERICA. 2 vols. Albany: Daniel Steele & Son, 1824; Waterton, N.Y.: Adams, 1825; Exeter: B. H. Mader, 1831.

CRITICISM

Anon. "The Collector [First Novel by a Canadian]." CANADIAN BOOKMAN, 12 (September 1930), 194-95.

Bennett, C. L. "An Unpublished Manuscript of the First Canadian Novelist." DALHOUSIE REVIEW, 43 (Autumn 1963), 317-32.

Beyea, George P. "The Canadian Novel Prior to Confederation." Thesis, University of New Brunswick, 1950.

    See chapter I.

Carnochan, Janet. "Rare Canadian Books." CANADIAN MAGAZINE, 43 (July 1914), 236-38.

Hart, Julia C.
_____

Gagnon, Phileas. "Le Premier roman canadien de sujet par un auteur canadien et emprime en Canada." PROCEEDINGS AND TRANSACTIONS OF THE ROYAL SOCIETY OF CANADA, 2nd ser., 6 (1900-01), 121-32.

Maxwell, Lillian M. Beckwith. "The First Canadian Born Novelist." DALHOUSIE REVIEW, 31 (April 1951), 59-64.

Morgan, H. R. "Mrs. Julia Beckwith Hart: Author of the First Canadian Novel." SATURDAY NIGHT, 40 (October 3, 1955), 23.

HEAVYSEGE, CHARLES (1816-1876)

Having already published a long epic, THE REVOLT OF TARTARUS, before emigrating to Canada in 1853, Heavysege continued to write stolid, long-winded plays and poetry, chiefly on Biblical themes, with no direct reference to his adopted land. If, however, we accept Northrop Frye's view (LITERARY HISTORY OF CANADA, p. 843), Heavysege was unconsciously influenced by the Canadian landscape, a characteristic discernible in his writing.

POETRY

THE REVOLT OF TARTARUS. A POEM. Liverpool: Hamilton, 1852. Reprint ed. Montreal: n.p., 1853.

SONNETS. Montreal: Rose, 1855.

THE DARK HUNTSMAN. Montreal: Witness Press, 1864.

THE OWL. Montreal: n.p., 1864.

JEPHTHAH'S DAUGHTER. Montreal: Dawson, 1865.

JEZEBEL: A POEM IN THREE CANTOS. Montreal: Golden Dog Press, 1972. Reprinted from NEW DOMINION MONTHLY, 1 (January 1868), 224-31.

FICTION

THE ADVOCATE: A NOVEL. Montreal: R. Worthington, 1865. Reprinted in facsimile. Toronto: University of Toronto Press, 1973.

DRAMA

SAUL: A DRAMA IN THREE PARTS. Montreal: Rose, 1857. Rev. ed. Boston: Fields, Osgood, 1869. Reprinted in facsimile. Toronto: University of Toronto Press, 1973.

COUNT FILIPPO; OR, THE UNEQUAL MARRIAGE. A DRAMA IN FIVE ACTS. Montreal: Privately printed, 1860. Reprinted in facsimile. Toronto: University of Toronto Press, 1973.

CRITICISM

Anon. "Charles Heavysege." DOMINION ILLUSTRATED, 2 (April 1889) 263-66.

Baker, Ray Palmer. "Charles Heavysege." In A HISTORY OF ENGLISH-CANADIAN LITERATURE TO THE CONFEDERATION, pp. 168-76. Cambridge: Harvard University Press, 1920.

Burpee, Lawrence J. "Charles Heavysege." PROCEEDINGS AND TRANSACTIONS OF THE ROYAL SOCIETY OF CANADA, 2nd ser., 7 (1901), 19-60.

Clark, Daniel. "The Poetry of Charles Heavysege." CANADIAN MONTHLY AND NATIONAL REVIEW, 10 (August 1876), 127-34.

Dale, T. R. "The Life and Works of Charles Heavysege, 1817-1876." Thesis, University of Chicago, 1951.

_____. "Our Greatest Poet--A Century Ago." CANADIAN FORUM, 37 (February 1958), 245-46.

_____. "The Revolt of Charles Heavysege." UNIVERSITY OF TORONTO QUARTERLY, 22 (October 1952), 35-42.

Greenshields, E. B. "A Forgotten Poet." UNIVERSITY MAGAZINE, 7 (October 1908), 343-59.

Montgomery, M. J. "Charles Heavysege." CANADIAN POETRY MAGAZINE, (September 1940), 5-12.

Murray, Louisa. "Heavysege's 'Saul.' " CANADIAN MONTHLY, 10 (July-December 1876), 250-54.

HOWE, JOSEPH (1804-1873)

In the political history of Canada the figure of Joseph Howe looms large. His leadership in Nova Scotia's fight for responsible government, his able defence of the freedom of the press, and his outstanding oratory ensure for him a permanent place in that history. Yet, as Howe wrote in a frequently quoted statement, writing poems was his chief delight: "Poetry was my first love, but politics was the hag I married." And, in spite of the fact that his poetry is inferior to his prose, there is enough of it to engage the student of early patriotic verse in many hours of pleasurable reading.

POETRY

POEMS AND ESSAYS. Montreal: Lovell, 1874. Reprint ed. with introduction by M. G. Parks. Toronto: University of Toronto Press, 1973.

PROSE

Only Howe's collected major prose is listed below. For a more comprehensive listing see Watters' CHECKLIST OF CANADIAN LITERATURE AND BACKGROUND MATERIALS, 1628-1960 (Toronto, 1972).

THE SPEECHES AND PUBLIC LETTERS OF THE HON. JOSEPH HOWE. Ed. William Annand. 2 vols. London: Sampson, Low, 1858. Rev. by Joseph Chisholm. Halifax: Chronicle Publishing Co., 1909.

THE HEART OF HOWE: SELECTIONS FROM THE LETTERS AND SPEECHES. Ed. D. C. Harvey. Toronto: Oxford University Press, 1939.

CRITICISM

Baker, Ray Palmer. "Joseph Howe and the 'Nova Scotian.'" In A HISTORY OF ENGLISH-CANADIAN LITERATURE TO THE CONFEDERATION, pp. 57-67. Cambridge, Mass.: Harvard University Press, 1920.

Beck, J. M. "Joseph Howe: Opportunist or Empire-Builder." CANADIAN HISTORICAL REVIEW, 41 (September 1960), 185–202.

_____. "Joseph Howe." In OUR LIVING TRADITION: FOURTH SERIES, pp. 3–30. Ed. R. L. McDougall. Toronto: University of Toronto Press, 1962.

Carman, Francis A. "The Howe Papers." CANADIAN MAGAZINE, 45 (September 1915), 365–69.

Chisholm, Joseph Andrew. "Hitherto Unpublished Letters of Joseph Howe." DALHOUSIE REVIEW, 12 (October 1932), 309–14.

Hassard, Albert R. "Great Canadian Orators: II: Joseph Howe." CANADIAN MAGAZINE, 53 (September 1919), 423–30.

Logan, J. D. "Joseph Howe." CANADIAN MAGAZINE, 62 (November 1923), 19–25.

Lumsden, Susan. "Joseph Howe: Editor of the 'Novascotian.' " Thesis, Carleton University, 1966.

Monroe, David. "Joseph Howe as Man of Letters." DALHOUSIE REVIEW, 20 (January 1941), 451–57.

Rhodenizer, V[ernon] B[lair]. "Who's Who in Canadian Literature: Joseph Howe (1804–1873)." CANADIAN BOOKMAN, 8 (May 1926), 139–41.

Roy, James Alexander. JOSEPH HOWE: A STUDY IN ACHIEVEMENT AND FRUSTRATION. Toronto: Macmillan, 1935.

Thomas, W. K. "Canadian Political Oratory in the Nineteenth Century." DALHOUSIE REVIEW, 39 (Autumn 1959), 377–89.

HUNTER-DUVAR, JOHN (1821-1899)

Had John Hunter (later Hunter-Duvar) settled in Upper Canada instead of Prince Edward Island, his poetry and plays would probably be better known than they are. His poetry exhibits an originality and a degree of accomplishment which place it among the best of the minor poetry of his time. Hunter-Duvar, however, did not care much for public attention: he preferred the life of a country squire, carefully cultivated at his estate at Hernewood, Prince Edward Island. That he was well-read, erudite, skilled in rhetoric, and loved his mode of life in Canada becomes clear in the few poems and plays which he left us.

Since it is likely that the original editions of his work will not be available in many libraries, the interested reader will find an excellent sampling of Hunter-Duvar's poetry, and a good introduction, in A. J. M. Smith's THE BOOK OF CANADIAN POETRY (Toronto: W. J. Gage, 1957), pp. 111-18.

BIBLIOGRAPHY AND MANUSCRIPTS

Campbell, Stephen Coady. "John Hunter-Duvar: A Biographical Introduction, Check List of his Works and Selected Bibliography." Thesis, University of New Brunswick, 1966.

> Contains a comprehensive list of unpublished manuscripts, letters, publications in periodicals, and other Hunter-Duvar material.

POETRY

JOHN A'VAR: HIS LAIS. East Boston: H. F. Hodges & Co., 1874.

"The Emigration of the Fairies" and "The Triumph of Constancy: A Romaunt."

> Published with his drama DE ROBERVAL (see below).

DRAMA

THE ENAMORADO. Summerside, P.E.I.: Graves, 1879.

DE ROBERVAL. Saint John, N.B.: McMillan, 1888.
Contains "The Emigration of the Fairies" and "The Triumph of Constancy: A Romaunt," poems.

PROSE

ANNALS OF THE COURT OF OBERON. London: Digby Long, 1895.

CRITICISM

Burpee, Lawrence J. "John Hunter-Duvar." In A LITTLE BOOK OF CANADIAN ESSAYS, pp. 65-72. Toronto: Musson, 1909.

Cogswell, Fred[erick W.] "John Hunter-Duvar." In LITERARY HISTORY OF CANADA: CANADIAN LITERATURE IN ENGLISH, pp. 114-15, 123-24. Ed. Carl F. Klinck. Toronto: University of Toronto Press, 1965.

Payzant, J. A. "John Hunter-Duvar." DOMINION ILLUSTRATED, 5 (August 23, 1890), 127.

JOHNSON, EMILY PAULINE (1862-1913)

Probably no other Canadian poet, except Robert Service, has enjoyed such out-standing popular success as Pauline Johnson. Born on the Iroquois Reserve near Brantford, Ontario, to the chief of the Six Nations Confederacy and an English Mother, "Tekahionwake" received a formal education and began to write poetry early but did not receive recognition until she gave her first public reading in 1892. Thereafter, dressed in her Indian-princess costume, she gave hundreds of poetry recitals in Canada, England, and the United States. The popularity of her readings and her cause (the elevation of her native people), and the curiosity attached to the person, accounted for her reputation. She did, how-ever, write a few fine lyrics and these, such as "The Song My Paddle Sings," can be found in nearly every anthology and schoolbook published in Canada.

POETRY

THE WHITE WAMPUM. London: Lane, 1895.

CANADIAN BORN. Toronto: Morang, 1903.

FLINT AND FEATHER. COLLECTED POEMS. Toronto: Musson, [1912]. Rev. and enl. ed. with introduction by Theodore Watts-Dunton. Toronto: Musson, 1913. Reprint ed. in paperback. Toronto: Paperjacks, 1972.

PROSE

LEGENDS OF VANCOUVER. Vancouver: Thompson Stationery Co., 1911.

> These first appeared in the Vancouver "Daily Province." The
> LEGENDS enjoyed immediate success, and a seventh edition ap-
> peared in 1913.

THE SHAGGANAPPI. Introduction by Ernest Thompson Seton. Toronto: Briggs, 1912.

> Chiefly autobiographical sketches.

THE MOCCASIN MAKER. Introduction by Sir Gilbert Parker and "appreciation" by Charles Mair. Toronto: Briggs, 1913.

Chiefly Indian tales.

CRITICISM

Ayre, Robert. "Pauline Johnson." CANADIAN FORUM, 14 (October 1933), 17.

Charlesworth, Hector W. "Miss Pauline Johnson's Poems." CANADIAN MAGA-ZINE, 5 (September 1895), 478-80.

Foster, Mrs. W. G. THE MOHAWK PRINCESS. Vancouver: Lion's Gate Publishing Co., 1931.

_____. "The Lyric Beauty of Pauline Johnson's Poetry." CANADIAN BOOK-MAN, 16 (March 1934), 37, 43.

_____. "Pauline Johnson's Gift to Vancouver." CANADIAN BOOKMAN, 18 (June 1936), 6-7.

Hammond, M[elvin] O. "Who's Who in Canadian Literature: E. Pauline Johnson." CANADIAN BOOKMAN, 8 (February 1926), 41-43.

Loosely, E. "Pauline Johnson." In THE CLEAR SPIRIT: TWENTY CANADIAN WOMEN AND THEIR TIMES, pp. 74-90. Ed. Mary Q. Innis. Toronto: University of Toronto Press, 1966.

Mackay, Isabel E. "Pauline Johnson: A Reminiscence." CANADIAN MAG-AZINE, 41 (July 1913), 273-78.

McRaye, Walter. "East and West with Pauline Johnson." CANADIAN MAG-AZINE, 60 (March 1923), 381-89; (April 1923), 494-502.

_____. "Pauline Johnson." In LEADING CANADIAN POETS, pp. 88-97. Ed. W. P. Percival. Toronto: Ryerson, 1948.

_____. PAULINE JOHNSON AND HER FRIENDS. Toronto: Ryerson, 1947.

Mair, Charles. "Pauline Johnson: An Appreciation." CANADIAN MAGA-ZINE, 41 (July 1913), 281-83.

Scott, Jack. "The Passionate Princess." MACLEAN'S MAGAZINE, 64 (April 1, 1952), 12-13, 54, 57.

Shrive, Norman. "What Happened to Pauline?" CANADIAN LITERATURE, 13 (Summer 1962), 25-38.

Stevenson, O. J. "Tekahionwake." In A PEOPLE'S BEST, pp. 141-52. Toronto: Musson, 1927.

Van Steen, Marcus. PAULINE JOHNSON: HER LIFE AND WORK. Toronto: Musson, 1965.

Biography, pp. 1-42; poems, pp. 43-175; prose, pp. 175-278.

Waldie, Jean H. "The Iroquois Poetess, Pauline Johnson." ONTARIO HISTORICAL SOCIETY PAPERS, 40 (1948), 65-75.

Yeigh, Frank. "Memories of Pauline Johnson." CANADIAN BOOKMAN, 11 (October 1929), 227-29.

KIRBY, WILLIAM (1817-1906)

A United Empire Loyalist from Ohio (where his family had settled in 1832), Kirby came to Canada in 1839, settled in Niagara, worked as a tanner and teacher, edited the Niagara MAIL (1850-1863) and was collector of customs for the last twenty-four active years of his life (1871-1895). During that time he wrote a great deal of political prose (not listed below), some bad patriotic poetry, a few inferior sonnets, and one good novel, THE GOLDEN DOG, on which his literary fame precariously rests.

LETTERS

ALFRED, LORD TENNYSON AND WILLIAM KIRBY: UNPUBLISHED CORRE-SPONDENCE, TO WHICH ARE ADDED SOME LETTERS FROM HALLAM, LORD TENNYSON. Ed. Lorne Pierce. Toronto: Macmillan, 1929.

POETRY

THE U.E.: A TALE OF UPPER CANADA. Niagara: The Mail, 1859. Re-printed in NINETEENTH CENTURY NARRATIVE POEMS. Ed. David Sinclair. Toronto: McClelland & Stewart, 1972, pp. 81-114.

CANADIAN IDYLLS. Welland, Ont.: n.p., 1888. 2nd rev. ed. Welland: n.p., 1894.

> The poems in this "collected" edition had previously been published separately at various times between 1876 and 1894. For a detailed list of these and of poems published in periodicals see Riddell, William R., WILLIAM KIRBY, under Criticism, below, pp. 167-72.

FICTION

THE GOLDEN DOG (LE CHIEN D'OR). Montreal: Lovell, 1877. Illustrated "authorized" edition. Montreal: Montreal News Co., 1897. Modem edition. Ed. with introduction by Derek Crawley. Toronto: McClelland & Stewart, 1969.

OTHER PROSE

Britannicus [pseud.] COUNTER MANIFESTO TO THE ANNEXATIONISTS OF MONTREAL. Niagara: Davidson, 1849. Reprinted in THE EVOLUTION OF CANADIAN LITERATURE IN ENGLISH: BEGINNINGS TO 1867, pp. 208-21. Ed. Mary Jane Edwards. Toronto: Holt, Rinehart & Winston, 1973.

ANNALS OF NIAGARA. Welland, Ont.: The Tribune, 1896. Reprint ed. with introduction by Lorne Pierce. Toronto: Macmillan, 1927.

REMINISCENCES OF A VISIT TO QUEBEC, JULY, 1839. Niagara: Privately printed, 1903. Reprinted in WILLIAM KIRBY. By Lorne Pierce. Toronto: Macmillan, 1929.

CRITICISM

Carnochan, Janet. "Reminiscences of William Kirby, F.R.S.C." UNITED EMPIRE LOYALISTS' ASSOCIATION TRANSACTIONS, 6 (1914), 49-56.

Pierce, Lorne [Albert]. "Who's Who in Canadian Literature: William Kirby." CANADIAN BOOKMAN, 11 (February 1929), 35-39.

_____. WILLIAM KIRBY: THE PORTRAIT OF A TORY LOYALIST. Toronto: Macmillan, 1929.

Riddell, William R. WILLIAM KIRBY. Toronto: Ryerson, [1923].

Sandwell, B. K. "Debunking THE GOLDEN DOG." SATURDAY NIGHT, October 2, 1930, p. 2.

Sinclair, David. "William Kirby and the Production of THE U.E." PAPERS OF THE BIBLIOGRAPHICAL SOCIETY OF CANADA, 9 (1970), 30-35.

Sorfleet, John Robert. "Fiction and the Fall of New France: William Kirby vs. Gilbert Parker." JOURNAL OF CANADIAN FICTION, 2 (Summer 1973), 132-46.

von Guttenberg, A. C. "William Kirby." REVUE DE L'UNIVERSITE LAVAL, 9 (December 1954), 337-45.

_____. "William Kirby." In EARLY CANADIAN ART AND LITERATURE, pp. 34-44. Liechtenstein: Europe Printing Establishment, 1969.

LEPROHON (MULLINS), ROSANNA ELEANOR (1829-1879)

One of the most frequent contributors to THE LITERARY GARLAND between 1846 and 1851 (when it folded) was Rosanna Mullins, with more than a dozen poems and five serialized novels. She was, in 1851, just twenty-two years old. Born in Montreal, the daughter of an Irish businessman, she married a French-Canadian doctor, M. Leprohon, in 1851. Thereafter she moved in upper-class circles and continued to write popular prose and poetry. But whereas her LITERARY GARLAND prose had dealt with high society in a melodramatic manner, her published novels, on which her reputation stands, saw her turning to strictly Canadian subjects. She was, indeed, the first English-Canadian writer to explore the French-Canadian way of life. Testimony to her success is the fact that LE MANOIR DE VILLERAI, though originally written in English, was long considered a French novel. Her poetry is generally poor stuff and deserves little critical attention.

POETRY

THE POETICAL WORKS. Montreal: Lovell, 1881.

NOVELS

THE MANOR HOUSE OF DE VILLERAI: A TALE OF CANADA UNDER THE FRENCH DOMINION. In THE FAMILY HERALD [Montreal], no. 1. (November 16, 1859), no. 13 (February 8, 1860).

ANTOINETTE DE MIRECOURT; OR, SECRET MARRYING AND SECRET SORROW-ING. A CANADIAN TALE. Montreal: Lovell, 1864. Reprint ed. with introduction by Carl F. Klinck. Toronto: McClelland & Stewart, 1973.

ARMAND DURAND; OR, A PROMISE FULFILLED. Montreal: Lovell, 1868.

"Clive Weston's Wedding Anniversary." CANADIAN MONTHLY AND NA-TIONAL REVIEW, 2, no. 2 (August 1872), 2, no. 3 (September 1872). Reprinted in THE EVOLUTION OF CANADIAN LITERATURE IN ENGLISH:

BEGINNINGS TO 1867, pp. 266-301.   Ed. Mary Jane Edwards.   Toronto: Holt, Rinehart & Winston, 1973.

For a list of novels published serially in THE LITERARY GARLAND, see Mary Markham Brown, AN INDEX TO THE "LITERARY GARLAND" (MONTREAL, 1838-1851).   Toronto: Bibliographical Society of Canada, 1962.

CRITICISM

Beyea, George P. "The Canadian Novel Prior to Confederation." Thesis, University of New Brunswick, 1950, chapter III.

Deneau, Henri (Brother Adrian). "The Life and Works of Mrs. Leprohon." Thesis, University of Montreal, 1948.

LIGHTHALL, WILLIAM DOUW (1857-1954)

Justifiably, William Lighthall will be longer remembered as an anthologist than as a poet and novelist. His SONGS OF THE GREAT DOMINION, with its nationalistic manifesto, is indeed a landmark in Canadian literary history, and for this alone he deserves recognition. His own poetry is undistinguished and often quite bad, but it achieved some popularity because of the patriotic sentiment. His novels are all romances of the chivalric kind, even when they have only Indians as their characters. They survive as good examples of a school of early Canadian writing which consciously strove to renew a sense of the nation's past, mainly by idealizing French-Canadian history in a Dumas-like fashion.

POETRY

THOUGHTS, MOODS AND IDEALS. Montreal: The "Witness," 1887.

THE LAND OF MANITOU. Montreal: Desbarats, 1916.

OLD MEASURES: COLLECTED VERSE. Montreal: A. T. Chapman; Toronto: Musson, 1922.

ANTHOLOGIES

SONGS OF THE GREAT DOMINION: VOICES FROM THE FORESTS AND WATERS, THE SETTLEMENTS AND CITIES OF CANADA. London: Walter Scott, 1889. Reprint ed. in facsimile. Toronto: Coles Publishing Co., 1971.

> See annotation to main entry, under Lighthall, William Douw, in Chapter 3, above.

CANADIAN POEMS AND LAYS. SELECTIONS OF NATIVE VERSE. London: Walter Scott, 1893.

CANADIAN POETS OF THE GREAT WAR. Ottawa: The Royal Society, n.d.

FICTION

Chateauclair, Wilfrid [pseud.] THE YOUNG SEIGNEUR; OR, NATION-MAKING. Montreal: Drysdale, 1888.

THE FALSE CHEVALIER; OR, THE LIFEGUARD OF MARIE ANTOINETTE. Montreal: Grafton, 1898.

HIAWATHA, THE HOCHELAGAN. Montreal: n.p., 1906.

THE MASTER OF LIFE. A ROMANCE OF THE FIVE NATIONS. Toronto: Musson, 1908.

OTHER PROSE

For a list of Lighthall's other prose see Watters' CHECKLIST OF CANADIAN LITERATURE AND BACKGROUND MATERIALS, 1628-1960 (Toronto, 1972), pp. 532, 624, 880, 926, 970.

CRITICISM

Elson, John Melbourne. "Who's Who in Canadian Literature: William Douw Lighthall." CANADIAN BOOKMAN, 12 (August 1930), 151-54.

Gibbon, John Murray. "William Douw Lighthall." In LEADING CANADIAN POETS, pp. 107-16. Ed. W.P. Percival. Toronto: Ryerson, 1948.

Smith, A[rthur] J[ames] M[arshall]. "Canadian Anthologies New and Old." UNIVERSITY OF TORONTO QUARTERLY, 11 (July 1942), 457-74.

Somerville, R. S. "Canadian Celebrities, 69: Mr. W. D. Lighthall." CANADIAN MAGAZINE, 26 (April 1906), 552-55.

Surveyer, E. F. "William D. Lighthall, 1857-1954." PROCEEDINGS AND TRANSACTIONS OF THE ROYAL SOCIETY OF CANADA, 3rd ser., 49 (1955), 113-15.

McCULLOCH, THOMAS (1776-1843)

As Fred Cogswell has pointed out in THE LITERARY HISTORY OF CANADA (p. 93), McCulloch belongs in that history on the basis of one book, LETTERS OF MEPHIBOSHETH STEPSURE (1860), and the same is true for this bibliography. He did publish some sermons and two short novels, but none of those would have gained him a literary reputation. The LETTERS, however, styled somewhat on the essays of Addison and Steele, published serially in THE ACADIAN RECORD-ER and later in book form, are engaging and witty, and exhibit a sure control of subtle understatement:

> Our sherriff is a very hospitable gentleman; and, when any
> of his neighbours are in hardship, he will call upon them,
> and even insist upon their making his house their home. Nor
> did I ever know any shy folks getting off with an excuse. (LETTERS,
> p. 14)

In each letter the foibles and greed of the Pictou people are laid bare, often with a sure, Swiftian touch. The whole adds a new dimension to Colonial writing and anticipates (perhaps even influences) the later success of Haliburton. Only the creative writing is listed below; for the sermons see Watters' CHECK-LIST OF CANADIAN LITERATURE AND BACKGROUND MATERIALS, 1628-1960 (Toronto, 1972), p. 808.

FICTION

COLONIAL GLEANINGS. . . . WILLIAM AND MELVILLE. Edinburgh: Oliphant, 1826.

Two short, soporific novels.

LETTERS OF MEPHIBOSHETH STEPSURE. Halifax: Blackader, 1860. Reprinted as THE STEPSURE LETTERS. Ed. with introduction by Northrop Frye. Toronto: McClelland & Stewart, 1960. Originally published in THE ACADIAN RECORD-ER, 9, no. 51 (December 22, 1821); 10, no. 19 (May 11, 1822).

McCulloch, Thomas

CRITICISM

Edwards, Mary Jane. "Thomas McCulloch." In THE EVOLUTION OF CANADIAN LITERATURE IN ENGLISH: BEGINNINGS TO 1867, pp. 51-53. Holt, Rinehart & Winston, 1973.

Harvey, Daniel Cobb. "Thomas McCulloch." In CANADIAN PORTRAITS, pp. 22-28. Ed. R. G. Riddell. Toronto: Oxford University Press, 1940.

Irving, John A. "The Achievement of Thomas McCulloch." In THE STEPSURE LETTERS, pp. 150-56. Ed. Northrop Frye. Toronto: McClelland & Stewart, 1960.

Lochhead, Douglas G. "A Bibliographical Note." In THE STEPSURE LETTERS, pp. 156-59. Ed. Northrop Frye. Toronto: McClelland & Stewart, 1960.

McCulloch, William. THE LIFE OF THOMAS McCULLOCH. Truro, N.S.: The Albion, 1920.

MacIntosh, F. C. "Some Nova Scotian Scientists." DALHOUSIE REVIEW, 10 (July 1930), 199-213.

McGEE, THOMAS D'ARCY (1825-1868)

McGee will be remembered as one of the "Fathers of Confederation." An exiled Irish nationalist, he redirected his fervor and oratorical genius towards the task of helping Canada become an independent nation in 1867. He was assassinated just one year later.

But McGee will also be remembered for his prose oratory and his poetry, chiefly because he used poetry, as the Irish have often done, "to advance the cause of nationality." His CANADIAN BALLADS (1858) were written for that purpose, and celebrated such historical figures as Jacques Cartier and Sebastian Cabot. It might be claimed, of course, that these poems are as political as his prose, insofar as McGee, in need of support, had been in Canada for only one year when he wrote them. Still, they remain interesting and readable mementos of the era in which the Canadian nation was born.

McGee, a prolific contributor to newspapers, edited several as well. He also made many speeches during his career. Only his major Canadian writing is listed below.

POETRY

CANADIAN BALLADS, AND OCCASIONAL VERSES. Montreal: Lovell, 1858.

THE POEMS OF THOMAS D'ARCY McGEE. Ed. with notes and biography by Mrs. J. Sadlier. New York: Sadlier, 1869.

DRAMA

SEBASTIAN; OR, THE ROMAN MARTYR. A Drama. New York: n.p., 1861.

PROSE

EMIGRATION AND COLONIZATION IN CANADA. Quebec: Hunter, 1862.
Speech given in the House of Assembly, April 25, 1862.

THE CROWN AND THE CONFEDERATION. THREE LETTERS BY A BACK-
WOODSMAN. Montreal: Lovell, 1864.

SPEECHES AND ADDRESSES CHIEFLY ON THE SUBJECT OF BRITISH AMERICAN
UNION. London: Chapman & Hall, 1865.

TWO SPEECHES ON THE UNION OF THE PROVINCES. Quebec: Hunter,
Rose, 1865.

THE IRISH POSITION IN BRITISH AND IN REPUBLICAN NORTH AMERICA.
Montreal: Longmoore, 1866.

"The Mental Outfit of the New Dominion." GAZETTE (Montreal), 93 Novem-
ber 5, 1867. Reprinted in THE EVOLUTION OF CANADIAN LITERATURE IN
ENGLISH: BEGINNINGS TO 1867, pp. 254-64. Ed. Mary Jane Edwards.
Toronto: Holt, Rinehart & Winston, 1973.

1825 - D'ARCY McGEE - 1925. A COLLECTION OF SPEECHES AND AD-
DRESSES. Ed. Charles Murphy. Toronto: Macmillan, 1937.

CRITICISM

Brady, Alexander. THOMAS D'ARCY McGEE. Toronto: Macmillan, 1923.

Burns, Robin B. "D'Arcy McGee and the New Nationality." Thesis, Carleton
University, 1966.

Clarke, Henry J. A SHORT SKETCH OF THE LIFE OF THE HON. D'ARCY
McGEE. Montreal: Lovell, 1968.

Cross, Ethelbert F. H. "An Exile from Erin." In FIRE AND FROST, pp. 78-
88. Toronto: Bryant, 1898.

Harvey, Daniel Cobb. THOMAS D'ARCY McGEE: THE PROPHET OF CANA-
DIAN NATIONALITY. Winnipeg: University of Manitoba, 1923.

_____. "The Centenary of D'Arcy McGee." DALHOUSIE REVIEW, 5 (April
1925), 1-10.

Hassard, A[lbert] R. "Great Canadian Orators: D'Arcy McGee." CANADIAN MAGAZINE, 53 (August 1919), 263-69.

Henderson, John. "Thomas D'Arcy McGee." In GREAT MEN OF CANADA, pp. 205-18. Toronto: Southam, 1928.

Keep, G. R. C. "D'Arcy McGee and Montreal." CULTURE, 12 (March 1951), 16-28.

Louise, Sister Mary. "Thomas D'Arcy McGee as a Man of Letters." Thesis, University of New Brunswick, 1960.

Markey, John. "Thomas D'Arcy McGee: Poet and Patriot." CANADIAN MAGAZINE, 46 (November 1915), 67-72.

O'Donnell, Kathleen. "Thomas D'Arcy McGee's Irish and Canadian Ballads." Thesis, University of Western Ontario, 1956.

O'Neill, K. "Thomas D'Arcy McGee: Statesman, Journalist, Poet." CATHOLIC WORLD, 130 (March 1930), 681-86.

Phelan, Josephine. THE ARDENT EXILE: THE LIFE AND TIMES OF THOS. D'ARCY McGEE. Toronto: Macmillan, 1951.

_____. THE BALLAD OF D'ARCY McGEE: REBEL IN EXILE. Toronto: Macmillan, [1967].

Skelton, Isabel. THE LIFE OF THOMAS D'ARCY McGEE. Gardenvale, Que.: Garden City Press, 1925.

_____. THOMAS D'ARCY McGEE. Toronto: Ryerson, n.d.

Slattery, Timothy Patrick. THE ASSASSINATION OF THOMAS D'ARCY McGEE. Toronto: Doubleday, 1968.

Spaight, George. TRIAL OF PATRICK J. WHELAN FOR THE MURDER OF THE HON. D'ARCY McGEE. Ottawa: Desbarats, 1868.

MACHAR, AGNES MAULE ("FIDELIS") (1837-1927)

Didactic to a fault, Agnes Machar nevertheless represents that curious blend of British-Canadianism which dominates much of the minor writing of her time, the period of "high-colonialism" in Canada. On the one hand she exhorts her readers to love Canada, learn its history, and protect its traditions; on the other, she constantly refers to Canada as a "lesser Britain," a position neatly embodied in "The Queen's Jubilee Canadian Poem."

All of her writing (several novels, a few hundred poems, histories, and essays) is, considered critically, second-rate. Yet her espousal of the cause of humane studies, her fervid patriotism, her prolific contributions to Canadian periodicals (where "Fidelis" became a familiar watchward), and her accurate portrayal of post-confederation attitudes, made her a legend in her time.

POETRY

LAYS OF THE 'TRUE NORTH' AND OTHER CANADIAN POEMS. London: Elliot Stock, 1899; 2nd enl. ed. 1902.

THE THOUSAND ISLANDS. Toronto: Ryerson, 1935.

FICTION

KATIE JOHNSTONE'S CROSS: A CANADIAN TALE. Toronto: Campbell, 1870.

FOR KING AND COUNTRY: A STORY OF 1812. Toronto: Adam, Stevenson & Co., 1874. First published in CANADIAN MONTHLY, 5 (January-June 1874).

MARJORIE'S CANADIAN WINTER: A STORY OF THE NORTHERN LIGHTS. Boston: Luthrop, 1892; Toronto: Briggs, 1906.

ROLAND GRAEME, KNIGHT: A NOVEL OF OUR TIMES. Montreal: Drysdale, 1892; Toronto: Briggs, 1906.

DOWN THE RIVER TO THE SEA. New York: Home Book Co., 1894.

THE HEIR OF FAIRMOUNT GRANGE. London: Digby, Long, [1895].

LUCY RAYMOND; OR, THE CHILDREN'S WATCHWORD. Toronto: Campbell, [1902].

OTHER PROSE

For a list of Machar's other prose see Watters' CHECKLIST OF CANADIAN LITERATURE AND BACKGROUND MATERIALS, 1628-1960 (Toronto, 1972), pp. 540, 628, 705, 884.

CRITICISM

Cumberland, R. W. "Agnes Maule Machar." QUEEN'S QUARTERLY, 34 (January 1927), 331-39.

———. "Agnes Maule Machar." WILLISON'S MONTHLY, 3 (June 1927), 34-37.

Guild, Leman A. "Canadian Celebrities: Agnes Maule Machar." CANADIAN MAGAZINE, 27 (October 1906), 499-501.

MacCallum, F. L. "Agnes Maule Machar." CANADIAN MAGAZINE, 62 (March 1924), 354-56.

MacMurchy, Archibald. "Agnes Maule Machar." In HANDBOOK OF CANADIAN LITERATURE, pp. 134-35. Toronto: Briggs, 1906.

McLACHLAN, ALEXANDER (1818-1896)

When Dewart, in the introduction to his SELECTIONS FROM CANADIAN POETS (1864), called McLachlan "the most intensely human of all our Canadian bards" (p. xvii), he was obviously thinking of McLachlan's preoccupation with poetry of the "common man," which was a decided departure from the usual descriptions of natural beauty and the classical subjects of his contemporaries. This is perhaps the chief reason for his popularity in Canada: he celebrates the freedom to be found in the new country and voices the disappointments as well as the joys of the emigrant's struggle for economic security (McLachlan himself tried farming but went back to his old profession of tailoring). "His memory," writes MacMurchy, "would be cherished with more honor and fervor if he had diligently weighed and polished what he had written" (HANDBOOK OF CANADIAN LITERATURE, p. 54). Perhaps.

POETRY

THE SPIRIT OF LOVE, AND OTHER POEMS. Toronto: Cleveland, 1846.

POEMS. Toronto: Geikie, 1856.
    Scottish dialect poems.

LYRICS. Toronto: Armour, 1858.

POEMS AND SONGS. Toronto: Hunter, Rose, 1874.

THE POETICAL WORKS OF ALEXANDER McLACHLAN. Ed. with introduction by Edward Hartley Dewart. Toronto: Briggs, 1900. Reprinted in facsimile, with introduction by E. Margaret Fulton. Toronto: University of Toronto Press, 1974.

CRITICISM

Begg, W. P. "Alexander McLachlan's Poems and Ballads." CANADIAN

MONTHLY, 12 (October 1877), 355–62.

Burton, Jean. "Alexander McLachlan. The Burns of Canada." WILLISON'S MONTHLY, 3 (December 1927), 268–69.

Duff, James. "Alexander McLachlan." QUEEN'S QUARTERLY, 8 (October 1900), 132–44.

Lande, Lawrence M. "Alexander McLachlan.: In OLD LAMPS AGLOW, pp. 298–99. Montreal: Privately printed, 1957.

McCaig, D. "Alexander McLachlan." CANADIAN MAGAZINE, 8 (November 1897), 520–23.

MacMurchy, Archibald. "Alexander McLachlan." In HANDBOOK OF CANADIAN LITERATURE, pp. 53–56. Toronto: Briggs, 1906.

MAIR, CHARLES (1838-1927)

As a founding member of the "Canada First" movement, one significantly involved in the Red River Rebellion and the subsequent hanging of Louis Riel, Charles Mair is one of many Canadian literary figures (McGee is another) whose lives are more exciting than their writing. Mair's long verse drama, "Tecumseh," is marred by too much national sentiment; but his shorter poems--particularly his CANADIAN POEMS--are still quite readable. These, plus his ardent nationalistic activities (excellently presented in Norman Shrive's book, listed under Bibliography, below), are enough to ensure him a prominent position in the history of Canadian life and letters.

BIBLIOGRAPHY

Shrive, Norman. CHARLES MAIR: LITERARY NATURALIST. Toronto: University of Toronto Press, 1965.

   Pages 290-91 contain a detailed list of the poems and incidental prose published in newspapers and other serial publications.

COLLECTED WORKS

TECUMSEH, A DRAMA, AND CANADIAN POEMS. Toronto: Briggs, 1901. Reprint ed. of CANADIAN POEMS. Toronto: Canadiana House, 1968.

TECUMSEH, A DRAMA, AND CANADIAN POEMS; DREAMLAND AND OTHER POEMS; THE AMERICAN BISON; THROUGH THE MACKENZIE BASIN; MEMOIRS AND REMINISCENCES. Ed. John W. Garvin. Introduction Robert Norwood. Toronto: Radisson Society, 1926.

POETRY

DREAMLAND AND OTHER POEMS. Montreal: Dawson; London: Sampson Low, 1868.

DRAMA

TECUMSEH, A DRAMA. Toronto: Hunter, Rose, 1886.

CRITICISM

Bailey, A. G. "Literature and Nationalism after Confederation." UNIVERSITY OF TORONTO QUARTERLY, 25 (July 1956), 409-24.

Charlesworth, Hector W. "Patriots and the Poets of the West." In MORE CANDID CHRONICLES, pp. 18-36. Toronto: Macmillan, 1928.

Copp, E. A. "Canada First Party (Charles Mair)." Thesis, Queen's University, 1926.

Denison, George T. THE STRUGGLE FOR IMPERIAL UNITY: RECOLLECTIONS AND EXPERIENCES. London: Macmillan, 1909.

Dooley, D. J., and F. N[orman] Shrive. "Voice of the Burdash." CANA- DIAN FORUM, 37 (July 1957), 80-82.

Fraser, A. E. "A Poet-Pioneer of Canada." QUEEN'S QUARTERLY, 35 (May 1928), 440-50.

Garvin, John W. "Who's Who in Canadian Literature: Charles Mair." CA- NADIAN BOOKMAN, 8 (November 1926), 335-37.

Guttenberg, A[ntoine] Ch[arles von]. "Charles Mair." In EARLY CANADIAN ART AND LITERATURE, pp. 63-82. Liechtenstein: Europe Printing Establish- ment, 1969.

Mackay, Isabel E. "Charles Mair, Poet and Patriot." CANADIAN MAGA- ZINE, 59 (June 1922), 162-65.

Matthews, John P. "Charles Mair." In OUR LIVING TRADITION, FIFTH SERIES, pp. 78-101. Ed. R. L. McDougall. Toronto: University of Toronto Press, 1965.

Morgan, H. R. "Dr. Charles Mair." WILLISON'S MONTHLY, 2 (August 1926), 110-11.

Norwood, Robert. "Charles Mair." In LEADING CANADIAN POETS, pp. 152-57. Ed. W. P. Percival. Toronto: Ryerson, 1948.

Shrive, [F.] Norman. "Poet and Politics: Charles Mair at Red River." CA-NADIAN LITERATURE, 17 (Summer 1963), 6-21.

_____. "Poets and Patriotism: Charles Mair and Tecumseh." CANADIAN LITERATURE, 20 (Spring 1964), 15-26.

_____. CHARLES MAIR: LITERARY NATURALIST. Toronto: University of Toronto Press, 1965.

Tait, Michael. "Playwrights in a Vacuum: English-Canadian Drama in the Nineteenth Century." CANADIAN LITERATURE, 16 (Spring 1963), 3-18.

MARQUIS, THOMAS GUTHRIE (1864-1936)

Marquis is an admirable representative of the new breed of Canadian who came to prominence at the turn of the century: the "Canadian man of letters," whose writings ranged all the way from belles-lettres to biography. In all, he could be described as quite competent: his poem, "The Cathedral," was described by Charles G. D. Roberts as "one of the most satisfying in our Canadian literature"; MARGUERITE DE ROBERVAL is a readable, if somewhat stilted, romance; THE KING'S WISH is an unusual fairy story; and the other published works (essays, biographies, and literary criticism) all testify to a career of continual involvement in and influence on the development of Canadian letters.

POETRY

THE CATHEDRAL AND OTHER POEMS. With a foreword by Charles G. D. Roberts. Toronto: Musson, [1936].

FICTION

MARGUERITE DE ROBERVAL: A ROMANCE OF THE DAYS OF JACQUES CARTIER. Toronto: Copp Clark, 1899.

THE KING'S WISH. Toronto: Ryerson, [1924].

OTHER PROSE

STORIES OF NEW FRANCE: BEING TALES OF ADVENTURE AND HEROISM FROM THE EARLY HISTORY OF CANADA. 2nd Series. Boston: Lothrop, 1890.

The first series was written by Agnes Maule Machar.

STORIES FROM CANADIAN HISTORY. Toronto: Copp Clark, 1893; reprint ed. 1936.

Contributions to CANADA AND ITS PROVINCES. Eds. Adam Shortt and Arthur G. Doughty. Toronto: Publishers' Association of Canada, 1913.

"The 'Adventurers' of Hudson Bay," vol. 1, 159-98; "English-Literature," vol. 12, 493-589, "The Period of Exploration," vol. 21, 13-74.

ENGLISH-CANADIAN LITERATURE. Toronto: Glasgow, Brook, 1915. Reprinted from CANADA AND ITS PROVINCES, vol. 12.

THE WAR CHIEF OF THE OTTAWAS: A CHRONICLE OF THE PONTIAC WAR. Toronto: Glasgow, Brook, 1915.

THE JESUIT MISSIONS: A CHRONICLE OF THE CROSS IN THE WILDERNESS. Toronto: Glasgow, Brook, 1916.

THE VOYAGES OF JACQUES CARTIER IN PROSE AND VERSE. Toronto: T. Allen, 1934.

Includes prose sketches by Marquis and sonnets by S. C. Swift.

CRITICISM

Anon. "Shepherd of Canadian Poets." CANADIAN BOOKMAN, 17 (September 1935), 106.

Burpee, Lawrence J. "Canadian Novels and Novelists." SEWANEE REVIEW, 11 (October 1903), 385-411.

Swift, S. C. "Thomas Guthrie Marquis." CANADIAN BOOKMAN, 18 (May 1936), 2, 6.

O'HAGAN, THOMAS (1855-1939)

Thomas O'Hagan is typical of many other minor poets, rich in volume but poor in quality. Born in Ontario, he became a pedagogue and never managed to divorce pedagogy from poetry. Many of his poems have an explicit moral and are reminiscent of Bunyan's EMBLEMS. Yet the fact that he was published by William Briggs indicates that O'Hagan was considered a good poet in his own time, and the number of volumes published seems to indicate that he was popular. He was also a prolific essayist, of the chatty variety.

POETRY

A GATE OF FLOWERS, AND OTHER POEMS. Toronto: Briggs, 1887.

IN DREAMLAND, AND OTHER POEMS. Toronto: Williamson, 1893.

SONGS OF THE SETTLEMENT, AND OTHER POEMS. Toronto: Briggs, 1899.

IN THE HEART OF THE MEADOW, AND OTHER POEMS. Toronto: Briggs, 1914.

SONGS OF HEROIC DAYS. Toronto: Briggs, 1916.

COLLECTED POEMS. Toronto: McClelland & Stewart, 1922.

ESSAYS

CANADIAN ESSAYS, CRITICAL AND HISTORICAL. Toronto: Briggs, 1901.

ESSAYS, LITERARY, CRITICAL, AND HISTORICAL. Toronto: Briggs, 1909.

CHATS BY THE FIRESIDE. A STUDY IN LIFE, ART AND LITERATURE. Somerset, Ohio: Rosary Press, [1911].

ESSAYS ON CATHOLIC LIFE. Baltimore: Murphy, 1916.

WITH STAFF AND SCRIP. Toronto: Ryerson, 1924.

INTIMACIES IN CANADIAN LIFE AND LETTERS. Ottawa: Graphic Press, 1927.

SPAIN AND HER DAUGHTERS. Toronto: Hunter, Rose, 1931.

CRITICISM

McManus, Emily. "O'Hagan's Poems: A Study." CANADIAN MAGAZINE, 1 (October 1893), 665-68.

Stevenson, Lionel. "Who's Who in Canadian Literature: Thomas O'Hagan." CANADIAN BOOKMAN, 11 (May 1929), 107-9.

OXLEY, JAMES MACDONALD (1855-1907)

Born in Nova Scotia, Oxley was educated in law and became quite successful
in that field. In addition, he became one of the most popular writers of boys'
adventure stories of his day, being widely read both in the United States and
Great Britain. In his usual naive fashion MacMurchy writes (in his HANDBOOK
OF CANADIAN LITERATURE), with regard to Oxley's work: "It is a good thing
that Canadian writers are rising up who are willing to make a study of the manners and customs of the denizens of the wide Dominion" (p. 161). Quite to
the contrary, it was novels like Oxley's which gave so many outsiders that long-
accepted stereotype of the Canadian way of life: ice, snow, brave rustics encountering savage natives, and always lots of adventure and excitement. This
is probably the only reason for which one would now read Oxley's work.

FICTION

BERT LLOYD'S BOYHOOD. A STORY OF NOVA SCOTIA. Philadelphia:
American Baptist Publishing Co., 1889.

UP AMONG THE ICE-FLOES. Philadelphia: American Baptist Publishing Co.,
1890. Reprint ed. London: Nelson, 1901.

THE CHORE-BOY OF CAMP KIPPEWA. Philadelphia: American Baptist Publishing Co., 1891. Reprinted as THE YOUNG WOODSMAN. London: Nelson, 1904.

THE WRECKERS OF SABLE ISLAND. Philadelphia: American Baptist Publishing
Co., 1891. Reprint ed. London: Nelson, 1904.

DONALD GRANT'S DEVELOPMENT. Philadelphia: American Baptist Publishing Co., 1892.

FERGUS McTAVISH; OR, PORTAGE AND PRAIRIE. A STORY OF THE HUD-
SON'S BAY CO. Philadelphia: American Baptist Publishing Co., 1892.

ARCHIE OF ATHABASCA. Boston: Lothrop, 1893. Reprinted as ARCHIE McKENZIE, THE YOUNG NOR'WESTER. London: Religious Tract Society, 1894; and as THE YOUNG NOR'WESTER. London: Religious Tract Society, 1908.

DIAMOND ROCK; OR, ON THE RIGHT TRACK. London: Nelson, 1893. Published as THE GOOD SHIP GRYPHON. Philadelphia: American Baptist Publishing Co., 1893.

MY STRANGE RESCUE AND OTHER STORIES OF SPORT AND ADVENTURE IN CANADA. London: Nelson, 1895.

IN THE WILDS OF THE WEST COAST. New York: Nelson, 1895; reprint ed. 1905.

BAFFLING THE BLOCKADE. London: Nelson, 1896.

THE BOY TRAMPS; OR, ACROSS CANADA. New York: Crowell, 1896. Published as TWO BOY TRAMPS. London: Chambers, 1896.

THE HERO OF START POINT AND OTHER STORIES. Philadelphia: American Baptist Publishing Co., 1896.

ON THE WORLD'S ROOF. London: Nisbet, 1896; Philadelphia: American Baptist Publishing Co., 1897; Toronto: Musson, n.d.

IN THE SWING OF THE SEA. Philadelphia: American Baptist Publishing Co., 1898; Toronto: Musson, n.d.

STANDING THE TEST. London: Religious Tract Society, [1898].

FROM RUNG TO RUNG. London: Kelly, 1899.

FIFE AND DRUM AT LOUISBOURG. Boston: Little, Brown, 1899.

TERRY'S TRIALS AND TRIUMPHS. London: Nelson, 1899.

L'HASA AT LAST. Philadelphia: American Baptist Publishing Co., 1900; London: Ward, Lock, 1902.

NORMAN'S NUGGET. London: Partridge, 1901; Toronto: Musson, n.d.

NORTH OVERLAND WITH FRANKLIN. London: Religious Tract Society, 1901; Toronto: Musson, n.d.

DONALDBLANE OF DARIEN. London: Partridge, 1902; Toronto: Musson, n.d.

WITH ROGERS ON THE FRONTIER. New York: Wessels, 1902.

IN PATHS OF PERIL. A BOY'S ADVENTURE IN NOVA SCOTIA. London: Partridge, 1903; Toronto: Musson, n.d.

WON IN WESTERN CANADA. N.p.: n.pag., 1903.

THE FAMILY ON WHEELS. New York: Crowell, 1905.

THE SPECIMEN HUNTERS. London: Religious Tract Society, 1907; Toronto: Musson, n.d.

TI-TI-PU. A BOY ON RED RIVER. Toronto: Musson, n.d.

CRITICISM

Brodie, Allan Douglas. "Canadian Short-Story Writers." CANADIAN MAGAZINE, 4 (February 1895), 334-44.

MacMurchy, Archibald. "James Macdonald Oxley." In HANDBOOK OF CANADIAN LITERATURE, pp. 160-61. Toronto: Briggs, 1906.

PARKER, GILBERT (1860-1932)

Like Sara Jeannette Duncan and others, Gilbert Parker (born at Camden East, Ontario) became successful as a writer only after leaving Canada, yet is still regarded as a "Canadian" writer. Perhaps the fact that half his novels are set in Canada is enough to justify this, though these settings have little thematic relevance to his plots. In any event, Parker, like the hero of his THE TRES-PASSER (1893), set out to prove that a colonial could successfully assume the role of an English gentleman: he became a member of the British parliament, was knighted in 1902, was made a member of the Privy Council, and became a very successful (though not a good) novelist, publishing more than thirty works of fiction. He is the only Canadian writer to have had his collected works published in a single edition (the Imperial edition, twenty-three volumes) and, in spite of their shallow plots and sentimental style, his fast-paced works are quite readable. Published in large quantities, they are also readily available.

COLLECTED WORKS

THE WORKS OF GILBERT PARKER. Imperial Ed. 23 vols. New York: Scribner's, 1912-23.

SELECTED WORKS OF SIR GILBERT PARKER. Pocket ed. 10 vols. London: Harrap & Co., 1926.

POETRY

A LOVER'S DIARY. SONGS IN SEQUENCE. London: Methuen, 1894; Toronto: Copp Clark, 1898.

EMBERS; BEING A BOOK OF VERSES. Plymouth: Brendon, 1908.

EMBERS; A LOVER'S DIARY. New York: Scribner's, 1913.

Parker, Gilbert

FICTION

THE CHIEF FACTOR. A TALE OF THE HUDSON'S BAY COMPANY. New York: Trow Directory Co., 1892.

PIERRE AND HIS PEOPLE. TALES OF THE FAR NORTH. London: Methuen; Toronto: Copp Clark, 1893.

> See annotation to AN ADVENTURE OF THE NORTH, below.

THE TRANSLATION OF A SAVAGE. New York: Appleton, 1893; Toronto: Copp Clark, 1898.

THE TRESPASSER. New York: Appleton, 1893; Toronto: Copp Clark, 1898.

THE TRAIL OF THE SWORD. New York: Appleton, 1894; Toronto: Copp Clark, 1898.

AN ADVENTURE OF THE NORTH. London: Methuen; New York: Stone & Kimball, 1895; Toronto: Copp Clark, 1898.

> In 1896 Stone & Kimball issued these stories and PIERRE AND HIS PEOPLE in two volumes as AN ADVENTURE OF THE NORTH and A ROMANY OF SNOWS. The latter title was used by Parker for all of these stories in the Imperial Edition.

WHEN VALMOND CAME TO PONTIAC. THE STORY OF A LOST NAPOLEON. London: Methuen, 1895; Toronto: Copp Clark, 1898.

THE POMP OF THE LAVILETTES. Boston: Lamson, Wolffe, 1896.

THE SEATS OF THE MIGHTY. London: Methuen, 1898. Modern paperback ed. with introduction by Elizabeth Waterston. Toronto: McClelland & Stewart, 1971.

THE BATTLE OF THE STRONG. A ROMANCE OF TWO KINGDOMS. London: Methuen; Toronto: Copp Clark, 1898.

BORN WITH A GOLDEN SPOON. London & New York: Doubleday, 1899.

THE HILL OF PAINS. Boston: Badger, 1899.

> Short stories.

THE LIAR. Boston: Brown, 1899.

> Three long stories: "The Liar," "The Red Patrol," "The House with the Broken Shutter."

184

THE LANE THAT HAD NO TURNING, AND OTHER ASSOCIATED TALES CONCERNING THE PEOPLE OF PONTIACS. New York: Doubleday; Toronto: Morang, 1900.

AN UNPARDONABLE LIAR. Chicago: Sergel, 1900.

THE MARCH OF THE WHITE GUARD. New York: Fenno, 1901.

THE RIGHT OF WAY. BEING THE STORY OF CHARLEY STEELE, AND ANOTHER. London: Heinemann; Toronto: Copp Clark, 1901.

DONOVAN PASHA, AND SOME PEOPLE OF EGYPT. London: Heinemann; Toronto: Copp Clark, 1902.

> Short stories.

A LADDER OF SWORDS. A TALE OF LOVE, LAUGHTER, AND TEARS. London: Heinemann; Toronto: Copp Clark, 1904. Reprinted as MICHEL AND ANGILE. New York: Scribner's, 1923.

THE WEAVERS. A TALE OF ENGLAND AND EGYPT OF FIFTY YEARS AGO. New York: Harper; Toronto: Copp Clark, 1907.

NORTHERN LIGHTS. London: Methuen; New York: Harper; Toronto: Copp Clark, 1909.

> Short stories.

CUMNER'S SON AND OTHER SOUTH SEA FOLK. London: Heinemann; Toronto: Copp Clark, 1910.

> Short stories.

THE JUDGEMENT HOUSE. A NOVEL. New York: Harper; Toronto: Copp Clark, 1913.

YOU NEVER KNOW YOUR LUCK. BEING THE STORY OF A MATRIMONIAL DESERTER. New York: Doran; Toronto: Bell & Lockburn, 1914.

THE MONEY MASTER. BEING THE CURIOUS HISTORY OF JEAN JACQUES BARBILLE, HIS LABOURS, HIS LOVES AND HIS LADIES. New York: Harper; Toronto: Copp Clark, 1915.

THE WORLD FOR SALE. New York: Harper; Toronto: Copp Clark, 1916.

WILD YOUTH, AND ANOTHER. Philadelphia: Lippincott; Toronto: Copp Clark, 1919.

The other story is "Jordan is a Hard Road."

NO DEFENCE. Toronto: Copp Clark, 1920.

CARNAC. London: Methuen; Toronto: Copp Clark, 1922. Published as CARNAC'S FOLLY. Philadelphia: Lippincott, 1922.

THE POWER AND THE GLORY. A ROMANCE OF THE GREAT LA SALLE. New York: Harper; Toronto: Copp Clark, 1925.

TARBEE. THE STORY OF A LIFE. New York: Harper; Toronto: Copp Clark, 1927.

THE PROMISED LAND. A STORY OF DAVID IN ISRAEL. London: Cassell; Toronto: Copp Clark, 1928.

OTHER PROSE

ROUND THE COMPASS IN AUSTRALIA. London: Hutchinson, 1892.

OLD QUEBEC, THE FORTRESS OF NEW FRANCE (with Claude G. Bryan). New York: Macmillan, 1903.

THE WORLD IN THE CRUCIBLE. AN ACCOUNT OF THE ORIGINS AND THE CONDUCT OF THE GREAT WAR. London: Murray, 1915.

CRITICISM

Adams, John Coldwell. "Sir Gilbert Parker as a Dramatist." CANADIAN AUTHOR AND BOOKMAN, 40 (Winter 1965), 5-6.

Anon. "The Northwest and Gilbert Parker." NATION, 96 (February 20, 1913), 181-82.

_____. "The Real Charley." BOOKMAN (New York), 37 (July 1913), 481-83.

Black, F. D. "He Made the Most of His Great National Gifts." CANADIAN MAGAZINE, 66 (August 1926), 14-15.

Carman, Bliss. "Gilbert Parker." THE CHAP-BOOK, 1 (November 1, 1894), 338-43.

Cogswell, Frederick W. "The Canadian Novel from Confederation to World War I." Thesis, University of New Brunswick, 1950.

Comer, Cornelia A. P. "The Novels of Gilbert Parker." CRITIC, 33 (October 1898), 271-74.

Cooper, J. A. "Canadian Celebrities: Sir Gilbert Parker." CANADIAN MAGAZINE, 25 (October 1905), 494-96.

Friden, Georg. THE CANADIAN NOVELS OF SIR GILBERT PARKER: HISTORICAL ELEMENTS AND LITERARY TECHNIQUE. Upsala: Lundenquistka Bokhandeln, 1953.

Garvin, John W. "Sir Gilbert Parker and Canadian Literature." CANADIAN BOOKMAN, 14 (September 1932), 92.

Horning, Lewis E. "Gilbert Parker." ACTA VICTORIANA, 11 (March 1896), 252-54.

Hume, Blanche. "Who's Who in Canadian Literature: Sir Gilbert Parker." CANADIAN BOOKMAN, 10 (May 1928), 131-34.

Ingraham, Mary Kinley. "Letters from Sir Gilbert Parker." CANADIAN BOOKMAN, 15 (January 1933), 3-4.

Logan, J. D. "Sir Gilbert Parker as Poet." CANADIAN MAGAZINE, 62 (January 1924), 179-82.

McArthur, James, et al. "Sir Gilbert Parker--The Man and the Novelist." BOOK NEWS, 27 (January 1908), 325-34.

MacPhail, Sir Andrew. "Sir Gilbert Parker: An Appraisal." PROCEEDINGS AND TRANSACTIONS OF THE ROYAL SOCIETY OF CANADA, 3rd ser., 33 (1939), 123-35.

Rutledge, J. L. "Gilbert Parker the Novelist." ACTA VICTORIANA, 27 (April 1904), 404-8.

Sorfleet, John Robert. "Fiction and the Fall of New France: William Kirby vs. Gilbert Parker." JOURNAL OF CANADIAN FICTION, 2 (Summer 1973), 132-46.

Thorold, W. J. "Gilbert Parker." MASSEY'S MAGAZINE, 3 (February 1897), 117-23.

SANGSTER, CHARLES (1822-1893)

Charles Sangster's first book, THE ST. LAWRENCE AND THE SAGUENAY, was hailed as a masterpiece and, in spite of the fact that only two other collections of his poems were ever published, he was long considered Canada's "first important national poet" (Lighthall, SONGS OF THE GREAT DOMINION, p. xxv). Current critical opinion, while acknowledging occasional flashes of poetic brilliance, especially in his sonnets, ranks Sangster as "a very minor Victorian versifier" (Pacey, TEN CANADIAN POETS, p. 23).

BIBLIOGRAPHY

Hamilton, W. D. CHARLES SANGSTER. New York: Twayne Publishers, 1971.

> Pages 108-34 contain an excellent bibliographical description of Sangster's unpublished work, preserved at McGill University Library.

COLLECTED WORKS

THE ST. LAWRENCE AND THE SAGUENAY, AND OTHER POEMS. HESPERUS AND OTHER POEMS. Ed. with introduction by George Johnston. Toronto: University of Toronto Press, 1972.

> A facsimile reprint of the original editions, cited below.

POETRY

THE ST. LAWRENCE AND THE SAGUENAY, AND OTHER POEMS. Kingston, Ont.: Creighton & Duff; New York: Miller, Orton & Mulligan, 1856.

HESPERUS AND OTHER POEMS AND LYRICS. Montreal: Lovell; Kingston, Ont.: Creighton & Duff, 1860.

OUR NORLAND. Toronto: Copp Clark, n.d.

Hamilton, W. D. "An Edition of Hitherto Uncollected Poems of Charles Sangster, together with a Biographical and Critical Introduction and Notes." Thesis, University of New Brunswick, 1958.

CRITICISM

Baker, Ray Palmer. "Charles Sangster." In A HISTORY OF ENGLISH-CANADIAN LITERATURE TO THE CONFEDERATION, pp. 159-65. Cambridge, Mass.: Harvard University Press, 1920.

Bourinot, Arthur S. "Charles Sangster." In LEADING CANADIAN POETS, pp. 202-12. Ed. W. P. Percival. Toronto: Ryerson, 1948.

Dewart, E[dward] H[artley]. "Charles Sangster, the Canadian Poet." CANADIAN MAGAZINE, 7 (May 1890), 28-34.

. "Charles Sangster, a Canadian Poet of the Last Generation." In ESSAYS FOR THE TIMES, pp. 38-51. Toronto: Briggs, 1898.

Gammon, Donald B. "The Concept of Nature in Nineteenth Century Canadian Poetry, with Special Reference to Goldsmith, Sangster and Roberts." Thesis, University of New Brunswick, 1948.

Hamilton, W. D. CHARLES SANGSTER. New York: Twayne Publishers, 1971.

Macklem, John. "Who's Who in Canadian Literature: Charles Sangster." CANADIAN BOOKMAN, 10 (July 1928), 195-96.

Morgan, Henry J. "Mr. Charles Sangster, the Poet." In SKETCHES OF CELEBRATED CANADIANS. Quebec: Hunter Rose, 1862, pp. 684-93.

Pacey, Desmond. "Charles Sangster." In TEN CANADIAN POETS, pp. 1-33. Toronto: Ryerson, 1958. Bibliography, p. 327.

Robb, W. H. "Charles Sangster, Canada's and Kingston's Poet." HISTORIC KINGSTON, 11 (1963), 30-34.

SAUNDERS, MARGARET MARSHALL (1861-1947)

In 1894 the American Humane Society offered a $200 prize for the best animal story similar to Anna Sewell's BLACK BEAUTY and illustrative of the American treatment of animals. The winner was Margaret Marshall Saunders, a Canadian born in Nova Scotia. The publication of the winner, BEAUTIFUL JOE, the autobiography of a dog, met with immediate success and was followed by another twenty-five book-length stories. Saunders was one of the first of the very few successful writers of children's books in Canada.

FICTION

MY SPANISH SAILOR. London: Ward, Lock, 1889. Rev. and enl. ed. published as HER SAILOR: A LOVE STORY. Boston: L. C. Page, 1900.

> Adult romance.

BEAUTIFUL JOE. AN AUTOBIOGRAPHY. Philadelphia: American Baptist Publishing Co.; London: Jarrold, 1894.

CHARLES AND HIS LAMB. Philadelphia: Banes, 1895.

FOR THE OTHER BOY'S SAKE, AND OTHER STORIES. Philadelphia: Banes, 1896.

THE HOUSE OF ARMOUR. Philadelphia: Rowland, 1897.

THE KING OF THE PARK. New York: Crowell, 1897.

ROSE A CHARLITTE. AN ACADIAN ROMANCE. Boston: L. C. Page; London: Methuen, 1898.

> Adult romance.

DEFICIENT SAINT. A TALE OF MAINE. Boston: L. C. Page, 1899.

DAISY. A TALE. Philadelphia: Banes, n.d.

FOR HIS COUNTRY; AND, GRANDMOTHER THE CROW. Boston: L. C. Page, 1900.

'TILDA JANE. AN ORPHAN IN SEARCH OF A HOME. Boston: L. C. Page, 1901.

BEAUTIFUL JOE'S PARADISE. Boston: L. C. Page, 1902; London: Jarrold, 1903.

THE STORY OF THE GRAVELEYS. Toronto: Briggs, 1903; London: Ward, Lock, 1905.

NITA. THE STORY OF AN IRISH SETTER. Boston: L. C. Page, 1904.

PRINCESS SUKEY. THE STORY OF A PIGEON AND HER HUMAN FRIENDS. New York: Eaton & Mains, 1905.

ALPATOCK. THE STORY OF AN ESKIMO DOG. Boston: L. C. Page, 1906. Published as THE STORY OF AN ESKIMO DOG. London: Hodder & Stoughton, 1906.

'TILDA JANE'S ORPHANS. Boston: L. C. Page, 1909.

THE GIRL FROM VERMONT. THE STORY OF A VACATION SCHOOL TEACH- ER. Boston: Griffith & Rowland, 1910.

PUSSY BLACK-FACE. Boston: L. C. Page, 1913.

THE WANDERING DOG. ADVENTURES OF A FOX TERRIER. New York: Doran, 1916.

"BOY" THE WANDERING DOG. New York: Grosset, 1916.

GOLDEN DICKY. THE STORY OF A CANARY AND HIS FRIENDS. New York: Stokes, 1919.

BONNIE PRINCE FETLAR. THE STORY OF A PONY AND HIS FRIENDS. Toronto: McClelland & Stewart, 1920.

JIMMIE GOLDCOAST; OR, THE STORY OF A MONKEY AND HIS FRIENDS. Toronto: Hodder & Stoughton, 1923.

ESTHER DE WARREN. THE STORY OF A MID-VICTORIAN MAIDEN. New York: Doran, 1927.

CRITICISM

Bowker, Kathleen K. "An Artist in Life." CANADIAN BOOKMAN, 5 (October 1923), 275, 279.

Elson, John Melbourne. "Who's Who in Canadian Literature: Miss Marshall Saunders." CANADIAN BOOKMAN, 12 (November 1930), 223-28.

Kirconnell, Watson. "Tribute to Marshall Saunders." CANADIAN AUTHOR & BOOKMAN, 30 (Spring 1954), 24-25.

Magee, William H. "The Animal Story: A Challenge in Technique." DALHOUSIE REVIEW, 44 (Summer 1964), 156-64.

Stevenson, O. J. "Lift Up Thy Voice for the Dumb." In A PEOPLE'S BEST, pp. 229-34. Toronto: Musson, 1927.

SCOTT, FREDERICK GEORGE (1861-1944)

A great many minor Canadian poets were clergymen and, indeed, the progress of letters in Canada owes a great deal to such churchmen as William Briggs (the publisher) and Edward Hartley Dewart. F. G. Scott was another whose poetry about God, nature, and patriotism was undistinguished but popular; his "Unnamed Lake" was a favourite selection in Canadian school texts for a few generations.

COLLECTED WORKS

COLLECTED POEMS. Vancouver: Clarke & Stuart, 1934.

POETRY

THE SOUL'S QUEST, AND OTHER POEMS. London: Kegan Paul, 1888.

MY LATTICE, AND OTHER POEMS. Toronto: Briggs, 1894.

THE UNNAMED LAKE, AND OTHER POEMS. Toronto: Briggs, 1897.

POEMS: OLD AND NEW. Toronto: Briggs, 1900.

A HYMN OF EMPIRE AND OTHER POEMS. Toronto: Briggs, 1906.

POEMS. London: Constable; Toronto: Musson, 1910.

THE GATES OF TIME, AND OTHER POEMS. London: Bagster, [1915].

IN THE BATTLE SILENCES. London: Constable, 1916.
    Poems written at the front.

BALLADS OF DISARMAMENT, AND OTHER POEMS. St. John, N.B.: "Globe" Publishing Co., 1923.

IN SUN AND SHADE. Quebec: Dussault & Proulx, 1926.

NEW POEMS. Quebec: Victor Lafrance, 1929.

SELECTED POEMS. Quebec: Emile Robitaille, 1933.

LIFT UP YOUR HEARTS. Toronto: Ryerson, 1941.

FICTION

ELTON HAZLEWOOD. New York: Whittaker, 1891.

DRAMA

THE KEY OF LIFE. A MYSTERY PLAY. Quebec: Dussault & Proulx, 1907.

OTHER PROSE

THE GREAT WAR AS I SAW IT. Toronto: Goodchild, 1922.
> Personal reminiscences of his career as a padre.

CRITICISM

Adams, Thomas. "Frederick G. Scott." CANADIAN MAGAZINE, 11 (June 1898), 160-64.

Brodie, Allan Douglas. "Canadian Short-Story Writers." CANADIAN MAGAZINE, 4 (February 1895), 334-44.

Cates, John. "Canon Scott, Beloved Padre of World War I." SATURDAY NIGHT, 59 (January 29, 1944), 16.

Evans, H. "Canon Scott." MacLEAN'S MAGAZINE, 51 (November 1, 1938), 15, 46-47.

Hammond, Melvin O. "The Poet of the Laurentians." CANADIAN MAGAZINE, 32 (March 1909), 456-60.

Lowe, A. "Beloved Companion." CANADIAN MAGAZINE, 74 (September 1930), 3-4.

Percival, W. P. "Frederick George Scott." In LEADING CANADIAN POETS, pp. 220-26. Toronto: Ryerson, 1948.

Raymond, W. O. "Frederick George Scott (1861-1944)." PROCEEDINGS AND TRANSACTIONS OF THE ROYAL SOCIETY OF CANADA, 3rd ser., 38 (1944), 119-23.

Stevenson, O. J. "Poet and Padre." In A PEOPLE'S BEST, pp. 177-84. Toronto: Musson, 1927.

Wetherell, J. E. "A New Book of Poems." CANADIAN MAGAZINE, 4 (January 1895), 287-88.

SHERMAN, FRANCIS JOSEPH (1871-1926)

While many of the poets of his time (Carman, Lampman, Roberts) were receiving adequate public recognition, Francis Sherman, whose best poetry is artistically equal to theirs, went unnoticed. As a matter of fact, he received even less notice than did most of the minor poets considered in this section, to whom he is vastly superior. Perhaps it was his affinity to Rossetti and Morris which dampened his appeal; perhaps it was the infrequency of publication; or perhaps few people could believe that an internationally known banking specialist could also be a good poet. Whatever, it remains a fact that his due place in anthologies is often preempted by poets of lesser ability.

In 1935 both Lorne Pierce and Charles G. D. Roberts attempted to rescue Sherman's work from obscurity. "Tomorrow," wrote Pierce in his introduction to the collected poems (p. 15), "Canada will place Sherman among her major poets." This, however, she has failed to do. Thus, as a reminder of what has been passed by, one moving lyric is reproduced below:

The Watch

Are those her feet at last upon the stair?
Her trailing garments echoing there?
The falling of her hair?
About a year ago I heard her come,
Thus; as a child recalling some
Vague memories of home.

Oh, how the firelight blinded her dear eyes!
I saw them open and grow wise.
No questions, no replies.

And now, to-night, comes the same sound of rain.
The wet boughs reach against the pane
In the same way, again.

In the old way I hear the moaning wind
Hunt the dead leaves it cannot find, --
Blind as the stars are blind.

She may come in at midnight, tired and wan.
Yet, --what if once again at dawn
I wake to find her gone?

COLLECTED WORKS

THE COMPLETE POEMS OF FRANCIS SHERMAN. Ed. with "memoir" by Lorne Pierce; foreword by Sir Charles G. D. Roberts. Toronto: Ryerson, 1935.

Contains an excellent bibliography listing Sherman's published works, MS. locations, poems in periodicals, poems in anthologies, reviews of his work, and quotations from numerous letters.

POETRY

MATINS. Boston: Copeland & Day, 1896.

IN MEMORABILIA MORTIS. Cambridge, Mass.: Harvard University Press, 1896.

THE DESERTED CITY: STRAY SONNETS WRITTEN BY F. S. AND RESCUED FOR THE FEW WHO LOVE THEM BY H. D. N.p.: Privately printed, 1899.

A CANADIAN CALENDAR: XII LYRICS. Havana: Privately printed, 1900.

AN ACADIAN SINGER. Ed. with introduction by H. G. Wade. Winnipeg: Stovel Co., 1930.

CRITICISM

Anon. "Francis J. Sherman: Poet and Banker." ROYAL BANK OF CANADA MAGAZINE, June–July, 1935, pp. 3-10.

Hathaway, R. H. "Francis Sherman: Canadian poet." WILLISON'S MONTH-LY, 2 (March 1927), 383-84.

Massey, Vincent. "Roberts, Carman, Sherman: Canadian Poets." CANADIAN AUTHOR AND BOOKMAN, 23 (Fall 1947), 29-32.

Pierce, Lorne [Albert]. "Francis Sherman." In THREE FREDERICTON POETS, pp. 25-30. Toronto: Ryerson, 1933.

Roberts, Charles G. D. "Francis Sherman." DALHOUSIE REVIEW, 14 (January 1935), 419-27.

Wilson, L. R. "A Biographical and Critical Study of Francis Sherman, 1871-1926." Thesis, University of New Brunswick, 1959.

THOMSON, EDWARD WILLIAM (1849-1924)

The bulk of Edward Thomson's writing is of the journalistic kind, since, between 1889 and 1901, he served as editor of the Toronto GLOBE and associate
editor of YOUTH'S COMPANION (Boston). He published only four books of
fiction, three of which are collections of sketches for juveniles; only one,
OLD MAN SAVARIN, a collection of stories dealing with Canadian pioneer
life, was intended for an adult audience. On the basis of that one book,
however, Thomson has gained deserved literary acclaim: he has been called
a master of the short story form and a pioneer of literary realism in Canada.
One of his stories, "Privilege of the Limits," has been reprinted in four modern
anthologies. His one book of poetry is undistinguished.

BIBLIOGRAPHY

Bourinot, A[rthur] S. EDWARD WILLIAM THOMSON (1849-1924): A BIBLIOG-
RAPHY WITH NOTES AND SOME LETTERS. Ottawa: Privately printed, 1955.

> Contains descriptions of the works listed below.

LETTERS

THE LETTERS OF EDWARD THOMSON TO ARCHIBALD LAMPMAN. Ed. A. S.
Bourinot. Ottawa: Privately printed, 1957.

POETRY

THE MANY-MANSIONED HOUSE AND OTHER POEMS. Toronto: Briggs,
1909. Published as WHEN LINCOLN DIED AND OTHER POEMS. Boston:
Houghton Mifflin, 1909.

> The format of the American edition was slightly altered and a few
> poems were deleted.

Thomson, Edward William

FICTION

OLD MAN SAVARIN AND OTHER STORIES. Toronto: Briggs, 1895.

SMOKY DAYS. New York: Crowell, 1896.

WALTER GIBBS, THE YOUNG BOSS, AND OTHER STORIES. Toronto: Briggs, 1896.

BETWEEN EARTH AND SKY AND OTHER STRANGE STORIES OF DELIVERANCE. Toronto: Briggs, 1897.

OLD MAN SAVARIN STORIES. TALES OF CANADA AND CANADIANS. New and enlarged edition. Toronto: Gundy, 1917. Reprinted with introduction by Linda Shesko. Toronto: University of Toronto Press, 1974.

CRITICISM

Hammond, Melvin O. "Edward William Thomson." QUEEN'S QUARTERLY, 38 (Winter 1931), 123-39.

M., W. E. "Topics of the Day." DALHOUSIE REVIEW, 2 (October 1922), 374-75.

McMullen, Lorraine. "Tales of Canada and Canadians: The Stories of Edward William Thomson." JOURNAL OF CANADIAN FICTION, 2 (Summer 1973), 191-94.

Peacock, H. R. "A Biographical and Critical Study of Edward William Thomson." Thesis, University of New Brunswick, 1949.

TRAILL, CATHERINE PARR

Older sister to Susanna Moodie, Catherine emigrated to Canada with the Moodies and her husband in 1832 and settled near Rice Lake, Ontario. THE BACK-WOODS OF CANADA (1836), published twelve years before Susanna's ROUGH-ING IT IN THE BUSH, was an instant success in England and was frequently reprinted. Her CANADIAN CRUSOES (1852), a mixture of fictional suspense, religious homily, and nature lore, remained popular reading with young people until well into the twentieth century. She was not, however, as skilled a stylist as her sister, nor so keen an observer of social mores; thus, even though her work was more popular in her own time than that of Susanna, she does not merit equal critical attention today.

FICTION

CANADIAN CRUSOES. A TALE OF THE RICE LAKE PLAINS. London: Hall, 1852; New York: Francis, 1853; Toronto: McClelland & Stewart, 1923. Several editions, beginning with that published by Nelson in London, 1882, are titled LOST IN THE BACKWOODS.

LADY MARY AND HER NURSE. London: Hall, 1856. Published as AFAR IN THE FOREST. London: Nelson, 1873. Published as IN THE FOREST; OR, PICTURES OF LIFE AND SCENERY IN THE WOODS OF CANADA. London: Nelson, 1894.

COT AND CRADLE STORIES. Ed. Mary Agnes Fitzgibbon. Toronto: Briggs, 1894.

THE YOUNG EMIGRANTS. New York: Johnson Reprint Corp., 1969.

> This is a facsimile reprint of an anonymous book published in London in 1826 and attributed to Traill by Ruth Marks of the Toronto Public Library. It is not listed in Watters' CHECKLIST or the British Museum Catalogue.

OTHER PROSE

THE BACKWOODS OF CANADA. BEING LETTERS FROM THE WIFE OF AN EMIGRANT OFFICER. London: Knight, 1836. Ed. E. S. Caswell. Toronto: McClelland & Stewart, 1929. Ed. Clara Thomas. Toronto: McClelland & Stewart, 1966. Reprint ed. in facsimile. Toronto: Coles Publishing Co., 1971.

THE FEMALE EMIGRANT'S GUIDE. Toronto: McClear, 1854. Published as THE CANADIAN SETTLER'S GUIDE (Toronto: The Old Countryman Office, 1855) and as THE CANADIAN EMIGRANT HOUSEKEEPER'S GUIDE (Toronto: Lovell & Gibson, 1862). Modern ed. THE CANADIAN SETTLER'S GUIDE. Ed. Clara Thomas. Toronto: McClelland & Stewart, 1969.

CANADIAN WILD FLOWERS. Montreal: Lovell, 1869. Reprint ed. in facsimile. Toronto: Coles Publishing Co., 1972.

STUDIES OF PLANT LIFE IN CANADA. Ottawa: Woodburn, 1885.

PEARLS AND PEBBLES; OR, NOTES OF AN OLD NATURALIST. Toronto: Briggs, 1894.

CRITICISM

Ballstadt, Carl. "The Literary History of the Strickland Family." Thesis, University of London, 1965.

Beyea, George P. "The Canadian Novel Prior to Confederation." Thesis, University of New Brunswick, 1950, chapter III.

Burham, Hampden. "Mrs. Traill." CANADIAN MAGAZINE, 4 (February 1895), 388-89.

Burpee, Lawrence J. "Catherine Parr Traill." In A LITTLE BOOK OF CANADIAN ESSAYS, pp. 56-64. Toronto: Musson, 1909.

_____. "Last of the Stricklands: Mrs. Catherine Parr Traill." SEWANEE REVIEW, 8 (April 1909), 207-17.

Eaton, Sara. LADY OF THE BACKWOODS. Toronto: McClelland & Stewart, 1969.

   A biographical study for juveniles.

Gairdner, William D. "Traill and Moodie: The Two Realities." JOURNAL OF CANADIAN FICTION, 1, no. 2 (Spring 1972), 35-42.

Hume, Blanche. "Grandmothers of Canadian Literature." WILLISON'S MONTH-LY, 3 (May 1928), 474-77.

_____. THE STRICKLAND SISTERS. Toronto: Ryerson, 1928.

Lande, Lawrence M. "The Strickland Sisters." In OLD LAMPS AGLOW, pp. 301-7. Montreal: Privately printed, 1957.

McNeil, J. L. "Mrs. Traill in Canada." Thesis, Queen's University, 1948.

Morris, Audrey Y. GENTLE PIONEERS: FIVE NINETEENTH-CENTURY CANA-DIANS. Toronto and London: Hodder & Stoughton, 1968.

   A study of Susanna Moodie, Samuel Strickland, John Moodie, Catherine Parr Traill, and Thomas Traill.

Needler, G. H. OTONABEE PIONEERS: THE STORY OF THE STEWARTS, THE STRICKLANDS, THE TRAILLS AND THE MOODIES. Toronto: Burns & MacEachern, 1953.

Scott, Lloyd M. "The English Gentlefolk in the Backwoods of Canada." DALHOUSIE REVIEW, 39 (Spring 1959), 56-59.

Thomas, Clara. "Journeys to Freedom." CANADIAN LITERATURE, 51 (Winter 1972), 11-19.

_____. "The Strickland Sisters." In THE CLEAR SPIRIT: TWENTY CANADI-AN WOMEN AND THEIR TIMES, pp. 42-73. Ed. Mary Q. Innis. Toronto: University of Toronto Press, 1966.

Weaver, Emily. "Mrs. Traill and Mrs. Moodie, Pioneers in Literature." CA-NADIAN MAGAZINE, 48 (March 1917), 473-76.

Chapter 6

LITERATURE OF EXPLORATION,
TRAVEL AND DESCRIPTION

Chapter 6
LITERATURE OF EXPLORATION,
TRAVEL AND DESCRIPTION

The arrangement of this chapter has been determined by three considerations: the geographical vastness of Canada; the long period of time between the earliest explorations of Eastern Canada in the eleventh century and those of Western Canada in the eighteenth century; and the large body of literature dealing with these expanses of space and time. Any consideration of so much demands some kind of meaningful breakdown of the whole, and this I have attempted to do.

In Section A, therefore, I have listed first-hand accounts of early exploration in Eastern Canada, Western Canada, and the North (Hudson Bay and the Northwest Passage). Section B comprises books of travel and description for six Canadian regions: Newfoundland, the Maritimes, the Canadas, the Prairies, British Columbia, and the Hudson Bay Territory. In Section C are included those books which do not fit into any of the foregoing categories or which are, quite intentionally, "nation-wide" in scope, such as George Grant's OCEAN TO OCEAN.

Because of the vast amount of descriptive literature which exists, the following is not an exhaustive list. My chief aim has been to expose an area of reading and research too often overlooked or ignored by the student of literature. I have omitted works which are too weighted with history, which are merely statistical guides and propaganda sheets for emigrants, which are too narrowly tourist guides, which have only a chapter or two on Canada, and which do not in my opinion offer any worthwhile insights into the Canadian way of life.

It is important to add that in recent years there have been many reprints of this kind of literature. This increased accessibility is yet another reason why an up-to-date listing of the literature of travel and description is needed. I have, therefore, noted the latest editions of these works. Within sections, items are arranged alphabetically by author. My annotations, should they disturb certain sensibilities, are designed to arouse the reader's curiosity and offer, as succinctly as possible, the essence of the work cited.

For an overview of the literature of exploration, travel, and description, the following are particularly helpful:

Craig, Gerald M., ed. EARLY TRAVELLERS IN THE CANADAS:
1791-1867. Toronto: Macmillan, 1955.

Klinck, Carl F., general ed. LITERARY HISTORY OF CANADA:
CANADIAN LITERATURE IN ENGLISH. Toronto: University of
Toronto Press, 1965, chapters 1-3, 5, 18.

Smith, A[rthur] J[ames] M[arshall], ed. THE BOOK OF CANADIAN
PROSE. Vol. 1: EARLY BEGINNINGS TO CONFEDERATION.
Toronto: W. J. Gage, 1965.

A. EARLY EXPLORATION

1. EASTERN CANADA

From the Sea

The first Europeans to discover North America were the Vikings Bjarni Herjolfsson
(ca. 985) and Leif Erikson (ca.1001). They were followed, almost 500 years
later, by a fleet of explorers hoping to find a "North-West Passage," men such
as Cabot, Gilbert, Frobisher, Davis, Hore, Cartier, and Roberval. Nearly all
of them left first-hand accounts of their voyages and frustrated attempts at colonization and their opinions of the land. Accounts of the Vikings are contained
in their sagas, newly collated and translated; those of the later major explorers
in Hakluyt and Purchas; accounts of Jacques Cartier's voyages are also contained
in Hakluyt, but since he is the greatest Canadian explorer from the sea, one
should also read the modern version. For all of these see:

Biggar, H. P., ed. THE VOYAGES OF JACQUES CARTIER. Ottawa: King's
Printer, 1924.

Hakluyt, Richard. THE PRINCIPAL NAVIGATIONS, VOYAGES, TRAFFIQUES
AND DISCOVERIES OF THE ENGLISH NATION. 2nd ed. 3 vols. London,
1598. Reprint ed. in 12 vols. Glasgow: MacLehose, 1903.

> This work, described as one of the "great English prose epics,"
> is the primary source of all first-hand accounts of English voyages
> to America.

Jones, Gwynn. THE NORSE ATLANTIC SAGA. London: Oxford University
Press, 1964.

Magnusson, Magnus, and Hermann Palsson. THE VINLAND SAGAS. Harmondsworth: Penguin, 1965.

Purchas, Samuel. HAKLUYTUS POSTHUMUS OR PURCHAS HIS PILGRIMES.

London, 1625. Reprint ed. in 20 vols. Glasgow: MacLehose, 1905-7.

By Land

The basic exploration of inland Canada, from the mouth of the St. Lawrence River to the Great Lakes, was undertaken and successfully carried out by the colonizers of New France. Most notable was Samuel de Champlain, principally responsible for the exploration of the St. Lawrence and its tributaries; equally enterprising were the Jesuit missionaries who explored much of the territory north and south of the River; a third important group was the courier de bois who opened up much of inland Canada, particularly in the region of the Hudson Bay, and were typified in their adventures by their exemplar, Pierre Esprit Radisson. The personal narratives of these explorers offer first-hand descriptions of the land and the natives and excitingly recount numerous encounters with sickness and death. Important editions are:

Adams, Arthur T., ed. THE EXPLORATIONS OF PIERRE ESPRIT RADISSON. Minneapolis: Ross & Haines, 1961.

Biggar, H. P., ed. THE WORKS OF SAMUEL DE CHAMPLAIN. 6 vols. Toronto: The Champlain Society, 1922-26.

Thwaites, R. G., ed. TRAVELS AND EXPLORATIONS OF THE JESUIT MISSIONARIES IN NEW FRANCE. 73 vols. Cleveland: Burrows Bros., 1896-1901.

2. WESTERN CANADA

From the Sea

Inspired by Captain Cook's account of his exploration of the North Pacific Coast (1778) and of the trading to be done around the Nookta Sound, many other explorers, adventurers, and fur-traders made their way to that little-known part of the world. Many of them also followed Cook's example in leaving written records of their voyages:

Cook, James. THE JOURNALS OF CAPTAIN JAMES COOK ON HIS VOYAGE OF DISCOVERY. Vol. III: THE VOYAGE OF THE 'RESOLUTION' AND 'DISCOVERY,' 1776-1780. Ed. J. C. Beaglehole. Cambridge: The Hakluyt Society, 1967.

_____. A VOYAGE TO THE PACIFIC OCEAN. UNDERTAKEN BY COMMAND OF HIS MAJESTY, FOR MAKING DISCOVERIES IN THE NORTHERN HEMISPHERE. 3 vols. London: Strahan, 1784.

Dixon, George. A VOYAGE ROUND THE WORLD; BUT MORE PARTICULARLY
TO THE NORTH-WEST COAST OF AMERICA. London, 1789. Reprint ed. in
facsimile. New York: De Capo Press, 1968.

See annotation to Portlock, Nathaniel, below.

Ledyard, John. JOHN LEDYARD'S JOURNAL OF CAPTAIN COOKS'S LAST
VOYAGE. Ed. James K. Mumford. Corvallis: Oregon State University Press,
1963.

Marchand, Etienne. A VOYAGE ROUND THE WORLD PERFORMED DURING
THE YEARS 1790, 1791 and 1792. Trans. C. P. C. Fleurieu. 2 vols. London:
Longman, 1801. Reprint ed. in facsimile. New York: De Capo Press, 1969.

Meares, John. VOYAGES MADE IN THE YEARS 1788 AND 1789...TO
THE NORTH-WEST COAST OF AMERICA. London, 1790. Reprint ed. in
facsimile. New York: De Capo Press, 1967.

Nicol, John. THE LIFE AND ADVENTURES OF JOHN NICOL, MARINER.
Ed. John Howell. London: Blackwood, 1822.

Nicol made his voyage to the Pacific coast with Captain Portlock
in 1785.

Portlock, Nathaniel. A VOYAGE ROUND THE WORLD; BUT MORE PARTIC-
ULARLY TO THE NORTH-WEST COAST OF AMERICA. London: Stockdale,
1798. Reprint ed. in facsimile. New York: De Capo Press, 1968.

Dixon and Portlock made their voyages together and wrote different
versions of the trip under the same title.

Rickman, John. JOURNAL OF CAPTAIN COOK'S LAST VOYAGE TO THE
PACIFIC OCEAN ON DISCOVERY, PERFORMED IN THE YEARS 1776, 1777,
1778, 1779. London: Newbery, 1781. Reprint ed. in facsimile. New York:
De Capo Press, 1967.

Vancouver, Captain George. A VOYAGE OF DISCOVERY TO THE NORTH
PACIFIC OCEAN, 1790-95. 3 vols. London, 1798. Reprint ed. in facsimile.
New York: De Capo Press, 1967.

Second only to Cook, Vancouver ranks as the major explorer and
cartographer of the North Pacific coast.

By Land

Six weeks after Captain George Vancouver visited the Bella Coola River, another famous explorer left his inscription on a nearby rock: "Alexander Mackenzie, from Canada by land, the twenty-second of July, one thousand seven
hundred and ninety-three." The East and West of the vast land had at last

been linked. Mackenzie, however, was but one of many explorers and fur-
traders who made this achievement possible, men who individually explored the
vast tract of land between the Great Lakes and the Rocky Mountains and then
challenged the mountains themselves.

Fraser, Simon. THE LETTERS AND JOURNALS OF SIMON FRASER, 1806-1808.
Ed. W. Kaye Lamb. Toronto: Macmillan, 1960.

Harmon, Daniel Williams. A JOURNAL OF VOYAGES AND TRAVELS IN THE
INTERIOUR OF NORTH AMERICA. Andover: Flagg & Gould, 1820; Toronto:
Courier, 1911. Reprinted as SIXTEEN YEARS IN THE INDIAN COUNTRY:
THE JOURNAL OF DANIEL WILLIAMS HARMON, 1800-1816. Ed. W. Kaye
Lamb. Toronto: Macmillan, 1957.

Henry, Alexander. JOURNAL, COVERING ADVENTURES AND EXPERIENCES
IN THE FUR TRADE ON THE RED RIVER, 1799-1801. Ed. Charles N. Bell.
Winnipeg: Free Press, 1888-89.

_____. NEW LIGHT ON THE EARLY HISTORY OF THE GREATER NORTH-
WEST: THE MANUSCRIPT JOURNALS OF ALEXANDER HENRY...AND OF
DAVID THOMPSON, 1799-1814. Ed. Elliott Coues. 3 vols. New York:
Harper, 1897.

Hind, Henry Youle. NARRATIVE OF THE CANADIAN RED RIVER EXPLORING
EXPEDITION OF 1857 AND OF THE ASSINIBOINE AND SASKATCHEWAN
EXPLORING EXPEDITION OF 1858. 2 vols. London: Longman, Brown, Green
& Longmans, 1860. Reprint ed. in facsimile. Edmonton: Hurtig, 1971.

Keating, W. H. NARRATIVE OF AN EXPEDITION TO THE SOURCE OF ST.
PETER'S RIVER, LAKE WINNEPEEK, LAKE OF THE WOODS, &c. PERFORMED
IN THE YEAR 1823. Boston, 1824; Minneapolis: Ross & Haines, 1959.

Kelsey, Henry. THE JOURNEY OF HENRY KELSEY (1691-1692), THE FIRST
WHITE MAN TO REACH THE SASKATCHEWAN RIVER FROM HUDSON BAY.
Ed. Charles N. Bell. Winnipeg: Dawson Richardson, 1928.

_____. THE KELSEY PAPERS. Eds. A. G. Doughty and Chester Martin.
Ottawa: Public Archives, 1929.

La Verendrye, Sieur. THE JOURNALS AND LETTERS OF PIERRE GAULTIER
DE LA VERENDRYE AND HIS SONS. Ed. L. J. Burpee. Toronto: The
Champlain Society, 1927.

La Verendrye, in attempting to reach the Western Sea, opened up
much of Western Canada in the 1730s and 40s.

Mackenzie, Alexander. VOYAGES FROM MONTREAL, ON THE RIVER ST.
LAURENCE, THROUGH THE CONTINENT OF NORTH AMERICA TO THE

FROZEN AND PACIFIC OCEANS IN THE YEARS 1789 and 1793. London: T. Cadell, 1801. Reprint ed. in facsimile. Edmonton: Hurtig, 1971.

_____. THE JOURNALS AND LETTERS OF SIR ALEXANDER MACKENZIE. Ed. W. Kaye Lamb. Toronto: Macmillan, 1970.

3. THE "NORTHWEST PASSAGE" AND THE ARCTIC

All the early explorers--Cabot, Gilbert, Columbus, and Cartier--had ostensibly one aim: to discover a Northwest Passage to the Pacific. Many of them were sidetracked by or were content with the more immediate discovery of fish-yielding waters and fur-bearing lands. Others, however, continued to explore the northern part of Canada and its adjacent waters in search of the "Passage." Henry Hudson did so several times between 1607 and 1616; William Baffin added new data to the charts in 1616; Samuel Hearne and Alexander Mackenzie reached the Arctic Ocean overland in 1771 and 1789 respectively; in the mid-1800s the existence of the "Passage" was proven; and in 1905 the first ship (commanded by Roald Amundsen) forced its way through. Primary literature of "Passage" exploration is therefore quite extensive, beginning with Hakluyt, reaching its most dramatic in the career of John Franklin, and continuing until the end of the century.

Back, Sir George. NARRATIVE OF THE ARCTIC LAND EXPEDITION TO THE MOUTH OF THE GREAT FISH RIVER, AND ALONG THE SHORES OF THE ARCTIC OCEAN, IN THE YEARS 1833, 1834 AND 1835. London: John Murray, 1836. Reprint ed. in facsimile. Edmonton: Hurtig, 1970.

Baffin, William. THE VOYAGES OF WILLIAM BAFFIN, 1612-1622. London: The Hakluyt Society, 1881.

Barrow, Sir John, ed. THE GEOGRAPHY OF THE HUDSON'S BAY: BEING THE REMARKS OF CAPTAIN W. COATS IN MANY VOYAGES TO THAT LOCALITY BETWEEN THE YEARS 1727 AND 1751. WITH AN APPENDIX CONTAINING EXTRACTS FROM THE LOG OF CAPT. MIDDLETON ON HIS VOYAGE FOR THE DISCOVERY OF THE NORTH-WEST PASSAGE IN H.M.S. 'FURNACE' IN 1741-42. London: The Hakluyt Society, 1852.

_____. VOYAGES OF DISCOVERY AND RESEARCH WITHIN THE ARCTIC REGIONS. New York: Harper, 1846.

Beechey, Captain F. W. A VOYAGE OF DISCOVERY TOWARDS THE NORTH POLE, PERFORMED IN HIS MAJESTY'S SHIPS 'DOROTHEA' AND 'TRENT', UNDER THE COMMAND OF CAPTAIN DAVID BUCHAN, R.N., 1818. London: Richard Bentley, 1843.

_____. NARRATIVE OF A VOYAGE TO THE PACIFIC AND BEERING'S STRAIT TO CO-OPERATE WITH THE POLAR EXPEDITIONS. 2 vols. London:

Richard Bentley, 1831. Reprint ed. in facsimile. New York: De Capo Press, 1968.

Davis, John. THE VOYAGES AND WORKS OF JOHN DAVIS. Ed. Sir A. H. Markham. London: The Hakluyt Society, 1880. Reprint ed. in facsimile. New York: Burt Franklin, n.d.

Ellis, Henry. A VOYAGE TO HUDSON'S BAY BY THE 'DOBB'S GALLEY' AND 'CALIFORNIA' IN THE YEARS 1746 AND 1747. London: Whitridge, 1748. Reprint ed. in facsimile. New York: Johnson Reprint Corp., 1967.

Foxe, Captain Luke. THE VOYAGES OF CAPTAIN LUKE FOXE OF HULL, AND CAPTAIN THOMAS JAMES OF BRISTOL IN SEARCH OF A NORTH-WEST PASSAGE, IN 1631-32. Ed. Miller Christy. 2 vols. London: The Hakluyt Society, 1894.

Franklin, John. NARRATIVE OF A JOURNEY TO THE SHORES OF THE POLAR SEAS IN THE YEARS 1819, 20, 21 AND 22. London: John Murray, 1823. Reprint ed. in facsimile. Edmonton: Hurtig, 1969.

_____. NARRATIVE OF A SECOND EXPEDITION TO THE SHORES OF THE POLAR SEAS IN THE YEARS 1825, 1826, AND 1827. London: John Murray, 1828. Reprint ed. in facsimile. Edmonton: Hurtig, 1971.

Franklin's first expedition was overland to the Coppermine River and the Coronation Gulf; on his second he worked westward along the coast from the Mackenzie River as far as Return Reef, but failed to reach Commander Beechey who was working eastward from the Bering Strait. In 1845 Franklin was again asked to command an expedition and on this was lost. He was last seen by a whaler who encountered his ships, 'Erebus' and 'Terror' in Baffin Bay on July 26, 1845. It was not until 1859, after almost continuous searching, that the mystery of Franklin's disappearance was finally solved. The literature of the search is as exciting as the literature of Franklin's original expeditions. The following nine items are "search" descriptions.

Armstrong, Alexander. A PERSONAL NARRATIVE OF THE DISCOVERY OF THE NORTHWEST PASSAGE...WHILE IN SEARCH OF THE EXPEDITION UNDER SIR JOHN FRANKLIN. London: Hurst & Blackett, 1857.

Collinson, Sir Richard. JOURNAL OF H.M.S. 'ENTER-PRISE' ON THE EXPEDITION IN SEARCH OF SIR JOHN FRANKLIN'S SHIPS BY BEHRING STRAIT, 1850-51. London: Sampson Low, 1889.

Hall, Charles Francis. LIFE WITH THE ESQUIMAUX: A NARRATIVE OF ARCTIC EXPERIENCE IN SEARCH OF

SURVIVORS OF SIR JOHN FRANKLIN'S EXPEDITION.
London: Sampson Low, 1864. Reprint ed. in facsimile.
Edmonton: Hurtig, 1970.

Kane, Elisha K. ARCTIC EXPLORATION: THE SECOND
GRINNELL EXPEDITION IN SEARCH OF SIR JOHN
FRANKLIN, 1853, '54, '55. 2 vols. Philadelphia:
Childs & Peterson, 1856.

McClintock, Sir. F. L. THE VOYAGE OF THE 'FOX'
INTO THE ARCTIC SEAS: A NARRATIVE OF THE DIS-
COVERY OF THE FATE OF SIR JOHN FRANKLIN AND
HIS COMPANIONS. London: John Murray, 1860.
Reprint ed. in facsimile. Edmonton: Hurtig, 1972.

Richardson, Sir John. ARCTIC SEARCHING EXPEDITION:
A JOURNAL OF A BOAT-VOYAGE THROUGH RUPERT'S
LAND AND THE ARCTIC SEA, IN SEARCH OF THE DIS-
COVERY SHIPS UNDER THE COMMAND OF SIR JOHN
FRANKLIN. 2 vols. London: Longman, Brown, Green
& Longmans, 1851.

Schwatka, Lt. Frederick. THE LONG ARCTIC SEARCH:
THE NARRATIVE OF LT. FREDERICK SCHWATKA, U.S.A.,
1878-1880, SEEKING THE RECORDS OF THE LOST
FRANKLIN EXPEDITION. Ed. Edouard A. Stackpole.
Mystic, Conn.: Marine Historical Association, 1965.

Sontagg, August. THRILLING NARRATIVE OF THE
GRINNELL EXPLORING EXPEDITION TO ARCTIC OCEAN,
IN THE YEARS 1853, 1854, AND 1855, IN SEARCH OF
SIR JOHN FRANKLIN. Philadelphia: James T. Lloyd,
1857.

Sutherland, Peter C. JOURNAL OF A VOYAGE IN
BAFFIN'S BAY AND BARROW STRAITS, IN THE YEARS
1850-51...IN SEARCH OF THE MISSING CREWS
OF H.M. SHIPS 'EREBUS' AND 'TERROR.' 2 vols.
London: Longman, Brown, Green & Longmans, 1852.

Greely, Adolphus W. THREE YEARS OF ARCTIC SERVICE: AN ACCOUNT
OF THE LADY FRANKLIN BAY EXPEDITION OF 1881-84. 2 vols. London:
Richard Bentley, 1886.

Hearne, Samuel. A JOURNEY FROM PRINCE OF WALES' FORT IN HUDSON'S
BAY, TO THE NORTHERN OCEAN...IN THE YEARS 1769, 1770, 1771 AND
1772. London: Strahan & Cadell, 1795. Reprint ed. in facsimile. Edmonton:
Hurtig, 1971.

_____. THE JOURNALS OF SAMUEL HEARNE AND PHILIP TURNOR. Ed.
J. B. Tyrell. Toronto: The Champlain Society, 1934.

King, Richard. NARRATIVE OF A JOURNEY TO THE SHORES OF THE ARCTIC
OCEAN, IN 1833, 1834, and 1835, UNDER THE COMMAND OF CAPTAIN
BACK. London: Richard Bentley, 1836.

Lyon, Captain G. F. AN ATTEMPT TO REACH REPULSE BAY IN HIS MAJES-
TY'S SHIP 'GRIPER' IN THE YEAR MDCCCXXIV. London: John Murray, 1825.
Reprint ed. in facsimile. Toronto: Coles Publishing Co., 1971.

McClure, Robert. DISCOVERY OF THE NORTHWEST PASSAGE BY H.M.S.
'INVESTIGATOR,' CAPT. ROBERT M'CLURE, 1850, 1851, 1852, 1853, 1854.
London: Longman, Green, 1856. Reprint ed. in facsimile. Edmonton: Hurtig,
1969.

Markham, Sir A. H. THE GREAT FROZEN SEA: A PERSONAL NARRATIVE
OF THE VOYAGE OF THE 'ALERT' DURING THE ARCTIC EXPEDITIONS OF
1875-76. London: Daldy, 1878.

Parry, William. JOURNAL OF A VOYAGE FOR THE DISCOVERY OF A
NORTHWEST PASSAGE...1819-22-23. London: John Murray, 1821.

_____. JOURNAL OF A SECOND VOYAGE FOR THE DISCOVERY OF A
NORTHWEST PASSAGE...1819-22-23. London: John Murray, 1824.

Rae, John. NARRATIVE OF AN EXPEDITION TO THE SHORES OF THE ARCTIC
SEA IN 1846 AND 1847. London: Boone, 1850. Reprint ed. in facsimile.
Toronto: Canadiana House, 1970.

Ross, John. A VOYAGE OF DISCOVERY...FOR THE PURPOSE OF EXPLOR-
ING BAFFIN'S BAY. London: John Murray, 1819.

_____. NARRATIVE OF A SECOND VOYAGE IN SEARCH OF A NORTH-
WEST PASSAGE. London: Webster, 1835.

Simpson, Thomas. NARRATIVE OF THE DISCOVERIES OF THE NORTH COAST
OF AMERICA. London: Richard Bentley, 1843. Reprint ed. in facsimile.
Toronto: Canadiana House, 1970.

B. TRAVEL AND DESCRIPTION

1. NEWFOUNDLAND AND LABRADOR

The island of Newfoundland, discovered in 1497, was claimed as an English

Colony in 1583 and first settled by John Guy in 1610. It was not until the nineteenth century, however, that permanent settlement was permitted, that the Colony became self-governing, and that travellers began to include it on their itineraries. The best descriptive literature comes from the pens of military men and missionaries, the former patrolling its shores and the latter tending the needs of the many fishermen scattered along a rocky coastline. The best travel literature (in reality, a literature of exploration) was written by the several amateur explorers who penetrated the unknown interior of Labrador which, with the island of Newfoundland, is part of Canada's newest province.

Bonnycastle, R. H. NEWFOUNDLAND IN 1843. 2 vols. London: Colburn, 1842.

> A British officer, Bonnycastle spent the greater part of his military career in Canada and Newfoundland and wrote several books about his experiences there (see Section B3: Travel and Description-- The Canadas). His book on Newfoundland is perhaps the most informative and intimate of these, offering detailed accounts of the history, geography, geology, and economy of the island and, more significantly, offering vivid pictures of the Newfoundlanders, dwelling extensively on their social customs, their occupations, and their domestic economy.

Bryant, Henry Grier. A JOURNEY TO THE GRAND FALLS OF LABRADOR. Philadelphia: n.p., [1895].

> Bryant, secretary of the Geographical Club of Philadelphia, was not the first to see but the first to describe the magnificent falls on the Hamilton River in Labrador, fifty-nine feet higher than Niagara. The arduous trip, with all its hardships and delights, on which they towed an eighteen-foot riverboat, is described in detail.

Cartwright, George. A JOURNAL OF TRANSACTIONS AND EVENTS DURING A RESIDENCE OF NEARLY SIXTEEN YEARS ON THE COAST OF LABRADOR. 3 vols. Newark: Allen & Ridge, 1792. Reprinted as CAPTAIN CARTWRIGHT AND HIS LABRADOR JOURNAL. Ed. J. W. Townsend. London: Williams & Norgate, 1911.

> Between 1770 and 1786 Cartwright, on half-pay pension from the British Army, lived in Labrador as trader, trapper, and explorer. His journal is a lively account of his encounters with the natives, with American privateers, and wild animals and offers many fine descriptions of the rugged, yet beautiful, country.

Chappell, Edward. VOYAGE OF HIS MAJESTY'S SHIP 'ROSAMOND' TO NEWFOUNDLAND AND THE SOUTHERN COAST OF LABRADOR. London: J. Mawman, 1818.

> When Lt. Chappell docked the "Rosamond" in St. John's harbour in 1818, the town was still nothing more than a supply depot for British fishermen. He describes minutely the streets, taverns, forts and "public reading-room." He also goes on to describe the state of vassalage in which the fishermen were held by the merchants.

In short, Chappell's book offers one of the most vivid pictures of
the colony in the period immediately preceding that of Representative Government (1832), when Newfoundland finally gained a modi-
cum of independence.

Cilley, Jonathan P. BOWDOIN BOYS IN LABRADOR. Rockland, Me.: Rockland Publishing Co., n.d.

A very interesting account of the 1891 Bowdoin College expedition
to study the natural history of Labrador. The most exciting part,
as it turned out, was the successful attempt by two members to reach
the hitherto unmeasured Grand Falls, on the Hamilton River, two
weeks before it was again reached by Henry Grier Bryant (see above).

Cormack, W. E. NARRATIVE OF A JOURNEY ACROSS THE ISLAND OF NEW-
FOUNDLAND IN 1822. Ed. F. A. Bruton. London: Longman, Green, 1928.

Originally published in the EDINBURGH PHILOSOPHICAL JOURNAL,
X, 1823-24, Cormack's narrative is the record of the first trans-
Newfoundland crossing by a white man. The object of the journey
was to make contact with any Beothucks who had survived the earlier massacres; this Cormack failed to do, but nevertheless left a
journal of rare excitement, particularly so to the student of Newfoundlandiana. A born Newfoundlander, Cormack later became a
world traveller and died in British Columbia in 1868.

Dashwood, Richard Lewes. CHIPLOQUORGAN; OR, LIFE BY THE CAMP FIRE
IN THE DOMINION OF CANADA AND NEWFOUNDLAND. London: Simpkin,
Marshall, 1872.

As the title suggests, Dashwood was delighted primarily by the
hunter's paradise in which he found himself when he reached the
island of Newfoundland. Moose-hunting and salmon-fishing were
his chief delights; there are, however, other engaging diversions,
notably the problems of travel, accommodation, and mosquitoes.
The "Dominion of Canada" referred to is, in reality, New Brunswick,
where Dashwood also did a good deal of hunting.

Davis, S. T. CARIBOU SHOOTING IN NEWFOUNDLAND. Lancaster, Pa.:
New Era Printing House, 1895.

Before Davis begins to describe his hunting holiday in Newfoundland, he offers his reader eight chapters of history taken from
Moses Harvey's works. After that, the book becomes much more
descriptive and engaging, particularly so for the reader interested
in the minutest details of a nineteenth-century hunting expedition.

De Boilieu, Lambert. RECOLLECTIONS OF LABRADOR LIFE. London: Saunders, Otley, 1861. Reprint ed. with introduction by Thomas Bredin. Toronto:
Ryerson, 1969.

A model of descriptive literature, combining the right proportions of personal anecdote and factual description, de Boilieu's book depicts the life and labour of the people of Labrador in the 1850s when the peninsula attracted thousands of people yearly to its fishing grounds. Varied descriptions of Christmas customs, hunting expeditions, Eskimo villages, and harrowing tales of frostbite and accidents are liberally spiced with colloquialisms.

Elliott, J. R. RAMBLES IN AN ANCIENT COLONY. Boston: Privately printed, 1900.

This is an account of a journey across Newfoundland by train; a slow, but pleasant journey, interspersed with fishing and hunting excursions. A large number of false generalizations about the colony pervade the book, but it remains valuable for its localized descriptions.

Feild, Bishop Edward. A JOURNAL OF THE BISHOP'S VISITATION OF THE MISSIONS ON THE WESTERN AND SOUTHEAST COAST, AUGUST TO SEPTEMBER, 1845. London: Society for the Propagation of the Gospel, 1849.

_____. JOURNAL...OF VOYAGE...IN CHURCH SHIP 'HAWK' IN THE YEAR 1848. London: Society for the Propagation of the Gospel, 1849.

See next item.

_____. JOURNAL OF VISITATION IN THE 'HAWK' CHURCH SHIP ON THE COAST OF LABRADOR, AND AROUND THE WHOLE ISLAND OF NEWFOUNDLAND, IN THE YEAR 1849. London: Society for the Propagation of the Gospel, 1850.

Edward Feild, whose name is still revered in Newfoundland episcopal circles, was the second Bishop of the Church of England on the island. For twenty-seven years he laboured among the people and during that time visited every parish in Newfoundland and Labrador. His major "voyages of discovery" (as he called them) are recorded in these journals and constitute a remarkable document of living conditions in the many remote villages where the fishermen, with only the barest of necessities, without teachers, doctors, or clergy, struggled to exist.

Grenfell, Wilfred. VIKINGS OF TODAY; OR, LIFE AND MEDICAL WORK AMONG THE FISHERMEN OF LABRADOR. London: Marshall Bros., 1895.

Grenfell, a legend along the Labrador coast, spent more than forty years as medical missionary among the natives and "livyeres" of Labrador. This is the first of many similar books (the rest written after 1900) published to gain public awareness of his work and the need for financial assistance. It runs the gamut of Labrador existence, from the hardships of the Newfoundland fishermen to the Moravian work among the Eskimos. Although Grenfell had only been in Labrador for three years in 1895, he had witnessed enough suffering to last most men a lifetime.

Harvey, Rev. Moses. ACROSS NEWFOUNDLAND WITH THE GOVERNOR.
St. John's, Newfoundland: "Morning Chronicle, 1879.

This work describes a trip from Hall's Bay to Grand Lake with the
Governor, Sir John Hawley Glover. Its minute descriptions of the
journey, the scenery, the wildlife and its expressions of optimism
for the future of the land, make it an exciting piece of writing.

_____. NEWFOUNDLAND AS IT IS IN 1894: A HANDBOOK AND TOURIST'S
GUIDE. St. John's, Newfoundland: Queen's Printer; London: Kegan Paul,
1894.

Harvey's book is a dull, "matter-of-fact" tourist's guide, with history thrown in; but it contains a great deal of trivia that might interest those who relish it: "Custom House officers meet steamers on
arrival to examine and pass the passengers' luggage. Cabs also
meet the steamers and trains. Fare to hotel, including ordinary
luggage, forty to fifty cents....Mail wagons run to Portugal Cove
daily in summer, by-weekly in winter; to Broad Cove by-weekly."
He does much the same things in three other books: NEWFOUND-
LAND AS IT IS IN 1899, NEWFOUNDLAND IN 1897, and NEW-
FOUNDLAND IN 1900.

Hind, Henry Youle. EXPLORATIONS IN THE INTERIOR OF THE LABRADOR
PENINSULA. 2 vols. London: Longman, Green, 1863.

Hind, a professor of chemistry at the University of Toronto, became
a government geologist in 1857 and carried out several geological
expeditions in Nova Scotia, New Brunswick, and Labrador. Though
he includes a great deal of technical data, he is nevertheless very
much aware of the scenery and the people with whom he comes in
contact. He offers extensive commentary on life in Labrador, its
fishery, its natives, the Moravian mission, and other church influences.

Howley, James P. THE BEOTHUCKS OR RED INDIANS: THE ABORIGINAL
INHABITANTS OF NEWFOUNDLAND. Cambridge: At the University Press,
1915.

Howley's book is basically a collection of references to Beothuck
culture which he had gathered in his research into their history.
Many of these, like Cormack's NARRATIVE (above), are journals
of travel into the interior of Newfoundland and some, such as
David Buchan's JOURNEY UP THE EXPLOITS IN SEARCH OF RED
INDIANS IN THE WINTER OF 1810-11 (printed in full), are una-
vailable elsewhere. Howley's is a most valuable document.

Jukes, J. B. EXCURSIONS IN AND ABOUT NEWFOUNDLAND, DURING
THE YEARS 1839 AND 1840. 2 vols. London: John Murray, 1842. Reprint
ed. in facsimile. Toronto: Canadiana House, 1969.

Ostensibly the official geologist for the Colony, Jukes was fascinated
by all aspects of Newfoundland life. His descriptions range from

those of natural scenery, geological formations, Newfoundland dogs and weddings, to those of personal acquaintances. In short, his volumes, among the best of Newfoundland descriptive literature, are goldmines of information.

Kennedy, W. R. SPORT, TRAVEL AND ADVENTURE IN NEWFOUNDLAND AND THE WEST INDIES. Edinburgh: Blackwood, 1885.

Kennedy's book is a record "of events which happened while the writer was senior officer on the coast of Newfoundland, or cruising in the West Indies," 1879-80. It is delightfully humorous, with vivid pictures of life in the outports. Kennedy has a sharp eye for detail, a witty style, and a keen sense of the absurb.

McCrea, Robert B. LOST AMID THE FOGS: SKETCHES OF LIFE IN NEW-FOUNDLAND. London: Sampson Low, 1869.

The title is indicative of McCrea's bemusement with life in New-foundland. Among his best descriptions are those of St. John's, which offers a shop-by-shop picture of a walk down the main street, and his story of an outing to Portugal Cove, with all its romantic intrigues. Highly engaging, this work rivals those of Kennedy and Jukes as being the most entertaining and informative piece of New-foundland descriptive literature.

Mason, Captain John. A BRIEFE DISCOURSE OF THE NEW-FOUND-LAND, WITH THE SITUATION, TEMPERATURE, AND COMMODITIES THEROF. London: Andro Hart, 1620.

Mason was governor of the Colony at Cupids for three and a half years (1615-19). His Discourse is one of the earliest pieces of descriptive literature, offering detailed lists of plants, animals, birds, and fish, along with reasons why the island should be colo-nized. The pamphlet is, however, highly propagandistic: "And albeit it be thus cold in the Winter season by acidentall means, contrarie to the naturall position therof in the Spheare, yet it is tollerable, as by experience, so that there needs no stoaves as in Germanie...as also our owne experience both in Wheate, Rye, Barlie, Oates and Pease, which have growen and ripened there as well as in Yorkshire in England."

Moreton, Rev. Julian. LIFE AND WORK IN NEWFOUNDLAND. London: Rivingtons, 1863.

Moreton, an Englishman, was a missionary with the Society for the Propagation of the Gospel at the northeastern community of Greens-pond. His very lively account of life there includes such day-to-day experiences as visiting his parishioners, engaging them in dis-cussions, and learning of their hardships. Also included are many humorous anecdotes and descriptions of local customs, one of the most fascinating being that of giving children Biblical names.

Mountain, Rev. J. G. SOME ACCOUNT OF A SOWING TIME ON THE RUG-
GED SHORES OF NEWFOUNDLAND. London: Society for the Propagation of
the Gospel, 1857.

> Mountain was also a missionary for the Society for the Propagation
> of the Gospel, being sent to Newfoundland in 1847. For seven
> years he was resident at Harbour Breton in Fortune Bay; in 1854 he
> was appointed principal of Queen's College in St. John's but died
> two years later. SOWING TIME was published as a memorial to
> his work and is a detailed and poignant journal of his visits to every
> poor fisherman of the coast.

Mullaly, John. A TRIP TO NEWFOUNDLAND; ITS SCENERY AND FISHERIES.
New York: Strong, 1855.

> Mullay was one of a group of sightseers and businessmen--among
> them Samuel Morse, Cyrus Field, and Bayard Taylor--who travelled
> to Newfoundland in 1855 to witness the laying of a transatlantic
> cable. While this objective was not achieved, the trip was never-
> theless "most successful," and Mullaly, in his little book, evinces
> all the enthusiasm of a tourist, taking in all the sights (Quidi Vidi,
> Signal Hill, Portugal Cove), being entertained at the Colonial Build-
> ing, but seeing little of the harshness of the country.

Noble, Louis L. AFTER ICEBERGS WITH A PAINTER: A SUMMER VOYAGE
TO LABRADOR AND NEWFOUNDLAND. New York: Appleton, 1861.

> A very breezy book, with a novel subject: after icebergs. Ice-
> bergs are indeed described (and painted), of all sizes, shapes and
> hues, but Noble has an eye for other, less majestic, sights. He
> describes towns, funerals, religious services, and dinner parties.

Packard, Alpheus S. THE LABRADOR COAST: A JOURNAL OF TWO SUMMER
CRUISES TO THE REGION. New York: Hodges, 1891.

> The account of a scientific expedition and not strictly a travel book,
> Packard's work nevertheless has its moments of general interest, as
> in his description of the Moravian settlements.

Stearns, W. A. LABRADOR: A SKETCH OF ITS PEOPLE, ITS INDUSTRIES,
AND ITS NATURAL HISTORY. Boston: Lee & Shepard, 1884.

> Primarily interested in northern flora, Stearns also exhibited a keen
> interest in the total way of life of the people who settled in that
> remote region. The running titles of one chapter indicate his range
> of interest: "Preparing the summer house to live in--Moving out
> --A Spring rescue--Seals on ice--Lake--A home scene--
> Spring duck shooting--Repairing the boats--Visit to the Indians ans
> --Indian canoes--Labrador mail--Natural scenery of Labrador
> --Visit to Esquimaux graves--Ornithological notes."

Taylor, Bayard. AT HOME AND ABROAD: A SKETCH OF LIFE, SCENERY

AND MEN. New York: Putnam, 1880.

Taylor, a novelist, poet, journalist, and world traveller, visited
Newfoundland to witness the laying of the transatlantic cable in
1855. He devotes three chapters of this book to a description of
his "Telegraphic Trip to Newfoundland," in which he chiefly discusses the sights of St. John's and neighbouring towns.

Thomas, Aaron. THE NEWFOUNDLAND JOURNAL OF AARON THOMAS.
Ed. Jean M. Murray. London: Longman, Green, 1968.

This journal was written during a voyage from England to Newfoundland (and back) in 1794-96. Thomas, an able seaman with
a propensity towards homely philosophy, is a keen observer and
has a witty style. This book represents the first printing of Thomas'
journal, which has been in the possession of the editor's family.

Tocque, Phillip. WANDERING THOUGHTS OR SOLITARY HOURS. London:
Richardson, 1846.

Tocque, a locally-born writer, spends a great deal of time correct-
ing foreign impressions of Newfoundland (in a conversation between
father and son) and the remainder in "recollecting in tranquility"
days spent in Newfoundland, before his move to Toronto. In spite
of this, however, WANDERING THOUGHTS is pleasant to read
and offers many interesting insights. Newfoundland is also mentioned in two of his other books: NEWFOUNDLAND AS IT WAS
AND AS IT IS IN 1877 (Toronto: Magurn, 1878) is factual and
dull; KALEIDOSCOPE ECHOES (Toronto: Hunter, Rose, 1895) has
but passing references.

Tucker, E. W. FIVE MONTHS IN LABRADOR AND NEWFOUNDLAND, DUR-
ING THE SUMMER OF 1838. Concord: Boyd & White, 1839.

Tucker is the sort of writer Tocque did not like: he finds New-
foundlanders and their "quaint and curious" customs (such as marriage) highly amusing and quite pagan. His analysis of Newfoundland customs, however, is very superficial.

Wilson, Rev. William. NEWFOUNDLAND AND ITS MISSIONARIES. Cambridge, Mass.: Dakin & Metcalf, 1866.

This is basically a history of the Methodist Church in Newfoundland
from 1765, but contains many first-hand accounts of missionary experiences in the communities which they served.

Wix, Edward. SIX MONTHS OF A NEWFOUNDLAND MISSIONARY'S JOUR-
NAL. London: Smith & Elder, 1836. Reprint ed. in facsimile. Toronto:
Canadiana House, 1971.

Wix was an Archdeacon in Newfoundland, then under the Bishop
of Nova Scotia, when he made a visit (in 1835) to the southern
shore, encountering men like James Miles of Fortune Bay, who had

been "fifty-six years in Newfoundland and had never before seen a clergyman." Wix's journal is a picture of spiritual and physical poverty and of the often fruitless attempts to alleviate these evils.

Whitbourne, Richard. A DISCOURSE AND DISCOVERY OF NEW-FOUND-LAND. London: William Barrett, 1620.

In 1615 Whitbourne, who had been sailing to Newfoundland since 1579, was sent there by the Admiralty to investigate complaints of rowdyism among the fishermen and later, in 1617 and 1618, was employed by William Vaughan to transport settlers to his colony in Trepassey Bay. Whitbourne's book, one of the earliest of its kind, was written to encourage further settlement and is, although quite engaging, suspiciously propagandistic: "The climate differs but little from England....The ayre is sweeter....We always met with a faire fresh river, or a sweet brooke of running water, where-of we freely dranke, and it did quench my thirst as well as any beere." Extracts from the 1622 edition were published under the title WESTWARD HOE FOR AVALON and the original is available on microfiche.

2. THE MARITIMES

The provinces of New Brunswick, Nova Scotia, and Prince Edward Island all have long and colourful histories and are among the oldest settled parts of Canada. All were originally settled by the French and comprised its territory of Acadia. In 1713 France ceded a greater part of its possessions to England, but retained Ile Royale (Cape Breton), where it built the fort called Louisburg, Ile-Saint-Jean (P.E.I.), and much of New Brunswick where the Acadians lived. In 1755, however, English troops invaded the New Brunswick area and expelled the Acadians. Their place was taken by farmers from New England and later by the United Empire Loyalists. In 1758 Louisburg finally fell, and both Ile Royale and Ile-Saint-Jean passed into English hands. New Brunswick became an independent province in 1784 and Prince Edward Island in 1799, when it gained its English name. Both Nova Scotia and New Brunswick were founding members of Confederation; Prince Edward Island became a Canadian province in 1873.

Like that about Newfoundland, some of the best descriptive literature from the Maritime Provinces was written by missionaries. Unlike Newfoundland literature, however, in which there is little first-hand description of historical events, there are several Maritime books which offer eye-witness accounts of such events as the taking of Louisburg. Indian raids and the Acadian explusion also have their share of commentary.

Alline, Henry. THE LIFE AND JOURNALS OF THE REV. MR. HENRY ALLINE. Boston: Gilbert & Dean, 1806.

Popularly referred to as "the apostle of Nova Scotia," Alline was born in Rhode Island, but came to Falmouth, Nova Scotia, in 1760 to occupy land left vacant by expelled Acadians. Following a dramatic conversion (described in LIFE AND JOURNALS) he became an itinerant preacher, travelling on horseback throughout the Maritime provinces.

Bagster, C. Birch. THE PROGRESS AND PROSPECTS OF PRINCE EDWARD ISLANDS, WRITTEN DURING THE LEISURE OF A VISIT IN 1861.

Bagster's book is, in many respects, just another "emigrant guide," but is redeemed by and included here for its captivating description of Charlottetown in 1861.

Bailey, Jacob. THE FRONTIER MISSIONARY: A MEMOIR OF THE LIFE OF THE REV. JACOB BAILEY. Ed. Wm. S. Bartlett. Boston: Ide & Dutton, 1853.

A missionary sent by the Society for the Propagation of the Gospel to Maine, Bailey opposed the revolution and was forced to flee to Halifax where he served as Anglican parson. His journal describes his life and work there.

Beavan, Mrs. F. SKETCHES AND TALES ILLUSTRATIVE OF LIFE IN THE BACKWOODS OF NEW BRUNSWICK. London: Routledge, 1845.

A resident of New Brunswick for seven years, Mrs. Beavan provides an intimate account of "ordinary people": a great deal of information regarding the people, their houses, food, and schools, punctuated by some very lively and entertaining anecdotes.

Churchill, Rev. Charles. MEMORIALS OF A MISSIONARY LIFE IN NOVA SCOTIA. London: Mason, 1845.

"There is nothing," writes Churchill, "which so peculiarly forces upon the mind of an individual that he is in a foreign land, as the differences which he remarks in the manners and customs of ordinary life in those around him." It is when Churchill attempts to describe those "manners and customs" that his book becomes worth reading; otherwise it is taken up mainly with clerical problems and church business.

Cozzens, Frederick S. ACADIA; OR, A MONTH WITH THE BLUE NOSES. New York: Derby & Jackson, 1859.

It is quite often difficult to be certain of the integrity of any travel book. The air of superficiality about this one, however, is not difficult to feel. Inspired by Longfellow's poem "Evangeline," Cozzens sets off in search of the genuine Acadian, laments the loss of such people, and discusses his travels--all in a very nonchalant manner.

Curtis, Thomas. "A Narrative of the Voyage of Thos Curtis to the Island of St. John's...in the year 1775." In JOURNEYS TO THE ISLAND OF ST.

JOHN OR PRINCE EDWARD ISLAND. Ed. D. C. Harvey. Toronto: Macmillan, 1955.

Printed here for the first time, with an excellent introduction.

Dennys, N. B. AN ACCOUNT OF THE CRUISE OF THE ST. GEORGE ON THE NORTH AMERICAN AND WEST INDIAN STATION, DURING THE YEARS 1861-62. London: Saunders, Otley, 1862.

Chapters VIII-XII deal with the ship's tour of the Maritimes (chiefly of Halifax), where, among other things, the performance of "balls and theatricals" (complete with programmes) are entertainingly described.

Frame, Elizabeth. DESCRIPTIVE SKETCHES OF NOVA SCOTIA, IN PROSE AND VERSE. Halifax: Mackinlay, 1864.

This work is both informative and penetrating, offering descriptions of many aspects of Nova Scotian life, in a colloquial style, interwoven with stories from the province's past (such as "Blandine or the Exile of Cobequid") and poems on such varied subjects as "Address to a Moose" and "The Siege of Louisburg."

Hardy, Campbell. SPORTING ADVENTURES IN THE NEW WORLD; OR, DAYS AND NIGHTS OF MOOSE-HUNTING IN THE PINE FORESTS OF ACADIA. 2 vols. London: Hurst & Blackett, 1855.

See next item.

_____. FOREST LIFE IN ACADIE: SKETCHES OF SPORT AND NATURAL HISTORY IN THE LOWER PROVINCES OF THE CANADIAN DOMINION. London: Chapman & Hall, 1869.

An inveterate hunter, Hardy describes in great detail the hunt, the thrill of the kill, and the habits of the moose. But he also describes, in similar detail, the provinces (chiefly Nova Scotia and New Brunswick), something of their history, scenery, and people, and his own experiences there. This book is extremely like SPORTING ADVENTURES; elements of natural history, however, outweigh those of sport. Each contains some very fine illustrations.

[Hollingsworth, S.] THE PRESENT STATE OF NOVA SCOTIA. Edinburgh: Creech, 1786.

This early piece of descriptive literature while chiefly factual, is abundantly stored with information about towns and harbours, the natural wealth, the natives, the trade, all written as a plea to the mother country to take better care of her colonial possessions.

Howe, Joseph. WESTERN AND EASTERN RAMBLES: TRAVEL SKETCHES OF NOVA SCOTIA. Ed. M. G. Parks. Toronto: University of Toronto Press, 1973.

Published originally in Howe's own NOVASCOTIAN between July,

1828 and October, 1831, his RAMBLES describes, in his inimitable style, trips to all parts of Nova Scotia, physical descriptions combined with personal reflections and commentary. This important document is accompanied by a long and useful introduction and by annotation.

Johnstone, Walter. A SERIES OF LETTERS, DESCRIPTIVE OF PRINCE EDWARD ISLAND. Dumfries: Privately printed, 1822.

See next item.

_____. TRAVELS IN PRINCE EDWARD ISLAND...IN THE YEARS 1820-21. Edinburgh: David Brown, 1823.

Johnstone, who travelled the length and breadth of the island, investigating its suitability for settlement, provides one of the most intimate and detailed pictures of it in his two books. The whole of the first and excerpts from the second are included in D. C. Harvey's JOURNEYS TO THE ISLAND OF ST. JOHN (Toronto: Macmillan, 1955), pp. 73-172.

Lawson, John. LETTERS ON PRINCE EDWARD ISLAND. Charlottetown: Hazard, 1851.

This series of letters first appeared in the ROYAL GAZETTE and are, as the writer admits, as "dull and prosy as a price current." Some, however, though they always remain factual and statistical, offer glimpses of the countryside and of the major occupations of the people.

McGregor, J. HISTORICAL AND DESCRIPTIVE SKETCHES OF THE MARITIME COLONIES OF BRITISH AMERICA. London: Longman, 1828.

These are straightforward and objective (somewhat dull) descriptions, listing towns, owners of land, quality of soil, native flora and fauna, and commenting on the climate of Nova Scotia, New Brunswick, Prince Edward Island, Bay de Chaleur, Anticosti, and Newfoundland.

Marsden, Joshua. THE NARRATIVE OF A MISSION TO NOVA SCOTIA, NEW BRUNSWICK, AND THE SOMERS ISLANDS. Plymouth-Dock, Eng.: J. Johns, 1816. Reprint ed. in facsimile. New York: Johnson Reprint Corp., 1966.

"The narrative of a Mission," writes Marsden, "should possess peculiar claims to public notice; it should be entertaining as a book of travels, and instructive as natural history." Marsden's own narrative admirably lives up to those aims; it is a diary of personal trials in a new colony, a source of local description and commentary on the times, to which is added a long poem titled "The Mission." Marsden went to Nova Scotia as a Methodist Missionary in 1800. After having suffered "by exposures on the ice; in the swamp woods; in snow storms; by severe rains--damp clothes--damp

damp beds--log huts--travelling in the night; and laying upon the floor" for a period of seven years, he moved to the sun in Bermuda.

Moorsom, Capt. W. LETTERS FROM NOVA SCOTIA; COMPRISING SKETCHES OF A YOUNG COUNTRY. London: Colburn & Bentley, 1830.

Using the epistolary style, Moorsom acquaints his readers with the whole gamut of Nova Scotia society as he saw it: the climate, the currency, scenery, religion, education, amusements ("picnic parties in summer, and sleighing excursions in winter, complete the scale of divertissements"). He even adds a modern touch of sarcasm: "The address of your first Trans-Atlantic letter amused me much. Halifax-Canada. 'Tis well there is but one post-office route to British North America, otherwise the said epistle might have gone in search of me among the Chickasaws and Choctaws, in whose neighbourhood it would have stood much the same chance of finding me, as in Canada. Your mistake is pardonable, for it is quite a l'Anglaise."

[Pichon, T.] GENUINE LETTERS AND MEMOIRS, RELATING TO THE NAT-URAL, CIVIL, AND COMMERCIAL HISTORY OF THE ISLANDS OF CAPE BRETON, AND SAINT JOHN, FROM THE FIRST SETTLEMENT THERE TO THE TAKING OF LOUISBURG BY THE ENGLISH IN 1758. London: Nourse, 1760.

A series of letters describing the areas mentioned and the town of Louisburg. The most significant and interesting concern the siege and fall of Louisburg, written, as he says, by an impartial French-man.

Prenties, S. W. NARRATIVE OF A SHIPWRECK ON THE ISLAND OF CAPE BRETON, IN A VOYAGE FROM QUEBEC 1780. London, 1782. Reprint ed. with introduction by G. G. Campbell. Toronto: Ryerson, 1968.

In this Defoe-like tale of survival, Prenties describes being stranded on an uninhabited island and his rescue by the native Indians. A vivid, detailed, exciting but perhaps somewhat fictional account. The Ryerson edition includes an excellent introduction.

Roberts, Charles G. D. THE LAND OF EVANGELINE AND THE GATEWAY THITHER. Kentville, N.S.: Dominion Atlantic Railway Co., [1894].

This small booklet is primarily a tourist guide, but is enhanced by many fine descriptions and historical anecdotes.

Spedon, Andrew Learmont. RAMBLES AMONG THE BLUE-NOSES; OR, REM-INISCENCES OF A TOUR THROUGH NEW BRUNSWICK AND NOVA SCOTIA DURING THE SUMMER OF 1862. Montreal: Lovell, 1863.

Chiefly concerned with physical descriptions of such towns as St. John, Moncton, and Halifax, Spedon is best when offering more

personal observations on such things as the state of literature in
Nova Scotia or recording homely anecdotes about Yankee fishermen.

Springer, John S. FOREST LIFE AND FOREST TREES: COMPRISING WINTER
CAMP-LIFE AMONG THE LOGGERS. New York: Haprer, 1851.

>This soporific account of life in the lumbercamps of Maine and
>New Brunswick is occasionally redeemed by an interesting anecdote.

Warner, Charles Dudley. BADDECK AND THAT SORT OF THING. Boston:
Houghton Mifflin, 1884.

>This highly idiosyncratic and sometimes humorous account of a trip
>to the Maritimes concentrates chiefly on personalities and personal
>reactions. It is, therefore, often quite entertaining.

3. THE CANADAS

Although Ontario and Quebec are so obviously different from one another, their
contiguity has meant that often, especially in the nineteenth century, travellers
and writers failed to distinguish between them. Politically, the two provinces
were known as Upper and Lower Canada until 1841; in that year they became
one province by the Act of Union of 1840; in 1867 they reverted to their original separation from one another as the new provinces of Ontario and Quebec
in the new Dominion of Canada. Thus, while there is a great deal of descriptive literature which deals with each province separately, there is also
much which deals with both provinces at once (under the general name, "The
Canadas"). I have, therefore, further divided this chapter into three subsections as follows: books which describe life in (1) the Canadas, (2) in Lower
Canada or Quebec, and (3) in Upper Canada or Ontario.

The descriptive literature of this region is among the best stylistically and the
richest to be found in Canada. Detailed descriptions of such events as the
War of 1812, the Rebellions of 1837-38, and opinions about Confederation,
make this literature one of the primary sources for historians. Such works as
Susanna Moodie's ROUGHING IT IN THE BUSH and Catherine Parr Traill's
THE BACKWOODS OF CANADA have become Canadian classics; John Galt
and William Dunlop are names as well known as those of Charles G. D. Roberts
and Bliss Carman.

The Canadas

Bigsby, John J. THE SHOE AND THE CANOE; OR, PICTURES OF TRAVEL
IN THE CANADAS. 2 vols. London: Chapman & Hall, 1850. Reprint ed.
in facsimile. New York: Paladin Press, 1969.

>"Having in comparative leisure, for a period of six happy years,
>wandered, pencil and pen in hand, over the greater portion of

Canada, I purpose, in the following pages, to present to the reader
a group of popular pictures of their scenery and social condition."
This Bigsby does with great vividness, with scenes of Montmorency
and Niagara, descriptions of teaparties, and typhoid epidemics
from Quebec City to Rat Portage.

Bird, Isabella Lucy. THE ENGLISHWOMAN IN AMERICA. London: John
Murray, 1856. Reprint ed. in facsimile. Madison and Milwaukee: University
of Wisconsin Press, 1966.

This work includes several chapters devoted to Canada (Niagara
Falls being a vast disappointment) by an inveterate traveller and
writer of travel books.

Borrett, George Tuthill. LETTERS FROM CANADA AND THE UNITED STATES.
London: Adlard, 1865.

This is one of a large number of travel books which cover a vast
amount of territory. Only two chapters deal with Canada ("Montreal to Toronto" and "Niagara to Buffalo"), but they are worth
reading, primarily for their comments on Ottawa, recently selected
as capital of the new Dominion.

Brown, James B. VIEWS OF CANADA AND THE COLONISTS...BY A FOUR
YEARS' RESIDENT. Edinburgh: Black, 1844; 2nd ed., 1851.

The second edition adds four years' residence in Lower Canada to
the previous four in Upper Canada. Quite factual, the chief chapters of interest are those dealing with "Districts of Upper Canada"
(XI-XXI) where many descriptions of places and people (such as
Col. Talbot) are interspersed with historical sketches.

Day, Samuel Phillips. ENGLISH AMERICA; OR, PICTURES OF CANADIAN
PLACES AND PEOPLE. 2 vols. London: Newby, 1864.

Descriptions of Upper and Lower Canada with such telling titles as
"Kakouna, the Brighton of Canada," and comments on the social
conditions, the inter-colonial railway and on such unusual subjects
as "Sensational Puffing" (newspaper advertising), combine to make
this book a delightful one.

Dixon, James. PERSONAL NARRATIVE OF A TOUR THROUGH A PART OF
THE UNITED STATES AND CANADA. New York: Lane & Scott, 1849.

Dixon, staunch imperialist and Methodist clergyman, was chiefly
interested in Methodist institutions in Canada. Beyond that, there
is little of interest.

Duncan, John Morrison. TRAVELS THROUGH PART OF THE UNITED STATES
AND CANADA IN 1818 AND 1819. 2 vols. Glasgow: University of
Glasgow Press, 1823.

This work contains but a few chapters on the Canadas, the chief items of interest being his descriptions of Montreal and the "burning of York and Niagara."

Fidler, Rev. Isaac. OBSERVATIONS ON PROFESSIONS, LITERATURE, MANNERS AND EMIGRATION, IN THE UNITED STATES AND CANADA. London: Whittaker, 1833.

The seven chapters on Canada comment on such diverse topics as education, farming, prospects for the clergy, the Indians, cholera, and landladies.

Gray, Hugh. LETTERS FROM CANADA, WRITTEN DURING A RESIDENCE THERE IN THE YEARS 1806, 1807, AND 1808. London: Longman, 1809. Reprint ed. in facsimile. Toronto: Coles Publishing Co., 1971.

The most entertaining parts of this work are Gray's descriptions of winter travelling and summer picnics; his contemptuous remarks about French-Canadian culture were based on ignorance but were perhaps indicative of. a wide-spread feeling at the time.

[Grey, Lt.-Col. Charles.] CRISIS IN THE CANADAS 1838-1839: THE GREY JOURNALS AND LETTERS. Ed. William Ormsby. Toronto: Macmillan, 1964.

Grey, commanding officer of the 71st Regiment, had been ordered to Canada to ensure that further outbreaks of violence did not occur. In November and December of 1838, a second Rebellion did occur; Grey was present and helped suppress it. His letters and journals describe this event and his other duties during his year in Canada.

Hadfield, Joseph. AN ENGLISHMAN IN AMERICA, 1785. Ed. Douglas S. Robertson. Toronto: Hunter, Rose, 1933.

Hadfield's is an account of a brief trip to Upper and Lower Canada when the loyalists were flocking to the colonies. As a representative of an English trading firm, Hadfield had access to upper-class circles and thus describes the social customs of the more well-to-do in Canada.

Hall, Basil. TRAVELS IN NORTH AMERICA IN THE YEARS 1827 AND 1828. 3 vols. Edinburgh: Cadell, 1829.

Already famous as a writer of travel books, Hall visited North America with his wife and daughter. Most of his journey was in the United States, but he did visit Upper and Lower Canada (Volume I, chapters VI-XIII) and offers frank opinions about them.

Head, Sir Francis B. THE EMIGRANT. 4th ed. London: John Murray, 1846.

Decidedly a biased view of Canadian politics, but a very important first-hand account of such events as the Rebellion and the union of Upper and Lower Canada, by a man who was personally involved

(Head became Lieutenant-Governor of Upper Canada in 1835).
Here is his opinion of William Lyon Mackenzie: "first he wrote,
and then he printed, and then he rode, and then he spoke, stamped,
foamed, wiped his seditious little mouth, and then he spoke again;
and thus, like a squirrel in a cage, he continued with astonishing
assiduity the centre of a revolutionary career." There are also,
though less interesting, descriptions of Niagara and other scenic
spots.

Heriot, George. TRAVELS THROUGH THE CANADAS: CONTAINING A DES-
CRIPTION OF THE PICTURESQUE SCENERY ON SOME OF THE RIVERS AND
LAKES. London: Philips, 1807. Reprint ed. in facsimile. Toronto: Coles
Publishing Co., 1971.

A reviewer in the EDINBURGH REVIEW (XII, April 1808, pp. 212-
25) complained that Heriot's book contained too much detail: "We
have a detail of the lakes, rivers, and cataracts, the villages, farm-
houses, and townships of Canada, considerably more minute (need
we say how much less interesting) than we possess of the county of
Northumberland." It is Heriot's passion for detail, however, of
life in the Canadas (and among the Indians), illustrated by numerous
sketches, which makes his work so readable and important today.

Kingston, W. H. G. WESTERN WANDERINGS; OR, A PLEASURE TOUR IN
THE CANADAS. 2 vols. London: Chapman & Hall, 1856.

Another detailed descriptive account through Upper and Lower
Canada by a well-known author on his honeymoon. Most engag-
ing are his descriptions of the towns along the way: London,
Guelph, Galt, and others.

Kohl, J. G. TRAVELS IN CANADA, AND THROUGH THE STATES OF NEW
YORK AND PENNSYLVANIA. Trans. Mrs. Percy Sinnett. 2 vols. London:
Mainwaring, 1861.

This veteran German traveller offers many fine descriptions, with
numerous delightful anecdotes and discerning comments, such as
this (when describing a near-scalping): "The phrenologists have
not, I believe, yet recognized the scalping mania as one of the
original propensities of the human mind."

Lambert, John. TRAVELS THROUGH CANADA AND THE UNITED STATES OF
NORTH AMERICA, IN THE YEARS 1806, 1807, AND 1808. 2nd ed. London:
Cradock, 1813.

A goldmine of information about Upper and Lower Canada, Lambert's
work contains incisive commentary on all aspects of life, from drunk-
enness to genius.

Logan, James. NOTES OF A JOURNEY THROUGH CANADA, THE UNITED
STATES OF AMERICA AND THE WEST INDIES. Edinburgh: Fraser, 1838.

Only chapters II and III are relevant, but worth reading for the highly individualistic approach: "We had tea, in paying for which, the demand being 1s. 6d. currency, or 1s. 4 1/2d. sterling, Mr. Stewart, not having smaller change, gave a dollar, and was tendered the balance in halfpence, which he refused. On this M'Lean made his appearance, behaved in a most insolent manner, and refused to give silver, although Stewart politely stated that copper would be inconvenient for him to carry, and said he would be obliged to him for silver. Our host observed, insultingly, that we were no longer in Britain, and this was a land of liberty and equality."

Long, John. VOYAGES AND TRAVELS OF AN INDIAN INTERPRETER AND TRADER. London: Privately printed, 1791. Reprint ed. in facsimile. Toronto: Coles Publishing Co., 1971.

> In 1768 Long came to Canada as a clerk, was sent to live among the Six Nations Indians to learn their languages, became enthralled with their way of life and adopted it. He served thereafter as a scout for war parties and trader. His adventures and misadventures are vividly depicted, as are the Indian dances, games, and "manner of scalping."

Lyons, Sir Daniel. EARLY REMINISCENCES. London: John Murray, 1896.

> This well-written and humorous account of personal involvement in the Upper and Lower Canada Rebellions, is by an officer of the British militia. There are also many fine descriptions of people and pastimes.

Mackay, Charles. A TOUR IN THE UNITED STATES AND CANADA. 2 vols. London: Smith & Elder, [1859].

> An account of one of many "whirlwind" tours through both countries, Volume II being devoted to a cursory description of his impression of Canada.

Mactaggart, John. THREE YEARS IN CANADA: AN ACCOUNT OF THE COUNTRY IN 1826-7-8. 2 vols. London: Colburn, 1829.

> One of the most detailed descriptions of the Canadas in that era, this book includes captivating accounts of a wide variety of subjects such as "Canadian Cities," "Long Island Rapids," "System Proposed for Conducting the Works of the Rideau Canal," "Settlers and Squatters," "Winter Taverns," and 120 others.

Monck, Frances E. O. MY CANADIAN LEAVES. Dorchester: Dorset "County Express," [1873]. Reprint ed. in facsimile. Toronto: Canadian Library Service, 1967.

> Mrs. Monck, the wife of Col. Richard Monck (brother of the Governor-General, 1861-67), visited Canada in 1864-65. This very lively private journal is much more personal, with a greater

amount of name-dropping, than are the many public journals.
Country excursions, picnics, fashionable society, and play-going
formed the usual round of activities. This is a picture of Canadian
high society immediately preceding Confederation.

Moore, Thomas. A TOUR THROUGH CANADA IN 1879. Dublin: The "Irish
Farmer" Office, 1880.

This emigrant's guide, with special emphasis on farming, offers
interesting excursions into such peripheral areas as winemaking and
cheese-making and with illustrations of such institutions as the
Guelph Agricultural College.

Morris, William. LETTERS SENT HOME: OUT AND HOME AGAIN BY WAY
OF CANADA AND THE UNITED STATES; OR, WHAT A SUMMER'S TRIP TOLD
ME OF THE PEOPLE AND THE COUNTRY OF THE GREAT WEST. London:
Warne, n.d.

These letters, written during a two-month trip, first appeared in
the Swindon ADVERTISER in 1874. Chiefly composed of trivia:
"In 1872, the real and personal estate of the city [of Toronto]
was valued at $32,644,612." The book is very superifical, but
pleasant to read.

[Ogden, J. C.] A TOUR THROUGH UPPER AND LOWER CANADA....CON-
TAINING A VIEW OF THE PRESENT STATE OF RELIGION, LEARNING, COM-
MERCE, AGRICULTURE, COLONIZATION, CUSTOMS AND MANNERS, AMONG
THE ENGLISH, FRENCH, AND INDIAN SETTLEMENTS. Litchfield, Eng.:
n.p., 1799.

A relatively early account, this is quite interesting in its descriptions of travel (to Montreal in a flat-bottomed boat), the fortifica-
tion of such cities as Montreal, and the towns and scenes of Upper
Canada with Niagara as temporary seat of government.

Oliphant, Laurence. MINNESOTA AND THE FAR WEST. Edinburgh: Blackwood, 1855.

Oliphant, as superintendent of Indian affairs in Canada, had ample
opportunity to see the country. A great deal of his writing is devoted to a discussion of the social condition of the Indians, but he
is not blind to the physical beauty of the country. The title is
misleading: Part I is entitled "Canada" and includes such topics
as "The attractions of Quebec," "Scenery around Lake Simcoe" and
the like.

Preston, T. R. THREE YEARS' RESIDENCE IN CANADA, FROM 1837 TO 1839.
2 vols. London: Richard Bentley, 1840.

Preston describes life in Upper and Lower Canada, depicting such
social events as "charivaris," the political insurrections of Mackenzie and Papineau, and other, less exciting, affairs.

Rhys, Captain Horton [Morton Price]. A THEATRICAL TRIP FOR A WAGER! THROUGH CANADA AND THE UNITED STATES. London: Charles Dudley, 1861. Reprint ed. in facsimile. New York: Benjamin Blom, 1969.

In 1859 Rhys bet 500 pounds that he, a rank amateur, could make money by acting. He chose to test his abilities in the colonies. This entertaining and often funny account of his experiences describes his reception, his impressions of Upper and Lower Canada, and his numerous encounters with folk usually as eccentric as himself.

Shirreff, Patrick. A TOUR THROUGH NORTH AMERICA; TOGETHER WITH A COMPREHENSIVE VIEW OF THE CANADAS AND UNITED STATES. Edinburgh, n.p., 1835. Reprint ed. in facsimile. New York: Benjamin Blom, 1971.

In many respects this is a typical settler's guide, offering prices of land, etc. But it also offers many fine descriptions of such things as camp-meetings, Colonel Talbot's residence, and of such places as Goderich, London, and St. Thomas.

Talbot, Edward Allen. FIVE YEARS' RESIDENCE IN THE CANADAS. 2 vols. London: Longman, 1824.

Talbot, an Irishman, came to Canada in 1818 as one of a party of emigrants brought out by his father. He settled near London, Ontario, and later became a radical journalist and schoolmaster. His book was written, as he states, to give a realistic picture of Canada: "To tell an individual that he is about to be introduced to an earthly paradise, in which persons of both sexes are celebrated for their chaste converse and exemplary virtues, would be most egregiously to mislead. But when I offer him a few practical illustrations of Canadian morality, and show the proximate causes of the grossness of manners and of the semi-barbarism, which are much too prevalent, I guard the proposed settler against all misapprehensions on the subject." In Volume I he describes the transatlantic voyage and offers general descriptions of the Canadas and the usual scenic spots. In Volume II he becomes more specific, offering insights into such things as "Manners and customs of Upper Canada," "Their low idea of chastity," "Frequency of cases of seduction," "Happiness of Canadian Catholics," "The Charivari," and many others.

Theller, Edward A. CANADA IN 1837-38, SHOWING, BY HISTORICAL FACTS, THE LATE ATTEMPTED REVOLUTION, AND OF ITS FAILURE. 2 vols. Philadelphia: Anners, 1841.

A truly fascinating account of personal involvement in the Canada Rebellions by an American who styled himself "Brigadier General in the Canadian Republican Service," Theller describes the causes of the uprising, the various skirmishes, his arrest, trial, imprisonment, and escape to the United States.

Weld, Charles Richard. A VACATION TOUR IN THE UNITED STATES AND CANADA. London: Longman, 1855.

> By and large a superficial view of Canada, this work occasionally offers a curious insight: "A curious feature in the growth of Canadian towns merits notice. This is the progress which, with scarcely an exception, the houses make westward; thus following the course of the great human wave which, breaking on the eastern shores of North America, advances across the western wilderness at the rate of seventeen miles yearly."

Weld, Isaac. TRAVELS THROUGH THE STATES OF NORTH AMERICA AND THE PROVINCES OF UPPER AND LOWER CANADA, DURING THE YEARS 1795, 1796, AND 1797. 4th ed. London: Stockdale, 1800.

> In this remarkably comprehensive book, setting the tone for many subsequent travel books, Weld vividly describes many of the sights and events that would also occupy later books, such as travelling by canoe, the scenery, the towns, and the prospects for survival in Canada.

Wilkie, D. SKETCHES OF A SUMMER TRIP TO NEW YORK AND THE CANADAS. Edinburgh: Sherwood, 1837.

> Wilkie's is a thoroughly engaging and amusing (though not always favorable) picture of Canadian customs, hotels, religious habits, and so forth, with stories heard along the way. An example: "The orchards here [Niagara] are perhaps the best in Canada, and one could almost wish himself a pig, for a month or two, every autumn; it being a perfect paradise to the grunting gentry and their pretty sprigs. But in what degree of favour apple-fed pork stands, in the estimation of the consumers, I neglected to enquire."

Lower Canada (Quebec)

Abbott, Rev. Joseph. MEMORANDA OF A SETTLER IN LOWER CANADA. Montreal: Lovell & Gibson, 1842.

> Abbott's book describes "the adventures of a large family from the North of England, which emigrated in 1818." Designed chiefly for other emigrants, the detailed "account of everyday's doings upon a farm for a year" is interesting to the general reader as well.

Allan, Eric. MONTREAL BY WAY OF CHAZY AND DOWN THE ST. LAWRENCE RIVER TO QUEBEC. Boston: Willis & Co., 1899.

> An entertaining account of a bicycle trip from Boston to Montreal by the author and his wife. Excellent descriptions of Montreal: "It is a favourite pastime for cyclists of Montreal to ascend the mountain by the inclined railway, and then coast down on their wheels, round and round, winding to and fro over a splendid road, to the foot." Contains many photographs.

Cockloft, Jeremy. CURSORY OBSERVATIONS, MADE IN QUEBEC...IN THE
YEAR 1811. Bermuda: King's Printer, n.d. Reprint ed. with preface by
William Toye. Toronto: Oxford University Press, 1960.

"It was nine in the morning, of one of those fine warm days, that
so seldom bless this dreary Province of Canada, that I found myself
half leg deep in mud in a place called very properly the Cul de
Sac; in English, the bottom of the bag." Thus does the "eccentric
traveller," as Cockloft calls himself, commence his irreverent account of his visit to Quebec (chiefly to Quebec City); a rare account which, perhaps because of its whimsical style and frankness,
makes for delightful reading.

Davenport, Mrs. JOURNAL OF A FOURTEEN DAYS' RIDE THROUGH THE
BUSH FROM QUEBEC TO LAKE ST. JOHN. Quebec: "Daily Mercury," 1872.

"The history of the first journey made by a woman from Quebec to
Lake St. John for the most part on foot, through over a hundred
miles of wild, untravelled, wooded and mountainous country."
Slight (35 pages) but interesting and entertaining.

Fairchild, G. M. ROD AND CANOE, RIFLE AND SNOWSHOE IN QUEBEC'S
ADIRONDACKS. Quebec: "Daily Telegraph" Office, 1896.

Descriptions of Quebec's fishing and hunting delights ("the last
remaining kingdom of the angler-sportsman"), this work also includes commentary on the people, with numerous anecdotes and
illustrations.

Grant, George Monro. FRENCH CANADIAN LIFE AND CHARACTER. Chicago:
Belford, 1899.

This series of descriptive sketches (of Quebec, Montreal and Ottawa),
is more important for its excellent illustrations than for its commentary. Two similar books are J. M. Lemoine's PICTURESQUE QUEBEC
(Montreal: Dawson, 1882) and Mrs. Daniel MacPherson's OLD MEM-
ORIES (Montreal: Privately printed, 1890).

Greenough, William Parker. CANADIAN FOLK-LIFE AND FOLK-LORE. New
York: George H. Richard, 1897. Reprint ed. in facsimile. Toronto: Coles
Publishing Co., 1971.

The immediate focus of Greenough's interest is Quebec City and
its environs and habitants. After the first two chapters, of the
"natural history" type, he begins to illustrate his title by describing such habitant customs and institutions as "The Feudal System,"
"Chansons Canadiennes," "The Church," "A Winter Excursion";
the best of these sketches is "Amusements--Contes and Raconteurs."

Johnston, Thomas. TRAVELS THROUGH LOWER CANADA, INTERSPERSED WITH
CANADIAN TALES AND ANECDOTES. Edinburgh: J. Glass, 1827.

This journal of a trip made in 1814 describes the usual scenes

("Fall of Montmorency"), but is rescued from dullness by its many anecdotes: "Anecdote of a Canadian Superstition," "The English Officer and the Beautiful Nun," and so forth.

Oxendon, Rev. Ashton. MY FIRST YEAR IN CANADA. London: Hatchards, 1871.

These impressions of Lower Canada (winter in the Eastern Townships and summer in Montreal) were recorded during Oxendon's first year as Bishop of Montreal.

Sansom, Joseph. TRAVELS IN LOWER CANADA, WITH THE AUTHOR'S RECOLLECTIONS OF THE SOIL, AND ASPECT; THE MORALS, HABITS, AND RELIGIOUS INSTITUTIONS. London: Phillips & Co., 1820. Reprint ed. in facsimile. Toronto: Coles Publishing Co., 1970.

This is a picture of Quebec in 1817: its major cities (Quebec and Montreal), its religious life (the Grey Nuns) and its countryside. It is a well-written and engaging work.

Silliman, Benjamin. A TOUR TO QUEBEC, IN THE AUTUMN OF 1819. London: Phillips & Co., 1822. Reprint ed. in facsimile. Toronto: Canadiana House, 1968.

Silliman does not offer a very penetrating look at Quebec, for, as he says, it "is certainly a very peculiar place, [but] a stranger's residence of a few days is hardly sufficient to give him anything more than general views."

Upper Canada (Ontario)

Bâby, William Lewis. SOUVENIRS OF THE PAST: AN INSTRUCTIVE AND AMUSING WORK, GIVING A CORRECT ACCOUNT OF THE CUSTOMS AND HABITS OF THE PIONEERS OF CANADA. Windsor, Ontario: n.p., 1896.

A series of sketches, chiefly of historical events which the author witnessed, such as "The Destruction of Wm. L. McKenzie's Press," "The Old Family Compact," "Service on the Detroit Frontier During the Rebellion of '37 and '38." Illustrated.

Beavan, James. RECREATIONS OF A LONG VACATION; OR, A VISIT TO THE INDIAN MISSIONS IN UPPER CANADA. Toronto: Rowsell, 1846.

Excellent descriptions of Canadian roads and carriages, and of work among the natives, implicitly providing the reader with a display of nineteenth-century attitudes towards these people.

Boulton, D'Arcy. A SHORT SKETCH...OF UPPER CANADA. London: Rickaby, 1805. Reprint ed. with introduction by John Gellner. Toronto: Baxter Publishing Co., 1961.

A well-written and factual account, the book begins with a general description of the province, followed by more particular descriptions of the townships and of York (the seat of government).

Conant, Thomas. UPPER CANADA SKETCHES. Toronto: Briggs, 1898.

These "random sketches of life in the early settlements" of Upper Canada chronicle, in vivid detail, the life of the Conant family: its removal from the United States in 1777, its establishment in Canada, the murder of Thomas Conant (the writer's grandfather), the Rebellion of '37, the Fenian raids, daily life, charming anecdotes. Colored illustrations.

[Darling, W. S.] SKETCHES OF LIFE, LAY AND ECCLESIASTICAL. London: David Bogue, 1849.

Darling depicts the trials and tribulations of a fictional character, Rev. Harry Vernon, whose missionary zeal and British loyalty are constantly being tested in the Canadian backwoods. The character is fictional; the events real. Darling's loyalties are most evident in the chapter dealing with the Rebellion: "Canadian politics," he writes, after having loudly denounced the policy of amnesty for the rebels, "are by no means a pleasant subject to any true-hearted subject of the British Crown."

De Veaux, S. THE FALLS OF NIAGARA; OR, A TOURIST'S GUIDE TO THIS WONDER OF NATURE. Buffalo: Hayden, 1839.

This is not a run-of-the-mill tourist's guide: "It is intended to amuse as well as inform; to treat of some subjects not touched upon by previous publishers; to preserve from oblivion the names of some individuals of notoriety; and to furnish some incidents of border warfare, and descriptions peculiar to the country." Thus we get a picture of the Falls in a less congested era, glimpses of the kind of tourists, stories of some of the daredevils who had plunged over the Falls, and pictures of the nearby towns.

Dommett, Alfred. THE CANADIAN JOURNAL OF ALFRED DOMMETT (1833-1835). Eds. E. A. Horsman and Lillian Benson. London: University of Western Ontario, 1955.

Discussing the mode of life near Woodstock, Ontario, Dommett justifies the unusual nature of his journal (describing only those things which appealed to him) by the statement that he travelled not for information but to destroy ennui. This approach makes for engaging reading.

Drury, Thomas, et al. LETTERS AND EXTRACTS OF LETTERS FROM SETTLERS IN UPPER CANADA. London: Marchant, 1834.

Letters from seven settlers, some of whom were employed by and give details about the Canada Company. A twenty-page pamphlet.

[Dunlop, William.] STATISTICAL SKETCHES OF UPPER CANADA. London: John Murray, 1832. Reprinted together with RECOLLECTIONS OF THE AMERI-CAN WAR 1812-14 in TIGER DUNLOP'S UPPER CANADA. Ed. Carl F. Klinck. Toronto: McClelland & Stewart, 1967.

This is an emigrant guide with a vast difference: unique in its wit, its incisiveness, its originality of thought, Dunlop's SKETCHES ranks among the most enjoyable of any work written in Canada at that time: "When you arrive in the St. Lawrence, having been on shortish allowance of water, you will be for swallowing the river water by the bucketful. Now, if you have bowels of compassion for your intestinal canal, you will abstain from so doing;--for to people not accustomed to it, the lime that forms a considerable constituent part of the water of this country, acts pretty much in the same manner as would a solution of Glauber's salts, and often generates dysentery and diarrhoea; and though I have an unbounded veneration for the principles of the Temperance societies, I would, with all deference, recommend that the pure fluid be drunk in very small quantities at first, even then tempered with the most impalpable infusion possible of Jamaica or Cognac."

Green, Anson. THE LIFE AND TIMES OF ANSON GREEN. Toronto: Methodist Book Room, 1877.

This autobiography offers comments on such things as the Rebellion, political events, and Confederation, and insights into Church work between 1819 and 1877 in many parts of Upper Canada.

Haight, Canniff. COUNTRY LIFE IN CANADA FIFTY YEARS AGO: PERSONAL RECOLLECTIONS AND REMININSCENCES OF A SEXAGENARIAN. Toronto: Hunter, Rose, 1885.

Logging bees, charivaris, early newspapers, superstitions, religion, politics, candle-making, and night-fishing are only a few of the customs, occupations, and pastimes described in this entertaining book. Numerous illustrations.

Hamilton, Thomas. MEN AND MANNERS IN AMERICA. Edinburgh: Blackwood, 1743. Reprint ed. in facsimile. New York: Johnson Reprint Corp., 1968.

Chiefly about the United States, this work offers one long description of a visit to Canada: "They (the lower orders) have all the disagreeable qualities of the Americans, with none of that energy and spirit of enterprise which often convert a bad man into a useful citizen. They are sluggish, obstinate, ignorant, offensive in manner, and depraved in morals, without loyalty, and without religion."

Hilts, Joseph Henry. EXPERIENCES OF A BACKWOODS PREACHER. Toronto: Briggs, 1887.

A very intimate account, with special emphasis on clerical duties, religious services, and the hardships concomitant with backwoods preaching. It also contains elucidating comments on the everyday concerns of the preacher's existence. A well-written book.

Howison, John. SKETCHES OF UPPER CANADA, DOMESTIC, LOCAL AND CHARACTERISTIC. Edinburgh: Oliver & Boyd, 1821. Reprint eds. in facsimile. New York: Johnson Reprint Corp., 1965; Toronto: Coles Publishing Co., 1970.

Howison spent two and a half years in Upper Canada, 1818-20, residing "in various parts of the Province." The first part of his book describes his enchantment with the French-Canadians which left him unprepared for the "blunt and uncultivated" inhabitants of Upper Canada. He recovers, however, and after describing their life in detail, comments that "the man who is fond of a country life, who loves to be exempt from restrictions imposed by fashion and ceremony...might live very comfortably and very happily in Upper Canada."

Jameson, Mrs. [Anna]. WINTER STUDIES AND SUMMER RAMBLES IN CANADA. 3 vols. London: Saunders & Otley, 1838. Reprint ed. in facsimile. Toronto: Coles Publishing Co., 1970.

Anna Jameson came to Canada in December, 1836, stayed for seven months with her husband, then Upper Canada's Vice-Chancellor, found their marriage, which had been dissolving, to be unbearable and so returned to England. In her seven-month stay, however, she absorbed a great deal of the country. Her book, one of many such travel books she wrote, is intimate (but not overbearing), detailed and frank (her dislikes are many); and her reminiscences of Canadian life, in the months immediately preceding the Rebellion, are among the most incisive and enjoyable of their kind. See also Clara E. Thomas, LOVE AND WORK ENOUGH: THE LIFE OF ANNA JAMESON (Toronto: University of Toronto Press, 1967).

Langton, Anne. A GENTLEWOMAN IN UPPER CANADA. Ed. H. H. Langton. Toronto: Clarke, Irwin, 1950.

See next item.

Langton, John. EARLY DAYS IN UPPER CANADA. Ed. W. A. Langton. Toronto: Macmillan, 1926.

These two books comprise the letters and the journal of a brother and sister who settled at Fenelon Falls, Ontario, and they chronicle their daily lives between 1833 and 1845. Anne was also a very capable artist, and many of her drawings illustrate the texts.

Lett, William Pittman. RECOLLECTIONS OF BYTOWN AND ITS OLD INHABITANTS. Ottawa: "Citizen" Publishing Co., 1874.

This is an unusual work in that the whole is written in rhyme:

Now first among our old landmarks,
Comes Laird of Bytown, Nicholas Sparks,
Who came across in '26
From Hull, his lucky fate to fix
Upon a bush farm which he bought
For sixty pounds--and little thought
While grumbling at the price so high,
That fortune had not passed him by.

Magrath, T[homas] W. AUTHENTIC LETTERS FROM UPPER CANADA; WITH A
AN ACCOUNT OF CANADIAN FIELD SPORTS. Ed. T. Radcliff. Dublin:
Wm. Curry, 1833. Reprint ed. with introduction by James J. Tallman. Toron-
to: Macmillan, 1953.

> These letters, chiefly from Thomas Magrath, but also from Mr.
> and Mrs. William Radcliff and Bridget Lacy (a fictitious writer?)
> are meant to give the prospective emigrant a complete and detailed
> picture of what to expect in Canada: cost and kind of provisons,
> building houses and barns, the possibility of contracting cholera,
> Canadian expressions, the state of religion and the art of hunting
> are all discussed. The Magrath family settled on the Credit River;
> the Radcliffs settled in Adelaide Township, Middlesex County.

[Need, Thomas.] SIX YEARS IN THE BUSH; OR, EXTRACTS FROM THE
JOURNAL OF A SETTLER IN UPPER CANADA, 1832-1838. London: Simpkin,
Marshall, 1838.

> In this dated journal, Need describes the trip out, his first im-
> pressions of Canada, an attack of cholera, the business of purchas-
> ing a farm, life in Peterboro, his work and leisure activities,
> making it a very informative (as well as readable) work.

Ridout, Thomas. TEN YEARS IN UPPER CANADA IN PEACE AND WAR,
1805-1815: BEING THE RIDOUT LETTERS. Ed. with annotations by Matilda
Edgar. Toronto: Briggs, 1890.

> Thomas Ridout settled in York in 1797 and spent most of his life
> as a public servant. The letters, most of which say very little
> but which are annotated extensively, chronicle minor and major
> events in the lives of his family, the most notable being the War
> of 1812.

Simcoe, Elizabeth. THE DIARY OF MRS. JOHN GRAVES SIMCOE, WIFE
OF THE FIRST LIEUTENANT-GOVERNOR OF THE PROVINCE OF CANADA,
1792-6. With notes and a biography by J. Ross Robertson. Toronto: Briggs,
1911. Reprint ed. in facsimile. Toronto: Coles Publishing Co., 1973.

> This work derives its value from the fact that it is nothing more
> than "the simple recital of [Simcoe's] daily life in the pioneer
> days when Niagara was the centre of the military, civil and social
> life in the new province." The copious notes by a very knowl-
> edgeable editor and 237 illustrations considerably enhance this

already exciting work.

Strachan, James. A VISIT TO THE PROVINCE OF UPPER CANADA IN 1819. Aberdeen: Longman, 1820. Reprint ed. in facsimile. New York: Johnson Reprint Corp., 1968.

> After the initial description of the voyage out, Strachan's journal becomes quite factual and statistical, with brief respites such as the section entitled "Tranquility of Upper Canada." In the introduction to THE JOHN STRACHAN LETTER BOOK (Toronto: Ontario Historical Society, 1946), G. W. Spragge claims that John, the well-known Bishop of Toronto and James' brother, is the real author of A VISIT TO THE PROVINCE OF UPPER CANADA IN 1819.

Strickland, Samuel. TWENTY SEVEN YEARS IN CANADA WEST OR THE EXPERIENCES OF AN EARLY SETTLER. Ed. Agnes Strickland. London: Richard Bentley, 1853. Reprint ed. in facsimile with introduction by Carl F. Klinck. Edmonton: Hurtig, 1970.

> In 1826 the Canada Company, founded by John Galt, bought more than two million acres of land in Upper Canada, promising to settle it and build roads. Before the Company dissolved in 1843 the towns of Guelph, Galt, and Goderich had been settled. From 1828 to 1831 Samuel Strickland was an officer of the Company at Guelph and Goderich. Almost a third of his book is devoted to a description of this phase of his career. He was also a militia-man during the Rebellion; vividly described. In addition he offers numerous other anecdotes, descriptions, and personal comments on all aspects of life in Upper Canada.

Taylor, James. NARRATIVE OF A VOYAGE TO, AND TRAVELS IN UPPER CANADA. Hull: Nicholson, 1846.

> A resident between 1843 and 1845, Taylor absorbed a great deal of geographical facts, but was also keenly intrigued by local customs and social mores. His book is composed chiefly of descriptions of such events and customs as "Fire in Toronto," "Sleighing Amusements," "College Avenues," "Millerism," "Tavern Keepers," and "Journey to an Indian Village."

Thompson, Samuel. REMINISCENCES OF A CANADIAN PIONEER FOR THE LAST FIFTY YEARS [1833-1883]. Toronto: Hunter, Rose, 1884. Reprint ed. Toronto: McClelland & Stewart, 1968.

> In this book perhaps one of the most informative of its kind, are descriptions of such things as "Toronto During the Rebellion," "A First Day in the Bush," "Society of the Backwoods," and "Tories of the Rebellion Times."

4.   THE PRAIRIES AND NORTHWEST TERRITORIES

Compared with the eastern provinces of Canada, the western Prairie Provinces
(Alberta, Manitoba, and Saskatchewan) are mere youngsters: in 1867, the year
of Confederation, all three were simply parts of that vast, unknown territory
variously referred to as Rupert's Land or the North-West Territories.   Manitoba
became a part of the Dominion in 1870; Saskatchewan and Alberta remained
districts of the Territories until 1905.

In spite of those facts, however, the Prairie Provinces can boast of a history as
exciting as and marked by more dramatic events than that of their neighbours.
The invasion of the Selkirk settlers into the Red River area met with opposition
from the fur companies, and a great deal of bitterness, fighting, and death resulted; later (1869-70) the same area was the scene of the first Riel Rebellion,
which spread to include a larger area and greater strife in 1884.   The institu-
tion of the North-West Mounted Police, the building of Canadian Pacific Railway, the demise of the buffalo, the Indian treaties--these also gained their
share of publicity.   All these, and the obvious adventure to be had from simply
crossing such a vast land, resulted in a large amount of travel and descriptive
literature, among which are some of the world's classics in that genre.

Not listed below are the many hundreds of emigrant pamphlets which were so
common during the late nineteenth century.   For these and for a more comprehensive list of Prairie literature see Bruce Peel's BIBLIOGRAPHY OF THE PRAI-
RIE PROVINCES TO 1953.   (Toronto: University of Toronto Press, 1956; rev. ed.
1973).

Anon.   LETTERS FROM A YOUNG EMIGRANT TO MANITOBA.   London:
Kegan Paul, 1883.

> These are the personal letters of a nineteen-year-old emigrant who
> studied for a year at the Ontario Agricultural College before head-
> ing to Manitoba where he hired out to a farmer and later home-
> steaded.   They offer details concerning the cost of land, the kind
> of equipment needed, conditions of the land purchase, and com-
> ments on the personalities encountered.   Added to these are de-
> scriptions of his intimate feelings of loneliness and of the pride of
> achievement.

_____.   THE WINNIPEG COUNTRY; OR, ROUGHING IT WITH AN ECLIPSE
PARTY.   Boston: Cupples, 1886.

> This energetic work describes a trip to Cumberland House to view
> a total eclipse of the sun: "Three thousand miles of constant travel
> occupying five weeks, to reach by heroic endeavour the outer edge
> of the belt of totality; to sit in a marsh, and view the eclipse
> through the clouds!" The modern reader, however, is not disap-
> pointed; described in minutest detail, the trip comes alive.   Many
> fine illustrations are included.

Travel Literature

Begg, Alexander. ALEXANDER BEGG'S RED RIVER JOURNAL 1869-70. Ed. with introduction by W. L. Morton. Toronto: The Champlain Society, 1956. Reprint ed. in facsimile. New York: Greenwood Press, 1969.

> One of the very few firsthand accounts of critical days in Canadian history, Begg's journal describes the Metis resistance to the declaration of transfer of the Northwest Territories to the Dominion, the setting up of a provisional government under Louis Riel, the treatment of the prisoners, the death of Thomas Scott, and Riel's flight. Begg was a free trader at Red River and was sympathetic to the demands of the Metis (though not always with their methods). He later wrote a three-volume HISTORY OF THE NORTH-WEST.

Boulton, Major. REMINISCENCES OF THE NORTH-WEST REBELLIONS. Toronto: Grip, 1886.

> Totally biased and marked by inaccuracies, Boulton's memoirs nevertheless remain a valuable contribution to the literature of the North-West: he was a participant in both Rebellions (1869-70 and 1884-85). Minute, day-to-day record of events, with comments and statistics (e.g., a complete list of officers and men in the Canadian North-West Field Force).

Bryce, George. HOLIDAY RAMBLES BETWEEN WINNIPEG AND VICTORIA. Winnipeg: n.p., 1888.

> Divided into two parts, the first part of the book ("Prairie and Mountain") deals with the journey west and the second ("Lo! the Poor Indian") with the natives and their habits. Characteristic of Bryce's superficial attitude is one final sentence: "If both the government and the churches give their best thought to the subject the poor Indian may in time be civilized and christianized." The work nevertheless has its interesting moments.

Butler, William Francis. THE GREAT LONE LAND: A NARRATIVE OF TRAVEL AND ADVENTURE IN THE NORTH-WEST OF AMERICA. London: Sampson Low, 1872. Reprint ed. in facsimile. Edmonton: Hurtig, 1968.

> See next item.

_____. THE WILD NORTH LAND: BEING THE STORY OF A WINTER JOURNEY, WITH DOGS ACROSS NORTHERN AMERICA. London: Sampson Low, 1873. Reprint ed. in facsimile. Edmonton: Hurtig, 1968.

> Classics among western travel literature, Butler's books very entertainingly describe his hurried departure from England to join Wolseley's troops as they headed to quell Riel's insurrection (1870), his role as an advance scout, his lone entry into Red River (see also Begg's RED RIVER JOURNAL for July 20, 21, 1870), his interview with Riel, and his subsequent commission to tour the west, view conditions, and make recommendations for keeping the peace. His first work not only describes his adventures and such places as Fort Edmonton, but was also instrumental in bringing about the formation

of the North-West Mounted Police. In 1872 he was back in Canada on another adventure: a trip northward to Lake Athabasca, to the Peace River, through the mountains. A brilliantly told tale of perseverance and endurance.

D'Artigue, Jean. SIX YEARS IN THE CANADIAN NORTH-WEST. Trans. L. C. Corbett and S. Smith. Toronto: Hunter, Rose, 1882.

This work is divided into three parts: (1) the organization of the North-West Mounted Police in 1874 and the author's acceptance into the force; (2) his tour of duty in the west; (3) his return to the east via Saskatchewan, Red River, Lakes Winnipeg, Superior and Huron to Sarnia, by rail to Quebec, and on to Liverpool.

Donkin, John G. TRAPPER AND REDSKIN IN THE FAR NORTH-WEST: RECOLLECTIONS OF LIFE IN THE NORTH-WEST MOUNTED POLICE, 1884-1888. London: Sampson Low, 1889.

The chief chapters of interest in this book are those dealing with the second North-West Rebellion, the Battle of Batoche and this policeman's involvement.

Dwight, Charles P. LIFE IN THE NORTH-WEST MOUNTED POLICE AND OTHER SKETCHES. Toronto: National Publishing Co., 1892.

A delightful book, approaching the autobiographical novel in form and appeal. Setting out for Winnipeg with a desire to wander and failing as a door-to-door salesman, Dwight enlisted in the North-West Mounted Police. He describes the training period and his six-month tour of duty at considerable length and in great detail. Having earned enough money, he resigned and spent the remainder of a year touring the west and farming.

Elkington, W. M. FIVE YEARS IN CANADA. London: Whittaker, 1895.

Elkington describes life in western Canada as a common labourer, chiefly as farmer, rancher, and stonemason at Portage la Prairie and Fort Qu'Appelle. "The facts narrated here are but the everyday life of an emigrant; they are things that have happened to me and that are likely to happen to every young man who may leave his home in England to try his fortune 'out West!' "

Fitzgibbon, Mary. A TRIP TO MANITOBA; OR, ROUGHING IT ON THE LINE. Toronto: Rose Belford, 1880.

This very flattering picture of Manitoba is well told in a casual manner with plenty of anecdotes.

[Goodridge, R. E. W.] A YEAR IN MANITOBA: BEING THE EXPERIENCES OF A RETIRED OFFICER IN SETTLING HIS SONS. London: Chambers, 1882.

Intended for future emigrants, this little book details the journey out, first impressions of Winnipeg, state of the roads, their first farm and shanty, their social intercourse, some political events, and ends with this statement: "I think it may be fairly asserted that this country offers at the present time to any enterprising young man a better prospect of success that any other country or colony."

Gordon, Rev. Daniel M. MOUNTAIN AND PRAIRIE: A JOURNEY FROM VICTORIA TO WINNIPEG VIA PEACE RIVER PASS. London: Sampson Low, 1880.

Gordon accompanied the party sent by the Canadian government to explore one of the proposed Canadian Pacific Railway routes. "The following chapters, consisting chiefly of notes taken by the way, record [the author's] impressions of the country traversed from the Pacific to Winnipeg, across the 'sea of mountains,' and the more inviting sea of prairies." Many excellent descriptions, as of the trip from Athabasca Landing to Fort Edmonton. Many illustrations.

Gowanlock, Theresa, and Theresa Delaney. TWO MONTHS IN THE CAMP OF BIG BEAR. Parkdale: Times Office, 1885.

The husbands of both authors were murdered during the Frog Lake massacre (April 2, 1885), and the widows were taken prisoners by Big Bear's warriors. The massacre and subsequent experiences are vividly described.

Graham, Frederick Ulfric. NOTES ON A SPORTING EXPEDITION IN THE FAR WEST OF CANADA 1847. London: Privately printed, 1898.

A large folio production, elegantly prepared, this is basically a book of illustrations with commentary in diary form. The final impression is that it is a good example of the kind of attitudes, primarily the sportsman's disregard for conservation, which eventually helped bring about the demise of the buffalo.

Hall, Mrs. Cecil. A LADY'S LIFE ON A FARM IN MANITOBA. London: Allen, 1884.

"On the prairie! I cannot describe to you our first impression. Its vastness, dreariness, and loneliness is appalling." That was the first reaction of Mrs. Hall, a self-styled "English lady." Later, however, she admits "we have fallen into it wonderfully quickly; completely sunk the lady and become sort of maids-of-all-work." The diary of her six-month stay (in 1882) is fascinating in its detail of pioneer life and marked by a growing love of the country.

Hamilton, J. C. THE PRAIRIE PROVINCE: SKETCHES OF TRAVEL FROM LAKE ONTARIO TO LAKE WINNIPEG. Toronto: Belford, 1876.

This work contains detailed descriptions of the Red River area: Fort Garry, Winnipeg, Mennonites (who came in 1874), smaller settlements, the natives, natural history, and occupations, with frequent anecdotes.

Hargrave, Joseph James. RED RIVER. Montreal: Lovell, 1871.

"The history, present condition and recent current events of this municipality." The author arrived in 1861; he details the "annual routine," offers statistics, describes people and events to 1869, and offers a history of previous events. A valuable work for a memorable era.

Hill, A. Staveley. FROM HOME TO HOME: AUTUMN WANDERING IN THE NORTH-WEST IN THE YEARS 1881, 1882, 1883, 1884. New York: Judd, 1885.

"From home to home--from my old home of Oxley Manor in Staffordshire to the new Oxley in the foothills of the Rocky Mountains." An absentee landlord, Staveley owned a ranch, made several visits to it in Western Canada, and offers in his book many graphic descriptions of the prairies, the forts, the dangers and pleasures, the railway building, the Indians (Big Bear and Little Man), and his ranch.

Hind, Henry Youle. NARRATIVE OF THE CANADIAN RED RIVER EXPLORING EXPEDITION OF 1857 AND OF THE ASSINIBOINE AND SASKATCHEWAN EXPLORING EXPEDITION OF 1858. 2 vols. London: Longman, Green, 1860. Reprint ed. in facsimile. New York: Greenwood Press, 1969.

This work contains much of the factual material of the official reports, but offers in addition many excellent descriptions of the people met, the towns and the natives, along with comments and numerous illustrations.

Huyshe, G. L. THE RED RIVER EXPEDITION. London: Macmillan, 1871.

After the death of Thomas Scott (March 1870), the Canadian government decided to send troops to Red River to restore authority and peace. Huyshe describes the formation of a force of 1200 men, its movement west and its occupation of Red River (and the escape of Riel). An interesting work with details of daily routine and a long description of the Red River Settlement.

Johnstone, C. L. WINTER AND SUMMER EXCURSIONS IN CANADA. London: Digby Long, [1894].

This is a superficial view of life near such places an Qu'Appelle, Regina, Saskatoon, and Winnipeg, based on a two-month stay. It includes comments on the weather, terrain, the railway, the natives, and prairie fires, but offers no real insights into the lives of the settlers.

Legge, Alfred O. SUNNY MANITOBA: ITS PEOPLE AND ITS INDUSTRIES.
London: Unwin, 1893.

This travelogue was designed basically for the prospective emigrant.
It includes, therefore, a large number of statistics and much farming information, but is redeemed by some personal observations on
the prairies ("What is the prairie like?"), the natives, and the
winters. Illustrated.

MacBeth, Rev. R. G. THE MAKING OF THE CANADIAN WEST: BEING
THE REMINISCENCES OF AN EYE-WITNESS. Toronto: Briggs, 1898. Reprint
ed. in facsimile. Toronto: Coles Publishing Co., 1973.

A native of Red River District, MacBeth was a boy during the
first Rebellion and a young military officer during the second.
Nearly the whole work is taken up with his memories of those
two momentous events, with many names mentioned and with illustrations.

Macdonnell, Alexander. A NARRATIVE OF TRANSACTIONS IN THE RED
RIVER COUNTRY; FROM THE COMMENCEMENT OF THE OPERATIONS OF
THE EARL OF SELKIRK, TILL THE SUMMER OF THE YEAR 1816. London:
Macmillan, 1819.

The Red River Settlement was founded in 1812 by Lord Selkirk, at
the junction of the Red and Assiniboine Rivers, on a large tract of
land granted to him by the Hudson's Bay Company. The North-
West Company objected strenuously to the settling of this land,
believing that it would destroy the fur trade, and tried desperately
to get rid of the settlers, a policy which led to bloodshed in 1816
with the killing of Semple and twenty of his men. Macdonell's
is a pro-North-West Company version of the affair. For a pro-
Selkirk version see the anonymous STATEMENT RESPECTING THE
EARL OF SELKIRK'S SETTLEMENT UPON THE RED RIVER...ITS
DESTRUCTION IN 1815 AND 1816. (London: Murray, 1817;
reprint ed. in facsimile. Toronto: Coles Publishing Co., 1970).

McDougall, John. FOREST, LAKE, AND PRAIRIE: TWENTY YEARS OF FRON-
TIER LIFE IN WESTERN CANADA, 1843-62. Toronto: Methodist Mission Room,
1895.

See McDougall's ON WESTERN TRAILS IN THE EARLY SEVENTIES,
below.

_____. SADDLE, SLED AND SNOWSHOES: PIONEERING ON THE SASKAT-
CHEWAN IN THE SIXTIES. Toronto: Briggs, 1896.

See McDougall's ON WESTERN TRAILS ON THE EARLY SEVENTIES,
below.

_____. PATHFINDING ON PLAIN AND PRAIRIE: STIRRING SCENES OF
LIFE IN THE CANADIAN NORTH-WEST. Toronto: Briggs, 1898.

See McDougall's ON WESTERN TRAILS IN THE EARLY SEVENTIES, below.

_____. ON WESTERN TRAILS IN THE EARLY SEVENTIES. Toronto: Briggs, 1911.

Primarily a Methodist minister and son of the well-known George McDougall, John was fluent in the Cree language, helped negotiate Treaty No. 6, was with the Alberta Field Force during the Rebellion of 1885, and was, in many ways, the leading pioneer of Western Canada. His four books offer one of the most vivid and extensive pictures of life in that era.

McGillivray, Duncan. THE JOURNAL OF DUNCAN McGILLIVRAY OF THE NORTHWEST COMPANY AT FORT GEORGE ON THE SASKATCHEWAN, 1794-95. Ed. with introduction by A. S. Morton. Toronto: Macmillan, 1929.

This interesting document deals chiefly with the fur-trade. Copious annotations amplify the text.

Messiter, Charles Alston. SPORT AND ADVENTURES AMONG THE NORTH-AMERICAN INDIANS. London: R. H. Porter, 1890.

Setting out in 1862, Messiter spent his first autumn and winter in a small cabin in the Thickwood Hills (about ninety miles northwest of Fort Carleton), with only Indians as his neighbours. In the first seven chapters he describes his adventures: meeting Big Bear, some methods of torture, several hair-breadth escapes, and other, less exciting, escapades. The rest of the book is concerned with similar adventures in the United States.

[Mountain, J. G.] THE JOURNAL OF THE BISHOP OF MONTREAL DURING A VISIT TO THE CHURCH MISSIONARY SOCIETY'S NORTH-AMERICA MISSION. London: Seeley, 1845.

Descriptions of the journey, the state of the mission, the society of the Red River Settlement, the people in charge, and the forts, along with a history of the mission, are the chief concerns of Mountain's journal.

Mulvaney, Charles Pelham. THE HISTORY OF THE NORTH-WEST REBELLION OF 1885. Toronto: Hovey, 1885. Reprint ed. in facsimile. Toronto: Coles Publishing Co., 1971.

Although basically second-hand, this remarkable history incorporates many first-hand accounts and reports of such engagements as the Battle of Fish Creek, Cut Knife Creek, Batoche, and the Frog Lake Massacre.

Newton, William. TWENTY YEARS ON THE SASKATCHEWAN. London: Elliot Stock, 1897.

The chronicle of an Anglican priest in the North-West from 1875, Newton's story is colloquilly told and offers insights into many aspects of missionary life, with comments on other missionaries (e.g., the McDougalls), the forts, the causes of the Rebellion, the natives, and so forth.

Pennefather, John P. THIRTEEN YEARS ON THE PRAIRIES: FROM WINNIPEG TO COLD LAKE. London: Kegan Paul, 1892.

Even though this work contains a great deal of factual material, intended for emigrants, it nevertheless offers some fascinating firsthand descriptions of trips across the prairies, the most captivating of which describes his involvement in the Frog Lake Massacre (a description of the mutilated bodies and the search for the prisoners). Numerous illustrations.

Pocock, Sidney. ACROSS THE PRAIRIE LANDS OF MANITOBA AND THE CANADIAN NORTH-WEST: A WILTSHIRE MAN'S TRAVELS IN THE SUMMER OF 1882. London: E. & S. Herbert, [1883].

This, as the writer states, is "a plain, unvarnished story" of adventure in search of land to farm, entertainingly told with dialogue and vivid descriptions of river crossings, unsavoury meals, and prairie hazards. A delightful book to read.

Ralph, Julian. ON CANADA'S FRONTIER: SKETCHES OF HISTORY, SPORT AND ADVENTURE AND OF THE INDIANS, MISSIONARIES, FUR-TRADERS AND NEWER SETTLERS OF WESTERN CANADA. New York: Harper, 1892.

By 1892 a large number of Europeans had taken up land in the Peace River Country and the fur-traders had retreated. This is a series of sketches intended to capture both the old and new ways of life: pioneer settlers, Blackfoot Indians (and Chief Crowfoot), and Father Lacombe are discussed. Numerous illustrations.

Ross, Alexander. THE RED RIVER SETTLEMENT: ITS RISE, PROGRESS AND PRESENT STATE. London: Smith, Elder, 1856.

A definitive history of the Settlement, with a vast amount of detail, first-hand description, and history.

Saxby, Jessie M. WES-NOR'-WEST. London: James Nisbet, 1890.

The experiences of a Scottish writer who visited the prairies as a colonist are described: her trip by Canadian Pacific Railway, prairie homes, prairie Sundays, a chapter on the prairie Member of Parliament (Nicholas Flood Davin) and a plea to women to colonize the "Greater Scotland."

Southesk, James Carnegie, Earl of. SASKATCHEWAN AND THE ROCKY MOUNTAINS: A DIARY AND NARRATIVE OF TRAVEL, SPORT, AND ADVENTURE, DURING A JOURNEY THROUGH THE HUDSON'S BAY COMPANY'S

TERRITORIES IN 1859 AND 1860. Edinburgh: Edmonston & Douglas, 1875.

The title reveals the scope: the quality is outstanding--fine descriptions of such places as Fort Edmonton, with vivid accounts of the travel adventures. Several illustrations.

Sutherland, Rev. A. A SUMMER IN PRAIRIE-LAND: NOTES ON A TOUR THROUGH THE NORTH-WEST TERRITORY. Toronto: Methodist Book and Publishing House, 1881.

On a tour of the Methodist missions among the Indians of the Upper Saskatchewan region, Sutherland describes the routes to the west, the herds of buffalo, the Indians of the plains, a stay at Fort Edmonton with the McDougalls, and journey to Victoria and back, in vivid detail and in a pleasant manner. Several illustrations.

Trow, James. A TRIP TO MANITOBA. Quebec: Marcotte, 1875.

These letters by an English M.P. to the Stratford BEACON offer comments on Winnipeg, Mennonites, Indian massacres, grasshopper plagues, and on the suitability of the area for settlement.

[Ward, B. Peyton.] ROUGHING IT IN THE NORTH-WEST TERRITORIES OF CANADA TWENTY YEARS AGO. London: Worrall & Robey, 1896.

This description of a winter spent at Duck Lake (and of the journey to and from the lake) have such chapter headings as "Fur-Trading," "Buffalo, Sleigh-Dogs and Pain-Killer," "Visiting," "The Half-Breeds," and "Le Pere Pierre." It is very well told, offering unusual insights into life in that area.

West, John. THE SUBSTANCE OF A JOURNAL DURING A RESIDENCE AT THE RED RIVER COLONY...IN THE YEARS 1820, 1821, 1822, 1823. London: Seeley, 1824. Reprint ed. in facsimile. New York: Johnson Reprint Corp., 1966.

Chaplain to the Hudson's Bay Company, with headquarters at Red River, West came to know the settlers and natives intimately. His journal is a wide-ranging commentary on life in that time and place.

Williams, W. H. MANITOBA AND THE NORTH-WEST: JOURNAL OF A TRIP FROM TORONTO TO THE ROCKY MOUNTAINS. Toronto: Hunter, Rose, 1882.

Williams, a correspondent for the Toronto GLOBE, travelled with Governor Lorne on a trip west, July 21 - December 16, 1881, by railway to Winnipeg, to Carlton by horse and wagon, to Prince Albert by steamer, and on to Battleford, Calgary, Fort McLeod, and Pincher Creek. Quite detailed (for example, a list of the members of the North-West Mounted Police is included) and extremely entertaining.

Young, Rev. George. MANITOBA MEMORIES: LEAVES FROM MY LIFE IN THE PRAIRIE PROVINCE, 1868-1884. Toronto: Briggs, 1897.

> Young was a pioneer Methodist missionary whose most dramatic experience occurred during the 1869 Riel Rebellion. He was with Thomas Scott up to the moment of his death, an event which he graphically depicts.

5. BRITISH COLUMBIA

The world-resounding cry of "gold," emanating from the Cariboo region in 1858, finally helped place British Columbia on the map of Canada. Although the 49th parallel had been fixed as boundary in 1846 and an attempt was made to colonize Vancouver Island in 1849, prior to the discovery of gold the province had been a kind of no man's land, frequented only by fur-traders from Britain and the United States. With the discovery, however, settlement expanded, and when the gold petered out the other economic potentials of the land were recognized. In 1871, on the promise of a transcontinental railroad, British Columbia became a province of Canada.

Because of the region's late development, its travel and descriptive literature is not as extensive as that for other parts of Canada. The accounts that do exist are largely concerned with the natural scenery, the unparalleled hunting and fishing, and with encounters between settlers and natives. A few deal with the Cariboo gold-rush and still fewer with the building of the railroad through the mountains. Included here are several books about the Klondike gold-rush; though not directly related to British Columbia, they are included here to preclude the necessity of another separate section.

For a more comprehensive list of material dealing with the history of British Columbia, see A BIBLIOGRAPHY OF BRITISH COLUMBIA, compiled by Barbara J. Lowther (Victoria: University of Victoria, 1968).

Barrett-Lennard, C. E. TRAVELS IN BRITISH COLUMBIA, WITH THE NARRATIVE OF A YACHT VOYAGE ROUND VANCOUVER'S ISLAND. London: Hurst & Blackett, 1862.

> Capt. Barrett-Lennard, of the Royal Thames Yacht Club, spent two years on the Pacific Coast. Although primarily intended to entice emigrants, his book is largely taken up with descriptions of the natives, their attacks, and so-called "savagery." He also offers comments on the gold-rush and some general remarks on British Columbia in such sections as "The Harrison Lillooett Route Described."

Cornwallis, Kinahan. THE NEW EL DORADO: OR, BRITISH COLUMBIA. London: Newby, 1858.

> This work offers a curious blend of personal experiences of life in the gold-fields and of commentary on the status and role of British

Columbia as a British colony. Cornwallis was a British historian, poet and novelist.

Green, William Spotswood. AMONG THE SELKIRK GLACIERS. London: Macmillan, 1890.

A noted Alpinist and explorer, Green surveyed the Selkirks, testing the "fastnesses" in proximity to the new railroad. His account of the exploration is entertaining and detailed, dwelling on the human rather than the natural.

Hazlitt, William Carew. BRITISH COLUMBIA AND VANCOUVER ISLAND. London: Routledge, 1858. Reprint ed. in facsimile. New York: Johnson Reprint Corporation, 1966.

This compilation from various sources, consists chiefly of topographical and historical sketches, but offers one or two descriptive chapters (such as "A Trip to Vancouver").

Horetsky, Charles. CANADA ON THE PACIFIC: BEING AN ACCOUNT OF A JOURNEY FROM EDMONTON TO THE PACIFIC. Montreal: Dawson, 1874.

"The writer organized and conducted the overland expedition of Mr. Sandford Fleming, during the summer of 1872...and it was at the instance of that gentleman...that the journey about to be described, was undertaken." Detailed and lively descriptions of the Peace River Country, a trip through the Rockies and down the Naas River, and of such places as Hazelton, Fort Simpson, and Nanaimo.

Jewitt, John. THE ADVENTURES OF JOHN JEWITT, ONLY SURVIVOR OF THE CREW OF THE SHIP "BOSTON" DURING A CAPTIVITY OF NEARLY THREE YEARS AMONG THE INDIANS OF NOOTKA SOUND. Ed. with introduction by Robert Brown. London: Clement Wilson, 1896.

"The ostensible author of this work was a Hull blacksmith, the armourer of the 'Boston,' an American ship which was seized while lying in Nootka Sound, and the entire crew massacred, with the exception of Jewitt, who was spared owing to his skill as a mechanic being valuable to the Indians, and John Thompson, the sailmaker, who, though left for dead, recovered, and was saved by the tact of Jewitt in representing him to be his father." A graphic description of the massacre and of the two years' captivity (1803-5), with accounts of native rituals, customs, and language. First published in 1814, but extremely rare.

Johnson, R. Byron. VERY FAR WEST INDEED: A FEW ROUGH EXPERIENCES ON THE NORTH-WEST PACIFIC COAST. London: Sampson Low, 1872.

An English adventurer, Johnson went to British Columbia in 1862, worked the gold-fields of Williams Creek, wintered in Victoria, returned to the mines, toured the province, and returned to England.

His book is a highly entertaining, though quite likely embellished account of his experiences.

Kirk, Robert C. TWELVE MONTHS IN THE KLONDIKE. London: Heinemann, 1899.

This well-written and very valuable document describes a tortuous trek to the Klondike gold-fields. Illustrated.

Lees, J. A., and W. J. Clutterbuck. B.C. 1887: A RAMBLE IN BRITISH COLUMBIA. London: Longman, Green, 1888.

"Our object in exploring this little known country [the Kootenay region] was to test its capabilities as a home for some of the public-school and university young men who, in this overcrowded old England of ours, every year find themselves more de trop." Excellent illustrations add variety to this entertaining and informative work.

Lord, John Keast. THE NATURALIST IN VANCOUVER ISLAND AND BRITISH COLUMBIA. 2 vols. London: Richard Bentley, 1866.

A member of the British North American Boundary Commission, Lord became thoroughly acquainted with British Columbia. His chief interest was natural history, but his book is enlivened by accounts of such events as the misery of taking a bath and attendance at a miner's ball. Numerous illustrations.

[MacInnes, Donald.] NOTES OF OUR TRIP ACROSS BRITISH COLUMBIA. Hamilton: Spectator Printing Co., 1889.

This slight but interesting account of a journey through British Columbia on the Canadian and Northern Pacifics Railways is concerned chiefly with the people and places encountered.

MacNab, Frances. BRITISH COLUMBIA FOR SETTLERS. London: Chapman & Hall, 1898.

After the preliminary chapters, this work, though never losing sight of its utilitarian aim, becomes less factual and offers a few interesting insights in such chapters as "The Chinese" and "The Rush to the Klondyke."

Macfie, Matthew. VANCOUVER ISLAND AND BRITISH COLUMBIA. London: Longman, Green, 1865. Reprint ed. in facsimile. Toronto: Coles Publishing Co., 1972.

The work is heavily weighted with facts, natural history, and topography. The most "descriptive" chapter is that which describes "Society in Vancouver Island and British Columbia."

McNaughton, Margaret. OVERLAND TO CARIBOO: AN EVENTFUL JOURNEY OF CANADIAN PIONEERS TO THE GOLD-FIELDS OF BRITISH COLUMBIA IN

1862. Toronto: Briggs, 1896.

The author was the wife of one of the pioneers, 150 of whom left Fort Garry on June 2 and reached the Cariboo on October 11, with loss of stock and food, after enduring considerable hardship. Illustrated.

Mayne, R. C. FOUR YEARS IN BRITISH COLUMBIA AND VANCOUVER ISLAND. London: Murray, 1862.

A member of a ship's survey crew, Mayne saw much of British Columbia and describes it all, from the spot where they decided the 49th parallel to be, to New Westminster, Victoria, Nanaimo, and the northern coast. He offers detailed commentary on social customs, hunting expeditions, missions, natives, and other subjects. Hundreds of excellent illustrations.

Phillipps-Wolley, Clive. THE TROTTINGS OF A TENDERFOOT. London: Richard Bentley, 1884.

See next item.

_____. A SPORTMAN'S EDEN. London: Richard Bentley, 1888.

Phillipps-Wolley came to British Columbia in 1886, settled in Victoria, and wrote several novels with British Columbia settings. He was undoubtedly a better hunter than novelist, and these two books are chiefly concerned with hunting adventures; but he writes well and offers some descriptions of the country and customs.

Poole, Francis. QUEEN CHARLOTTE ISLANDS: A NARRATIVE OF DISCOVERY AND ADVENTURE IN THE NORTH PACIFIC. Ed. John W. Lyndon. London: Hurst & Blackett, 1812.

"The only educated Englishman who has ever lived on Queen Charlotte Islands is Mr. Francis Poole, Civil and Mining Engineer. The best portion of two years he spent, either in actual residence in that outlying dependency, or in laborious work closely connected with it." The book is based on Poole's diary and describes the islands, their natural history, the natives, the potential mineral wealth, and something of his personal experiences (Indian attacks, bear-hunting, and so forth).

Price, Julius M. FROM EUSTON TO KLONDIKE: THE NARRATIVE OF A JOURNEY THROUGH BRITISH COLUMBIA AND THE NORTH-WEST TERRITORY IN THE SUMMER OF 1898. London: Sampson Low, 1898.

A minutely detailed and fascinating account of the Klondike trip: to Skagway, up the Chilkoot Pass, downriver to Dawson City, and extensive description of the city itself, and on to the mouth of the Yukon. Numerous illustrations.

Roberts, Morley. THE WESTERN AVERNUS: OR, TOIL AND TRAVEL IN
FURTHER NORTH AMERICA. London: Smith, Elder, 1887.

An English author (obviously in search of real-life adventure),
Roberts worked on the railway through the Kicking Horse Pass, as
a farm labourer in Kamloops and at a sawmill in New Westminster.
Since "Avernus" is a type of hell, one gathers from the title itself that the book is not altogether favourable to the quality of
life in British Columbia.

St. John, Molyneux. THE SEA OF MOUNTAINS: AN ACCOUNT OF LORD
DUFFERIN'S TOUR THROUGH BRITISH COLUMBIA IN 1876. 2 vols. London:
Hurst & Blackett, 1877.

In 1871 British Columbia joined the Dominion; in 1876 the citizens
were having second thoughts about the union, since the Canadian
government was slow in implementing railroad promises. It was at
this point that the Governor-General, Lord Dufferin, decided to
visit the new province on a public-relations tour. St. John, a
reporter for the Toronto GLOBE, was with him; in this series of
letters, originally published in the GLOBE, he describes Dufferin's
reception, the country, and its people as the official party would
have seen them.

St. Maur, Mrs. Algernon. IMPRESSIONS OF A TENDERFOOT DURING A
JOURNEY IN SEARCH OF SPORT IN THE FAR WEST. London: Murray, 1890.

On this "journey in search of health, sport and pleasure" all three
were found and the search is vividly recreated: pictures of Banff,
Vancouver, and Victoria; of fishing and hunting; of mishaps and
mild excitements; of Kootenay Indians and panning for gold; and
much more.

Secretan, James H. E. TO THE KLONDYKE AND BACK: A JOURNEY DOWN
THE YUKON FROM ITS SOURCE TO ITS MOUTH. London: Hurst & Blackett,
1898.

"I have been advised," writes Secretan, "by several friends--and
some enemies--to write a book, describing the perils and pleasures
which may be encountered in a voyage to the now celebrated Klondyke." This he does in a very engaging manner.

Seton-Karr, H. W. BEAR-HUNTING IN THE WHITE MOUNTAINS. London:
Chapman & Hall, 1891.

Seton-Karr's season of "hunting, exploration, and adventure" took
place in the Chilcat country of British Columbia, which the writer
refers to as the last unknown territory in British North America.
See also his SHORES AND ALPS OF ALASKA (London: Sampson
Low, 1887), in which he describes his rail journey through British
Columbia and along its coasts on his way to Alaska.

Somerset, H. Somers. THE LAND OF THE MUSKEG. London: Heinemann, 1895.

In this tale of adventure Somerset describes a trip from Athabasca Landing to Dunvegan, along the Pine and Misinchinka Rivers and on to Quesnel along the Stuart River. Encounters with Indians, starvation and grizzlies; all vividly described. More than a hundred illustrations.

Wilcox, Walter Dwight. CAMPING IN THE CANADIAN ROCKIES: AN ACCOUNT OF CAMP LIFE IN THE WILDER PARTS OF THE CANADIAN ROCKY MOUNTAINS. New York: Putnam's Sons, 1896.

A member of the Appalachian Club, Wilcox made as many as twenty first ascents of mountains in the Rockies. His work contains a great deal of information and description of the British Columbia-Alberta border region around Banff and Lake Louise. Illustrated.

6. THE HUDSON'S BAY TERRITORY AND NORTHERN CANADA

On May 2, 1670, the Hudson's Bay Company was given a monopoly over the fur trade of Rupert's Land, all that area which drained into the Hudson Bay. For approximately two hundred years (until 1869), the Company maintained control of this territory, which included all of Western Canada. Its reign was broken only briefly in 1686 by French invasion and capture of its forts along the Bay.

Much of the descriptive literature of Western Canada has some mention or recognition of the Company's dominion, but there exists a large number of books which deal specifically with service in the employ of the Company or with travels within the region of the Bay. These deserve a section to themselves, for the Hudson's Bay Company is a major factor in Canadian history. Also included here are several first-hand accounts of travel through the Arctic and sub-Arctic regions of Canada.

Anderson, David. THE NET IN THE BAY; OR, THE JOURNAL OF A VISIT TO MOOSE AND ALBANY. 2nd ed. London: Hatchard's, 1873.

First Bishop of Rupert's Land (1849), Anderson travelled extensively throughout his diocese; his journey from Fort Garry to forts on the Hudson Bay is vividly described, with special emphasis on missions to the Indians.

Ballantyne, Robert M. HUDSON'S BAY OR EVERYDAY LIFE IN THE WILDS OF NORTH AMERICA, DURING SIX YEARS RESIDENCE IN THE TERRITORIES OF THE HONOURABLE HUDSON'S BAY COMPANY. London, 1848. Reprint ed. in facsimile. Edmonton: Hurtig, 1972.

Ballantyne, later famous as a writer of such boys' adventure stories as THE CORAL ISLAND, spent six years with the Hudson Bay Company (1841-47). This book is an account of those years: lively, personal and exciting, illustrating Ballantyne's flair for dramatic situations.

Dobbs, Arthur. AN ACCOUNT OF THE COUNTRIES ADJOINING TO HUDSON'S BAY. London: Robinson, 1744. Reprint ed. in facsimile. New York: Johnson Reprint Corp., 1967.

Basically an attack on the Hudson Bay Company, which refused to go along with Dobbs' wishes to search for a Northwest Passage, this book nevertheless offers some interesting descriptive information, chiefly based on what Dobbs was told by others.

M'Keevor, Thomas. A VOYAGE TO HUDSON'S BAY, DURING THE SUMMER OF 1812. London: Phillips, 1819.

The title goes on to say that the work contains "a particular account of the icebergs...and a description of the esquimaux." These are his two chief concerns, and he describes both in great detail and with a sense of humour. Excellent reading; fine illustrations.

M'Lean, John. NOTES OF A TWENTY-FIVE YEARS' SERVICE IN THE HUDSON'S BAY TERRITORY. 2 vols. London: Richard Bentley, 1849.

"It was one chief design of the writer to draw a faithful picture of the Indian trader's life,--its toils, annoyances, privations, and perils, when on actual service, or on a trading or exploring expedition; its loneliness, cheerlessness, and ennui, when not on actual service; together with the shifts to which he is reduced in order to combat that ennui." M'Lean entered the Hudson Bay Company service in 1820, spent time in all parts of the Territory (Athabasca, Okanagan, York Factory, Labrador, Chimo, Fort Liard) and offers a detailed and very engaging account of his experiences.

Moberly, Henry John. WHEN FUR WAS KING. London: Dent, 1929.

Moberly's eight years of service with the Hudson's Bay Company began in 1852. This book of reminiscences describes meetings and confrontations with Sir George Simpson, service at Fort Edmonton, Norway House, Jasper House, and Fort MacMurray and includes chapters of the Cariboo gold-rush and the opening of the Jasper Trail.

Pike, Warburton. THE BARREN GROUND OF NORTHERN CANADA. London: Macmillan, 1892.

See next item.

_____. THROUGH THE SUBARCTIC FOREST. New York: Arnold, 1896.

"The sole object of my journey [was] to try and penetrate this unknown land, to see the Musk-ox and find out as much as I could
about their habits, and the habits of the Indians who go in pursuit
of them every year." In 1889 Pike, an English big-game hunter,
ranged Northern Canada on his quest. In 1892 he was back on
an adventure which took him down the Yukon, by canoe, to the
Bering Sea. His two books vividly recount these experiences.

Robinson, H. M. THE GREAT FUR LAND; OR, SKETCHES OF LIFE IN THE
HUDSON'S BAY TERRITORY. London: Sampson Low, [1879].

This fascinating document, details the nature of the Hudson Bay
Company's operations, its hierarchy, life in the Company's forts,
travelling with the voyageurs, preparing for the winter (the great
fall hunt), and social life during the winter in an isolated post.
Illustrated.

Robson, Joseph. AN ACCOUNT OF SIX YEARS RESIDENCE IN HUDSON'S
BAY FROM 1733 TO 1736, AND 1744 TO 1747. London: Payne & Bouquet,
1752.

A surveyor and supervisor of building for the Hudson Bay Company,
Robson offers detailed descriptions of the forts and also of the high-
handed dealings of superior adminstrators with Company's servants
and natives. In 1749 Robson gave evidence before a Parliamentary
committee reviewing the Company's charter; it was unfavourable
and much of it shows through in this book.

Ryerson, John. HUDSON'S BAY; OR, A MISSIONARY TOUR IN THE TERRI-
TORY OF THE HON. HUDSON'S BAY COMPANY. Toronto: Sanderson,
1855.

This description of a tour of the Territory in 1854 by a Methodist
missionary is detailed and offers considerable insight into life in
the Bay area. Illustrated.

Simpson, Sir George. PEACE RIVER: A CANOE VOYAGE FROM HUDSON'S
BAY TO THE PACIFIC...IN 1828. Ed. with notes by Malcolm McLeod.
Ottawa: J. Durie, 1872.

See next item.

_____. FUR TRADE AND EMPIRE: GEORGE SIMPSON'S JOURNAL. Ed.
with introduction by Frederick Merk. Cambridge, Mass.: Harvard University
Press, 1931. Rev. ed. with new introduction, 1968.

Simpson, associated with the Hudson Bay Company since 1820, was
made Governor of the Company in 1839 and was one of its most
dynamic leaders. The first of these two books describes a 3,261
mile trip from Norway House to Langley, British Columbia. The
second is his journal for 1824-25.

Tyrrell, J. W. ACROSS THE SUB-ARCTICS OF CANADA: A JOURNEY OF 3,200 MILES BY CANOE AND SNOWSHOES THROUGH THE BARREN LANDS. Toronto: Briggs, 1897.

Tyrell's trip took him from Athabasca Landing to Lake Athabasca to Fort Churchill in 1893 on an official government survey. It is not, however, an official report but a tale of adventure. Illustrated.

Umfreville, Edward. THE PRESENT STATE OF THE HUDSON'S BAY; CONTAINING A FULL DESCRIPTION OF THE SETTLEMENT, AND THE ADJACENT COUNTRY. London: Stalker, 1790. Reprint ed. with introduction by W. Stewart Wallace. Toronto: Ryerson, 1954.

Eleven years in the service of the Hudson Bay Company and four as a free trader gave Umfreville a vast knowledge of the territory; his work is wide-ranging, detailed, and often uncomplimentary.

C. NATION-WIDE TRAVEL AND DESCRIPTION

The term "nation-wide" implies variable distances: in the eighteenth and early nineteenth centuries it often denoted a journey from Halifax to some place in Upper Canada; later it included journeys to a variety of places between St. John's and Victoria. Therefore, I have included in this section books which are intentionally "trans-Canada" travelogues and books which describe life in a number of different regions previously dealt with.

Alexander, Sir James. L'ACADIE; OR, SEVEN YEARS' EXPLORATIONS IN BRITISH AMERICA. 2 vols. London: Colburn, 1849.

L'ACADIE is a veritable storehouse of information and description, chiefly of New Brunswick and Upper Canada. As a high-ranking military officer, Alexander met many of the leading settlers such as William Dunlop and Thomas Talbot; he met Dickens at Kingston; was in Quebec during the fire of 1845; and offers comments on all sorts of activities from smuggling to military manoeuvres.

Bonnycastle, Sir R. H. THE CANADAS IN 1841. 2 vols. London: Colburn, 1841. Reprint ed. in facsimile. New York: Johnson Reprint Corp., 1968.

See next item.

_____. CANADA AND THE CANADIANS IN 1846. 2 vols. London: Colburn, 1846. Reprinted as CANADA AND THE CANADIANS, 1849. Reprint ed. in facsimile. Toronto: Canadiana House, 1969.

Bonnycastle had a long military career in Canada and saw service during the War of 1812 and the Upper Canada Rebellion. Both books offer lively accounts of living conditions, with personal remarks about the people and politics, based on extensive travel between Labrador and Upper Canada.

Buckingham, James S. CANADA, NOVA SCOTIA, NEW BRUNSWICK, AND
THE OTHER BRITISH PROVINCES IN NORTH AMERICA, WITH A PLAN OF
NATIONAL COLONIZATION. London: Fisher, [1843].

This work contains a great deal of historical information, but also
contains many fine descriptions of such things as "Differences in
English and American Churches," "Visit to Kingston Penitentiary,"
"Newspapers of Montreal," "Canadian Boat-Songs," "Distinction
Between Upper and Lower Canada," "Ladies of Halifax," and
"Literary Productions."

Campbell, J. F. A SHORT AMERICAN TRAMP IN THE FALL OF 1864. Edinburgh: Edmonston & Douglas, 1865.

"Attracted by icebergs, attached to glaciers, and anxious to choose
between them [i.e., to prove a theory of glacial drift]," writes
Campbell, "the writer set off for Yankee-doodledum in search of
cold hard facts." In the process his keen eye also observed a
large number of other North American peculiarities, on a journey
which took him from Labrador, through Newfoundland, Nova Scotia,
Quebec, and on to the United States.

Campbell, Patrick. TRAVELS IN THE INTERIOR INHABITED PARTS OF NORTH
AMERICA, IN THE YEARS 1791 AND 1792. Eds. W. F. Ganong and H. H.
Langton. Toronto: The Champlain Society, 1937.

Campbell travelled from St. John to Grand River, Upper Canada,
with the object of finding suitable land for Highland settlement.
Vivid descriptions of the country, embellished with hairraising
anecdotes. Excerpts are included in A. J. M. Smith's BOOK
OF CANADIAN PROSE (Toronto, 1965).

Christmas, Rev. Henry, ed. THE EMIGRANT CHURCHMAN IN CANADA.
2 vols. London: Richard Bentley, 1849.

"From a very early age," writes this pioneer, "the New World has
been a favourite subject of my fancies and daydreams. Its primaeval
forests, its boundless prairies, its exciting scenes of Indian prowess
and adventure were all unspeakably delightful to my youthful imagination." Like all emigrants, however, he found that the country
never lived up to those romantic notions; but it was the place for
those desiring a happy, peaceful life, particularly so if more clergymen could be persuaded to come out. To this end the writer describes in minute detail all that Canada had to offer: the scenery,
the wild-life, the people, the parishes, the schools, the towns of
Upper Canada, Quebec, Nova Scotia, and New Brunswick.

Coke, E. T. A SUBALTERN'S FURLOUGH: DESCRIPTIVE SCENES IN VARIOUS
PARTS OF THE UNITED STATES, UPPER AND LOWER CANADA, NEW BRUNS-
WICK, AND NOVA SCOTIA, DURING THE SUMMER AND AUTUMN OF 1832.
London: Saunders & Otley, 1833.

The Canadian part of the tour, like the American, is described in

a town-to-town fashion; offering brief glimpses of each town passed
through, with occasional diversions, like this: "Prescott contains
from 800 to 1000 inhabitants; and being the head of the small-
craft navigation with Lake Ontario, much business is carried on
in the forwarding of goods and travellers, and a vast deal more
in the smuggling line." Coke's Canadian tour took him from Halifax to Niagara.

Colmer, J. G. ACROSS THE CANADIAN PRAIRIES. London: European Mail,
1896.

This work consists of letters written during a two-month visit in
1894; the title is somewhat misleading, for Colmer's tour began at
Quebec; his prairie experiences, which constitute the bulk of the
book, begin in Chapter VII. This is a cursory treatment (and it
was a fast tour), but it offers a few valuable insights.

Cumberland, Stuart. THE QUEEN'S HIGHWAY: FROM OCEAN TO OCEAN.
London: Sampson Low, 1887.

This description of the first west-to-east trip on the Canadian
Pacific Railway, includes glimpses of scenery and history, interspersed with personal comments.

Dufferin, Marchioness of. MY CANADIAN JOURNAL 1872-78: EXTRACTS
OF MY LETTERS HOME WRITTEN WHILE LORD DUFFERIN WAS GOVERNOR-
GENERAL. London: Murray, 1891. Reprint ed. in facsimile. Toronto: Coles
Publishing Co., 1971.

This very lively and thoroughly engaging diary of social events
also offers many fine descriptions of tours to and through many
parts of Canada, from the Maritimes to British Columbia. Illustrated.

Elliott, Charles. A TRIP TO CANADA AND THE FAR NORTH-WEST. London:
W. Kent, n.d.

An account of a voyage made in 1886, this work offers minute
descriptions of such towns as Guelph, Hamilton, Toronto, Montreal
and of a trip to the prairies, with comments on horse-breeding,
experimental farms and prairie grasses.

Fleming, Sandford. ENGLAND AND CANADA: A SUMMER TOUR BETWEEN
OLD AND NEW WESTMINSTER. London: Sampson Low, 1884.

Fleming knew Canada very well. This coast-to-coast account offers
a great deal of history, but is interspersed with little bits of local
colour. For example: "We reached Moose Jaw before breakfast,
and received a copy of the MOOSE JAW NEWS. Amongst its
advertisements we learn that pianos are offered for sale, and that
these luxuries can be had side by side with buckboards, stoves,
and, what is of first importance in that country, lumber. The
paper, we learn, is published every Friday morning in the city of

Moose Jaw....The city is declared to be in all respects a better, larger and more promising city than its rival, Regina." Returning to the Rockies, Fleming retraces his previous steps in locating the railway line through the Illecillawaet gorge.

Grant, George Monro. OCEAN TO OCEAN: SANDFORD FLEMING'S EX-PEDITION THROUGH CANADA IN 1872. Toronto: Campbell; London: Sampson Low, 1873. Reprint ed. in facsimile. Toronto: Coles Publishing Co., 1970.

One of the most popular and widely-read travel books, OCEAN TO OCEAN is part adventure and part mythic chronicle, depicting the chief aspiration of post-Confederation Canada, the fulfilment of its motto "From Sea to Sea." Fleming, a Scottish-born engineer, was appointed to survey the new railway route; Grant was secretary to the expedition. The tone of his book is impossible to convey. T. G. Marquis best sums it up: "It was written from day to day at hotels, by camp fires, and in trading posts. It abounds in humour and pathos. Breadth of judgement and keenness of observation illuminate its pages; and in the presence of nature--vast, rugged and inspiring--Grant had a lyrical force and fire that make many of his pages ring like prose poems" (CANADA AND ITS PROVINCES, vol. 12).

_____, ed. PICTURESQUE CANADA: THE COUNTRY AS IT WAS AND IS. 2 vols. Toronto: Belden, 1882.

Some titles from this collection of essays will indicate its nature: "Ottawa," "French-Canadian Life and Character," and "The North-West: Manitoba." Illustrated.

_____, ed. OUR PICTURESQUE NORTHERN NEIGHBOUR. Chicago: Belden, 1899.

A shortened version of the preceding book, designed for an American audience.

Head, George. FOREST SCENES AND INCIDENTS IN THE WILDS OF NORTH AMERICA; BEING THE DIARY OF A WINTER'S ROUTE FROM HALIFAX TO THE CANADAS. London: Murray, 1829. Reprint ed. in facsimile. Toronto: Coles Publishing Co., 1970.

A vivid and intimate account, which describes a journey from Halifax to York, Upper Canada.

Henry, Alexander. TRAVELS AND ADVENTURES IN CANADA AND THE INDIAN TERRITORIES BETWEEN THE YEARS 1760 AND 1776. New York: Riley, 1809. Reprint ed. in facsimile. Edmonton: Hurtig, 1969.

Arriving in Canada immediately after the British takeover (ratified by the Treaty of Paris, 1763), Henry describes a country in which the French are still unwilling to accept British rule. In addition, he vividly describes such events as the massacre at Michilimackinac,

his year as a prisoner of the Indians and his later travels to the
Great Lakes and the prairies. This book could also have been
included in the section dealing with early inland explorers, for
Henry was the first white man to explore the Great Lakes territory. His book remains one of the most exciting and widely-read
pieces of Canadian travel literature.

Kane, Paul. WANDERINGS OF AN ARTIST AMONG THE INDIANS OF
NORTH AMERICA. London: Longman, 1859. Reprint ed. in facsimile.
Edmonton: Hurtig, 1968.

One of the best known and perhaps most diligent students of Canadian native culture, Kane set out to record in words and paintings
their way of life. His paintings (most of them now in the Royal
Ontario Museum) are priceless archives; his book is an equally
valuable ethnological and descriptive work. In 1845 he made his
first expedition to Western Ontario; in 1848-50 he travelled throughout western Canada and to British Columbia. The Hurtig edition
contains Burpee's introduction to the 1925 edition and a list of
Kane's paintings. Excellent illustrations.

Lanman, Charles. ADVENTURES IN THE WILDS OF THE UNITED STATES AND
BRITISH AMERICAN PROVINCES. 2 vols. Philadelphia: Moore, 1856.

One of the earlier books written by a sporting enthusiast, it is
concerned chiefly with the hunting potential (but also the natural
beauty) of such areas as the Restigouche, Saguenay, St. John,
and other Canadian rivers.

Levigne, Sir R. G. A. ECHOES FROM THE BACKWOODS; OR, SKETCHES
OF TRANSATLANTIC LIFE. 2 vols. London: Colburn, 1846.

Descriptions of Nova Scotia and New Brunswick, where the author
was stationed in 1835, and of Upper and Lower Canada, where
he was stationed during the Rebellions.

Lorne, The Marquis of. CANADIAN PICTURES: DRAWN WITH PEN AND
PENCIL. London: The Religious Tract Society, [1884].

More interesting for its illustrations than for its written commentary,
this work contains numerous pictures of artifacts, such as Indian
hunting equipment; ingenious inventions, such as snowshoes for
horses; natural scenery, such as the Montmorency Falls in winter;
means of travel, such as Red River carts; settlers' huts; Winnipeg
in 1882; Indian buffalo dances; Indian burial on the plains; a
North Saskatchewan steamer; and many others. The commentary
is mainly factual and historical.

M'Gregor, John. BRITISH AMERICA. 2 vols. Edinburgh: Blackwood, 1832.

M'Gregor combines history and description: the former being ex-
tracted from various "old records" and the latter based on personal

observations. Volume I deals with the country as a whole, with long chapters on Newfoundland, Prince Edward Island, and Cape Breton. Volume II deals with Nova Scotia, New Brunswick, and Canada (Upper and Lower). History far outweighs description.

Mackenzie, William Lyon. SKETCHES OF CANADA AND THE UNITED STATES. London: Effingham Wilson, 1833.

In this series of fascinating letters, newspaper articles, sketches, and anecdotes Mackenzie discusses such topics as "Methodism in Canada--A Camp Meeting," "Nova Scotia--Beating Legislators into Order," "A County Election at the Falls of Niagara," "Book-Selling in America," "Upper Canada Paper Mills," "Bundling," "A Free Press." The story of Mackenzie's life as newspaperman, social reformer, maverick MP, and instigator of the Upper Canada rebellion, is told by William Kilbourn in THE FIREBRAND (Toronto, 1956).

Milton, Viscount and W. B. Cheadle. THE NORTH-WEST PASSAGE BY LAND: BEING THE NARRATIVE OF AN EXPEDITION FROM THE ATLANTIC TO THE PACIFIC. London: Cassell, 1865. Reprint ed. in facsimile. Toronto: Coles Publishing Co., 1970.

Undertaken solely for pleasure in 1862-63, the expedition is described in vigorous detail with pictures of new western towns (many still forts) and of personalities, such as Father Lacombe. For a different look at the same trip, involving some of the less pleasurable aspects and the personality conflicts, see CHEADLE'S JOURNAL, edited by John Gellner, (Toronto: Baxter Publishing Co., n.d.).

Murray, Hugh. AN HISTORICAL AND DESCRIPTIVE ACCOUNT OF BRITISH AMERICA. 3 vols. London: Oliver & Boyd, 1839.

The full title of Murray's book continues: "comprehending Canada Upper and Lower, Nova Scotia, New Brunswick, Newfoundland, Prince Edward Island, the Bermudas, and the fur countries; their history from the earliest settlement; the statistics and topography of each district; their commerce, agriculture, and fisheries; their social and political condition; as also an account of the manners and present state of the aboriginal tribes: to which is added a full detail of the principles and best modes of emigration."

O'Leary, Peter. TRAVELS AND EXPERIENCES IN CANADA, THE RED RIVER TERRITORY, AND THE UNITED STATES. London: John B. Day, n.d.

O'Leary, an Irish working man, came to Canada shortly after Confederation to see for himself the condition of the emigrants. He describes his adventures as he sails across the Atlantic and travels across Canada from Quebec to Winnipeg.

Rae, W. NEWFOUNDLAND TO MANITOBA: A GUIDE THROUGH CANADA'S

MARITIME, MINING, AND PRAIRIE PROVINCES. London: Sampson Low, 1881.

> Though heavily weighted with history, this work contains many first-hand descriptions of such things as prairie hotels, western winters, Mennonites and insect infestations. Rae was a journalist with the London TIMES.

Ritchie, J. Ewing. TO CANADA WITH THE EMIGRANTS: A RECORD OF ACTUAL EXPERIENCES. London: Fisher Unwin, 1885.

> A totally engaging book, written in a casual, off-hand style which is both frank and refreshing. After staying a while at Calgary, "amongst the cowboys," he wrote: "I begin to doubt whether I am not relapsing into the wild life of those around me. Fortunately I have not yet acquired the habit of speaking through my nose, nor do I make that fearful sound--a hawking in the throat--which is the signal that your neighbour is preparing to expectorate, and which renders travelling, even in a first-class car, almost insupportable; but my hands are tanned. I sit with my waistcoast open, and occasionally in my shirtsleeves. I care little to make any effort to be polite; I am clean forgetting all my manners, and feel that in a little while I shall be as rough as a cowboy, or as the wild wolf of the prairie. It is clear I must not tarry in Calgary too long."

Roper, Edward. BY TRACK AND TRAIL: A JOURNEY THROUGH CANADA. London: Allen, 1891.

> In what is one of the best Canadian travel books, Roper combines anecdotal style (with ample dialogue) with a vast amount of detail regarding the transportation, the towns and the life-style. An example of one of his chapters: "Meadow's Neighbours--A Sunday Visitor--Friend Brown's Loquacity--Canadian Habits--Miserable System of Keeping Cattle--Shiftless Warp--A Prairie Walk --Fire-Guards--Want of Society--What Girls Can Do in the N.W.T." Twenty-five of the thirty chapters are about the prairies and British Columbia; the other five record his superficial impressions of Quebec and Ontario.

Rowan, John J. THE EMIGRANT AND SPORTSMAN IN CANADA: SOME EXPERIENCES OF AN OLD COUNTRY SETTLER. London: Edward Stanford, 1876. Reprint ed. in facsimile. Toronto: Coles Publishing Co., 1972.

> A pedestrian piece of writing, chiefly aimed at emigrants, this work contains a few interesting accounts of the fauna of the country.

Sladen, Douglas. ON THE CARS AND OFF: BEING THE JOURNAL OF A PILGRIMAGE ALONG THE QUEEN'S HIGHWAY TO THE EAST, FROM HALIFAX IN NOVA SCOTIA TO VICTORIA IN VANCOUVER'S ISLAND. London: Ward, Lock, 1895.

This large folio production is designed to capture the beauty of
Canada and the romance of its past, with such chapter titles as
"Nova Scotia: The Land of Evangeline." It is amply illustrated,
with an eye to the many tourists who would soon be flocking to
such scenic spots as Lake Louise.

Sleigh, Lt.-Col. B.W.A. PINE FORESTS AND HAMATACK CLEARINGS; OR,
LIFE, TRAVEL AND ADVENTURE IN THE BRITISH NORTH AMERICA PROVINCES.
2nd ed. London: Richard Bentley, 1853.

A high-ranking officer, stationed successively in Nova Scotia, Cape
Breton, and Lower Canada, Sleigh was highly conversant with upper-
class social customs and with politics: it is with these that he is
chiefly concerned in this work.

Warburton, George. HOCHELAGA; OR, ENGLAND IN THE NEW WORLD.
Ed. Eliot Warburton. 2 vols. London: Colburn, 1846.

Volume I deals with Canada. The title is quite revealing for, as
the editor states in his preface, "the author is far away, in the
lands of which these volumes treat, but every page will tell that
his heart is still at home." There are, however, many fine descriptions of places (from St. John's to Niagara Falls) and of people
(from Colonel Moodie to the anonymous man who unfortunately
plunged over the Falls).

Warre, Capt. H. SKETCHES IN NORTH AMERICA AND THE OREGON TER-
RITORY. Barre, Mass.: Imprint Society, 1970.

This collection of seventy-one sketches (with written descriptions),
including coloured and uncoloured drawings, was made by Warre on
a trip across Canada (Montreal to Vancouver) and back in 1845-46
with Sir George Simpson.

Willis, N. P., and W. H. Bartlett. CANADIAN SCENERY. 2 vols. London:
Virtue, 1843. Reprint ed. in facsimile. Toronto: Peter Martin Associates,
1967.

This collection of skillfully executed drawings by Bartlett depict
natural scenes from Halifax to Lake Ontario; the written descriptions were selected by Willis from other first-hand accounts (such
as Mrs. Traill's BACKWOODS OF CANADA) and include such
titles as "Impression of Canada Upon Emigrant Settlers" and "Conditions of the Inhabitants of Canada."

Chapter 7

SELECTED NINETEENTH-CENTURY JOURNALS

Chapter 7

SELECTED NINETEENTH-CENTURY JOURNALS

Early Canadian journals, belletristic and humanistic, constitute a large area of unexplored literary territory. They mirror, vividly at times, the epochs which spawned them; issues--political, religious and social--were debated with a fervour only infrequently recaptured today during election rallies. They provide, as David Arnason states, "an invaluable insight into our past, and in particular into the qualities of imagination that shaped this country" (JOURNAL OF CANADIAN FICTION, II, 3, 128). They also prove that Canadians were, contrary to certain expressed opinions, well aware of the world beyond their socalled garrisons. Obviously no serious research into Canadian literary history can ignore them.

Many of these journals, once so scarce, are now being made accessible in microfilm by the Donner Foundation at Simon Fraser University and other institutions. Numerous rare journals are becoming available and, as a result, they are the subjects of renewed examination.

What follows is a chronological listing of the major Canadian literary journals of the nineteenth century, those which are now accessible (either in original form or on microfilm), and which contain material of interest to the student of Canadian literature. For a more comprehensive list see Goggio, et al, A BIBLIOGRAPHY OF CANADIAN CULTURAL PERIODICALS (Toronto: The University, 1955).

THE LITERARY GARLAND. Vols. 1-4: December 1838-December 1842; new series, Vols. 1-9: January 1843-December 1851. Monthly. Montreal: Lovell, 1838-51. Edited by John Gibson.

> Gibson defines his editorial aims as follows: "Be the task ours to gather up of these native gems the most beautiful, and by giving them a 'local habitation and a name,' in the pages of The GARLAND, as well preserve them from oblivion, as assist in fostering the spirit of literary enterprise."
>
> THE LITERARY GARLAND was Canada's first major journal and the only one to that date to survive for more than three years. It was international in scope, offering the usual reprinted material, but concentrating on original Canadian writing with special emphasis on

273

poetry and historical fiction. Among its contributors were Rosanna
Leprohon, Mrs. Moodie, Catherine Parr Traill, John Richardson,
Charles Sangster. It was, as Mary Markham Brown states, one of
the first vital influences in establishing a Canadian literary tradition.
See her INDEX TO THE LITERARY GARLAND (Toronto, 1962).

THE VICTORIA MAGAZINE. Vols. 1-12: September 1847–August 1848.
Monthly. Belleville, Ontario: Joseph Wilson, 1847-48. Edited by Susanna
and J. W. D. Moodie.

Here is the Moodies' stated aim: "The farmer, of all others, should
be a reading man. Books should be his every-day companions....
To this class, no less than to the intelligent inhabitants of the Towns,
do we look for encouragement and support in our undertaking" (I, 1).

THE VICTORIA MAGAZINE was intended to bring cultural improve-
ment to rural Canada at a cheap price. Most of the material was
supplied by the Moodies themselves or by Mrs. Moodie's sisters,
Catherine Parr Traill and Agnes Strickland. The whole has been
reprinted (Vancouver: University of British Columbia Press, 1968),
with an introduction by William H. New.

THE ANGLO-AMERICAN MAGAZINE. Vols. 1-8: July 1852–November/Decem-
ber 1855. Monthly. Toronto: Thomas Maclear, 1852-55. Editor unknown.

Of minimal interest to the student of Canadian literature, this magazine, decidedly belletristic, contained very little original material
and gave space only to a very few Canadian writers, one being
Alexander McLachlan who contributed two bad poems.

THE BRITISH-CANADIAN REVIEW. Vols. 1-3: December 1862–February 1863.
Monthly. Quebec: Hunter, Rose, 1862-63. Editor unknown.

The editor's aim was to provide "a trustworthy source of information
and amusement, and a truthful repository of National Literature,
pure and undefiled....We claim it as one of our special privileges,
to assert (where we deem it necessary to do so, on any question
which may arise) the claims of this Province, as paramount to consideration among the often conflicting and jarring interests of the
Empire" (I, 1).

A short-lived journal, the BRITISH-CANADIAN REVIEW is nevertheless of considerable interest, particularly for its attempt to "foster
the growing spirit of Nationality." Its editorials stressed national
unity, its articles were distinctively Canadian, and its reviews concerned themselves with Canadian books (Sangster's "Hesperus," Mc-
Lachlan's "The Emigrant," and Frances Brooke's EMILY MONTAGUE
are three that receive attention).

THE BRITISH AMERICAN MAGAZINE. Vol. 1, nos. 1-2, no. 6: May 1863–
April 1864. Monthly. Toronto: Lovell and Gibson, 1863-64. Edited by
Henry Youle Hind and G. Mercer Adam.

Another distinctively nationalistic magazine, its chief features are its long editorials by such men as Thomas D'Arcy McGee. Its articles deal mainly with Canadian topics, such as "On the Cultivation of Flax and Hemp in Canada" and "Insect Life in Canada," and it contains a large body of original writing by such people as Mrs. Leprohon, Susanna Moodie, Charles Sangster, Charles Mair, Daniel Wilson and, most often, Charles Reade.

THE NEW DOMINION MONTHLY. Vol. 1, nos. 1-4: October 1867-June 1869; July 1869-January 1879, unnumbered. Montreal: John Dougall & Son, 1867-79. Editor unknown.

It is difficult to discover a consistent underlying philosophy for this journal. It consists chiefly of extracts from other journals, household hints, bad verse, and an occasional poem or article by a Canadian writer. It is without editorials and, in spite of its title, spoke little of the New Dominion. It is not a profitable source for the modern researcher.

THE CANADIAN MONTHLY AND NATIONAL REVIEW. Vols. 1-13: January 1872-June 1878; new series, vols. 1-8. July 1878-June 1882. Toronto: Adam, Stevenson & Co., 1872-78; Rose Belford, 1878-82. Edited by George Stewart and G. Mercer Adam.

From 1872 until June, 1878, when it absorbed BELFORD'S MONTHLY MAGAZINE, the periodical was entitled THE CANADIAN MONTHLY AND NATIONAL REVIEW. From July, 1878 until 1882, the title was ROSE BELFORD'S CANADIAN MONTHLY AND NATIONAL REVIEW.

"There has been of late," wrote G. Mercer Adam, "a general awakening of national life; ...to deal with Canadian questions and to call forth Canadian talent will be the first aim of the managers of THE CANADIAN MONTHLY" (I,1).

Both THE CANADIAN MONTHLY and BELFORD'S MONTHLY MAGAZINE were dedicated to the cause of national unity, at a time when Confederation itself was undergoing severe pressures. The former, under the direction of a very capable editor, was much more overt in this and was the first journal to promote the idea of a "Canadian literature." Both contain a great deal of original material and include among its contributors Sangster, Moodie, Grant Allen, "Fidelis," J. G. Bourinot, E. W. Thomson, McLachlan, and Traill.

After the merger, with Stewart as editor, the magazine languished but was re-invigorated when Adam again took over. THE CANADIAN MONTHLY, BELFORD'S MONTHLY MAGAZINE, and ROSE BELFORD'S CANADIAN MONTHLY comprise one of the most successful and influential ventures in Canadian journalistic history.

BELFORD'S MONTHLY MAGAZINE: A MAGAZINE OF LITERATURE AND ART. Vols. 1-3: December 1876-May 1878. Toronto: Belford Brothers, 1877-78.

See the annotation for the preceding entry.

THE WEEK: AN INDEPENDENT JOURNAL OF LITERATURE, POLITICS AND CRITICISM. Vol. 1, nos. 1-13: December 1883-November 1896. Weekly. Toronto: C. Blackett Robinson, 1883-96. Edited by Charles G. D. Roberts and, subsequently, by W. Phillip Robinson.

Primarily a commentator on world affairs, THE WEEK also included a great deal of reprinted and original creative writing. All aspects of Canadian life were treated, and such writers as Carman, D. C. Scott, F. G. Scott, Lampman, S. J. Duncan, Mrs. Harrison, and Agnes Maule Machar were contributors.

THE DOMINION ILLUSTRATED. Series I, vols. 1-7: July 1888-December 1891; series II, vols. 1-3: February 1892-1895. Weekly, 1888-91; monthly, 1892-95. Montreal: Desbarats, 1888-95. Literary editor, John Lesperance.

Title varies: Vols. 1-7 were entitled THE DOMINION ILLUSTRATED: A CANADIAN PICTORIAL WEEKLY; the new series, Vols. 1-3 was DOMINION ILLUSTRATED MONTHLY.

Stated aim: "We intend to illustrate the Dominion of Canada, its scenery, its industries, its cities, its attractions and resources, its great public works, its prominent men" (I, 1).

For seven years this magazine lived up to its prospectus and provided its readers with some excellent photographs of Canada's scenic spots, civic events, and people. It also offered a wide variety of comments on all aspects of Canadian life, including a section called "Literary Notes." Among its contributors were John Hunter-Duvar, William Lighthall, and William McLennan.

THE CANADIAN MAGAZINE OF POLITICS, SCIENCE, ART AND LITERATURE. Vols. 1-91: March 1893-April 1939. Monthly. Toronto: Canadian Magazines Ltd., 1893-1939. Editor unknown.

Title varies: 1893-1925: THE CANADIAN MAGAZINE OF POLITICS, SCIENCE, ART AND LITERATURE; February 1925-July 1937: THE CANADIAN MAGAZINE; August 1937-1939: CANADIAN (with a running title, THE CANADIAN MAGAZINE). October 1931 not published.

When THE CANADIAN MAGAZINE was established a "Canadian" literature was being taken for granted. The new journal therefore commenced by publishing the stories and poems of writers who had become known in Canada and abroad and also launched such new writers as Theodore Rand, A. J. Stringer, and Bernard McEvoy. In addition it was the first journal to act as an outlet for critical writing; Canada's writers and literature were examined in increasingly good articles as the journal progressed.

See also next item.

MASSEY'S MAGAZINE. Vols. 1-3: January 1896-June 1897. Monthly.
Toronto: Massey Press, 1896-97. Edited by F. W. Falls.

Absorbed by THE CANADIAN MAGAZINE (see above) in July 1897.
In terms of both style and content this was one of the finest magazines ever produced in Canada. It offered something for everyone,
with numerous beautiful illustrations in every issue: erudite articles
on "Shakespeare's Tragedies," descriptive pieces on Canterbury Cathedral and "University Life at Cambridge," social items such as
"Legal Evolution of Married Women in Canada," current news,
sports reports, Canadian-interest stories such as "The New Ship
Canal at Sault St. Marie," literary studies, and poems and stories
by such distinguished writers as W. H. Drummond, Charles G. D.
Roberts, E. Pauline Johnson, D. C. Scott, and Bliss Carman (each
item elegantly illustrated).

INDEXES

Author Index

Title Index

AUTHOR INDEX

This index is alphabetized letter-by-letter and numbers refer to page numbers. In the case of individual authors, underlined numbers refer to main entries. Also indexed are names of editors, translators, and names of historical figures germane to the background and development of Canadian literature.

Bodsworth, C.F.   102

Boilieu, Lambert de.   See De Boilieu, Lambert

Bond, W.H.   63

Bonnycastle, Sir R.H.   218, 262

Booth, Michael R.   21

Borrett, George Tuthill   231

Boswell, James   115

Boucher, Brother Laurent   90

Boulton, D'Arcy   239

Boulton, Major   246

Bourinot, Arthur S.   32, 93, 95, 121, 190, 201

Bourinot, John George   17, 66, 70, 275

Bowker, Kathleen K.   193

Brady, Alexander   164

Bredin, Thomas   219

Brennan, M.W.   70

Brierley, James G.   24

Briggs, William   177, 195

Britannicus [pseud.]   See Kirby, William

British Columbia   254-61

Broadus, Edmund Kemper   31

Broadus, Eleanor   31

Brodie, Allen Douglas   95, 181, 196

Brooke (Moore), Francis   viii, 22, 24, 115-17, 274

Brown, E.K.   17, 21, 69, 70, 93, 95

Brown, George W.   6

Brown, Harry W.   48

Brown, James B.   231

Brown, Mary Markham   8, 158, 274

Brown, Robert 255

Brown, W.J.   114

Bruton, F.A.   219

Bryant, Claude G.   186

Bryant, Henry Grier   218, 219

Bryce, George   246

Buchan, Captain David   214, 221

Buckingham, James S.   263

Bunyan, John   177

Burham, Hampden   204

Burness, Jean F.   57

Burns, Robin B.   164

Burpee, Lawrence J.   5, 21, 30, 41, 54, 65, 72, 114, 115, 121, 125, 130, 146, 150, 176, 204, 213

Burrell, Martin   95

Burton, Jean   70, 170

Burwash, Ida   81, 117

Burwell, Adam Hood   119

Butler, William Francis   146, 246

Author Index

C

C., J.A.   114

Cabot, John   210, 214

Cabot, Sebastian   163

Calnek, W.A.   66

Cameron, Charles J.   121

Cameron, George Frederick   30, 32, 121-22

Campbell, Brian R.   70

Campbell, Henry C.   8, 70

Campbell, J.F.   263

Campbell, John Hugh   90

Campbell, Patrick   263

Campbell, Stephen Coady   149

Campbell William Wilfred   viii, 11, 30, 31, 32, 39-42, 70, 73, 96

Canada: National Library   9; Public Archives   9, 10, 11

Canadian Library Association   10

Cappon, James   48, 90

Carleton, Cousin May [pseud.]   See Fleming, May Agnes

Carman, Bliss   viii, 11, 20, 30, 31, 32, 39, 43-51, 83, 89, 90, 91, 92, 93, 186, 199, 200, 230, 276, 277

Carman, Francis A.   148

Carnegie, James   252

Carnochan, Janet   143, 156

Carpenter, David C.   62

Carstairs, J.S.   81

Cartier, Jacques   163, 210, 214

Cartwright, George   218

Cary, Thomas   33

Casselman, A.C.   80

Caswell, Edward S.   31, 204

Cates, John   196

Champlain, Samuel de   211

Chapman, F.M.   102

Chappell, Lt. Edward   218

Charlesworth, Hector C.   152, 172

Chateauclair, Wilfred [pseud.]   See William Douw Lighthall

Cheadle, W.B.   267

Chisholm, Joseph Andrew   147, 148

Chisholm, M.F.P.   66

Chittick, V.L.O.   63, 64, 66-67

Christmas, Rev. Henry   263

Christy, Miller   215

Churchill, Rev. Charles   226

Cilley, Jonathan P.   219

Clark, Daniel   146

Clarke, George Herbert   95

Clarke, Henry J.   164

Clemens, Samuel L.   65

Morris, William 235

Morse, Samuel 223

Morse, William Inglis 43, 63

Morton, A.S. 251

Morton, W.L. 246

Mountain, Rev. J.G. 223, 251

Moyles, R.G. 5

Muddiman, Bernard 22, 41, 49, 72, 91, 96

Mullaly, John 223

Mullins, Rosanna. See Leprohon (Mullins) Rosanna Eleanor

Mumford, James K. 212

Mulvaney, Charles Pelham 251

Murphy, Charles 164

Murray, Hugh 267

Murray, Jean M. 224

Murray, Louisa 146

Myatt, Wilfred E. 137

N

Need, Thomas 243

Needler, G.H. 78, 205

Nesbitt, Bruce 73

New, William H. 76, 115, 117, 274

New Brunswick 225-230

New Brunswick University Library 11

Newfoundland 217-225

Newton, Norman 22

Newton, William 251

Nicol, John 212

Noble, Louis L. 223

Norman, Louis [pseud.] See Bliss Carman

Northwest Passage 214-217

Northwest Territories 245-254

Norwood, Robert 171, 172

Nova Scotia 225-230

O

O'Brien, Arthur Henry 63

O'Brien, Sister Patricia 54

O'Donnell, Kathleen 165

Ogden, J.C. 235

O'Hagan, Thomas 19, 130, 177-78

Oland, Sidney 26

O'Leary, Peter 267

Oliphant, Laurence 235

O'Neill, K. 165

Ontario 230-237, 239-244

Ower, John 41, 54

Oxendon, Rev. Ashton 239

Oxley, James Macdonald viii, 179-81

P

Pacey, Desmond   8, 19, 50, 72, 73, 81, 83, 91, 96, 117, 138, 190

Packard, Alpheus S.   223

Page, L.C.   85, 86

Palsson, Hermann   210

Papineau, Louis-Joseph   235

Park, Sheila A.   78

Parker, Sir Gilbert   viii, 24, 31, 55, 152, 156, 183-87

Parker, Jack H.   8

Parks, M.G.   147, 227

Parry, William   217

Partridge, F.G.   78

Paterson, Beth   62

Patterson, E. Palmer   96

Patterson, George   125

Payzant, J.A.   150

Peacock, H.R.   202

Peel, Bruce B.   6, 245

Pennefather, John P.   252

Percival, W.P.   7, 20, 96, 152, 160, 172, 190, 197

Phelan, Josephine   165

Phelps, Arthur L.   68, 73, 130

Phillipps-Wolley, Clive   257

Phillips, Walter J.   95

Pichon, T.   229

Pickthall, Marjorie   11

Pierce, Lorne Albert   11, 20, 31, 39, 43, 44, 47, 48, 50, 53, 91, 155, 156, 199, 200

Pike, Warburton   260, 261

Pocock, Sidney   252

Poirier, Michel   23, 91, 102

Polk, James   91, 102

Pomeroy, Elise M.   54, 91

Poole, E. Phillips   115, 117

Poole, Francis   257

Poole, William Frederick   8

Porteus, Janet   11

Portlock, Nathaniel   212

Povey, John   23

Prairies   245-254

Pratt, E.J.   23, 89

Prenties, S.W.   229

Preston, T.R.   235

Price, Julius M.   257

Prince Edward Island   225-230

Pritchard, Allen   23

Purchas, Samuel   210

Q

Quayle, Eric   109, 110

Quebec   230-239

Simpson, Sir George 260, 261, 269

Simpson, Thomas 217

Sinclair, David 33, 155, 156

Singleton, Mary, Spinster [pseud.]
See Brooke, (Moore) Frances

Skelton, Isabel 165

Sladen, Douglas 268

Slattery, Timothy Patrick 165

Sleigh, Ltd.-Col. B.W.A. 269

Smith, Arthur James Marshall 23,
29, 31, 32, 33, 49, 66, 70,
77-78, 97, 121, 122, 149, 160,
210, 263

Smith, S. 247

Somerset, H.Somers 259

Somerville, R.S. 160

Sontagg, August 216

Sorfleet, John Robert 50, 156, 187

Southesk, Earl of. See Carnegie,
James

Spaight, George 165

Spedon, Andrew Learmont 229

Spragg, G.W. 244

Springer, John S. 230

Stackpole, Edouard A. 216

Staton, Frances 11

Stearns, W.A. 223

Steel, Sir Richard 161

Stephen, A.M. 31, 91

Stephens, Donald 43, 51

Stevenson, Lionel 20, 97, 178

Stevenson, O.J. 20, 41, 92, 131,
153, 193, 197

Stevenson, Robert Louis 44

Stewart, George 234, 275

Story, Norah 20

Strachan, James 244

Strickland, Agnes 24, 75, 244, 274

Strickland, Catherine 75

Strickland, Elizabeth 24, 75

Strickland, Jane 75

Strickland, Samuel 78, 205, 244

Strickland, Susanna 75

Stringer, Arthur 71, 92, 276

Stuart-Stubbs, Basil 68

Surveyer, E.F. 160

Sutherland, Rev. A. 253

Sutherland, John 72

Sutherland, Peter C. 216

Swift, Jonathan 161

Swift, S.C. 176

Sykes, W.J. 41, 97

Sylvestre, Guy 7

T

Tait, Michael 23, 42, 173

Talbot, Col. Edward Allen 231, 235

TITLE INDEX

A

Title Index

Title Index

Title Index

Title Index

Title Index

Title Index